# Work Engagement and Employee Well-being



*Work Engagement and Employee Well-being* highlights the vital role of psychosocial support in building and stimulating work engagement. It is a response to the growing phenomenon of weakened employee attachment and engagement instability. The authors underscore the importance of creating a friendly work environment, which accommodates a variety of employee needs and elicits positive emotions, thus fostering the well-being and complete engagement of employees.

An in-depth literature review and empirical research conducted using combined qualitative and quantitative methods enabled the authors to present the issue from a wide range of theoretical perspectives. With a model acknowledging the multifaceted nature of work engagement and its association with well-being, the book introduces a selection of psychosocial means to enhance it. The analysis focuses on both systemic measures, that is, promoting a supportive organizational culture and protecting work–life balance, as well as a more individualized approach that not only facilitates the recognition and respect of employee needs but also helps cultivate their development. The book places emphasis on a transformational leadership style and a high level of emotional intelligence among managers, particularly their empathy. Further attention was paid to the various ways to support specific employee groups, such as remote workers and neurodivergent members of the workforce.

**Małgorzata Adamska-Chudzińska** is an associate professor at the Krakow University of Economics with a postdoctoral degree in the discipline of management and quality sciences and head of the Department of Psychology and Didactics at the Institute of Management, Krakow University of Economics. She has authored publications in the fields of employee engagement, professional performance, and human subjectivity in organizations.

**Justyna Pawlak**, PhD, is an assistant professor at the Krakow University of Economics. Her main areas of scientific interest are human subjectivity in organizations, human resources management, and self-creation. She is a member of the Editorial Board of the *Polish Journal of Economic Psychology* and the European Association of Work and Organization Psychology.

## Routledge Research in Human Resource Management

**Human Capital Management in the Contemporary Workplace**
Enhancing Organisation Sustainability
*Edited by Agata Sudolska and Kamil Zawadzki*

**Human Resource Management in Higher Education Institutions**
An International Perspective
*Sylwia Przytuła, Łukasz Sułkowski and Konrad Kulikowski*

**Remote Work, Internal Marketing and Human Resource Management**
Innovative Approaches and Fundamentals
*Teena Mishra*

**Work Engagement and Employee Well-being**
Psychosocial Support to Build Engaged Human Capital
*Edited by Małgorzata Adamska-Chudzińska and Justyna Pawlak*

# Work Engagement and Employee Well-being

## Psychosocial Support to Build Engaged Human Capital

**Edited by**
**Małgorzata Adamska-Chudzińska and Justyna Pawlak**

Routledge
Taylor & Francis Group
NEW YORK AND LONDON

First published 2025
by Routledge
605 Third Avenue, New York, NY 10158

and by Routledge
4 Park Square, Milton Park, Abingdon, Oxon, OX14 4RN

*Routledge is an imprint of the Taylor & Francis Group, an informa business*



ISBN: 978-1-032-71077-8 (hbk)
ISBN: 978-1-032-71539-1 (pbk)
ISBN: 978-1-032-71540-7 (ebk)

DOI: 10.4324/9781032715407

Typeset in Times New Roman
by Apex CoVantage, LLC

# Contents

# Tables

# Figures

# Contributors

**Magdalena Adamczyk-Kowalczuk** is an assistant professor in the Institute of Finance at the Krakow University of Economics. She holds an MSc in psychology from Jagiellonian University, Poland, and a second MSc in finance from Krakow University of Economics. Her research interests focus on economic psychology, perception of information, decision-making, organizational psychology, and mental health.

**Małgorzata Adamska-Chudzińska** is an associate professor at the Krakow University of Economics with a postdoctoral degree in the discipline of management and quality sciences and head of the Department of Psychology and Didactics at the Institute of Management. She has authored publications in the fields of employee engagement, professional performance, and human subjectivity in organizations.

**Norbert Andraszak** is a PhD specializing in the discipline of management and quality sciences. He has been a police officer for more than 20 years and has participated in many training courses and international engagements (including a mission in Kosovo). His research interests revolve around employee engagement and empowerment.

**Marian Bursztyn** holds a PhD in the field of pedagogy (Jagiellonian University). His main area of scientific interest is human subjectivity in the field of education through art, the importance of emotional intelligence in improving organizational structure, and the psychosocial area of business etiquette in building interpersonal professional and non-professional relationships.

**Maria Foryś** is a psychologist, neuro speech therapist, and assistant professor at the Kraków University of Economics. Her research interests include the issue of neurodiversity in the professional context, the application of knowledge from neurobiology in effective management, and the assessment of managerial potential. She is a honorary member of the Polish Dyslexia Society (part of the European Dyslexia Society).

**Lech Górniak** is an assistant professor in the Department of Psychology and Didactics, University of Economics, Krakow. He is an author of scientific papers in the field of social and management psychology, trust in organization, and engagement of employees. He has extensive experience in consulting programs for companies in the field of management psychology and teamwork.

**Joanna Krzyżak** holds a PhD in economic sciences from the Krakow University of Economics. Her research interests include problems related to human creative activity and the application of neuroscience knowledge to effective self-management. She has also contributed to the educational literature on the methodology of economic education.

**Mariusz Makowski** is a social psychologist. He is a graduate of the Jagiellonian University and holds a PhD in the discipline of psychology. His main areas of scientific interest include mass communication, media, attitude formation, entrepreneurship, health psychology, and photography as a medium of communication. He has also authored scientific articles and a textbook on psychological contexts of management. Furthermore, he is a certified Gestalt psychotherapist.

**Justyna Pawlak,** PhD, is an assistant professor at the Krakow University of Economics. Her main areas of scientific interest are human subjectivity in organizations, human resources management, and self-creation. She is a member of the Editorial Board of the *Polish Journal of Economic Psychology* and the European Association of Work and Organization Psychology.

**Ireneusz Rynduch** is affiliated with the Department of Labor Resource Management, Krakow University of Economics. He is an HR specialist interested in the labor market, multiculturalism, virtualization of teamwork, sustainable management, and leadership in organizations. He is also a member of the Students Club of Self Development.

**Alicja Szczygieł** holds a PhD in the field of management sciences (Krakow University of Economics) and is a graduate of the Institute of Psychology (Jagiellonian University). Her research interests include management and subjective treatment of employees, negotiation in business, and interpersonal communication. She conducts trainings for managers on creative problem-solving, business negotiations, and psychological measurement.

**Robert Szydło** is an assistant professor in the Department of Labor Resource Management at the Krakow University of Economics. He is an HRM specialist and psychologist. His research interests include employability, competence development, gamification, and the usage of psychology in business. Furthermore, as the leader of the science-based NGO SEED, he enagages in various scientific, didactic, and voluntary activities.

**Małgorzata Tyrańska** is an associate professor at the Krakow University of Economics with a postdoctoral degree in economic science in the discipline of management sciences. Her research interests include employment restructuring, organizational structure improvement, job evaluation, and competency profile assessment. She is a member of the experts' team for the evaluation of projects implemented as part of European programs.

**Jolanta Walas-Trębacz** holds a PhD in economic science and is an assistant professor in the Department of Management Process at the Krakow University of Economics. She is the author of publications on the following issues: human resource management, strategic management, crisis management, and the use of concepts and methods in organizational improvement. She is also involved in organizational consulting and conducts training.

**Renata Winkler** is an assistant professor of management at the Kraków University of Economics. Her research interests focus on organizational behavior with particular emphasis on managing cultural diversity, buidling effective communication within the team, and the development of social potential in organizations. She has 20 years of experience in conducting training, workshops, and seminars.

**Sylwia Wiśniewska** holds a PhD in economics in the discipline of management sciences and is an assistant professor in the Department of Labor Resources Management, Krakow University of Economics. Her research interests include employability, sustainable employability, competencies, and quality of life. She also collaborates with business practices and nongovernmental organizations, including as an expert.

**Kamil Wiśniewski** is a PhD in economics in the field of management and an assistant professor in the Department of Management at Jan Kochanowski University in Kielce. He obtained a doctoral degree at the Kraków University of Economics. His research interests focus on knowledge management, organisational learning, and sales psychology. He cooperates with business practice, among others, as an expert.

# Introduction

*Małgorzata Adamska-Chudzińska and Justyna Pawlak*

Faced with the dynamic and ever-changing conditions in which today's organizations operate, managers have increasingly come to recognize the true benefits of having an engaged workforce whose willingness to learn constantly and creatively approach tasks accelerates the pace at which organizations adapt to new circumstances. Engaged employees also tend to display greater flexibility, which facilitates the implementation of structural and operational changes, essential for maintaining competitiveness. The decrease of absence and turnover rates reduces recruitment and training costs, thus enhancing operational efficiency. Employees who are engaged contribute to process optimization and improved resource utilization. Instances of companies that successfully navigate crises highlight the role of employee engagement. In a dynamic and changeable business environment, engaged employees are indispensable for long-term organizational success.

At the same time, the ongoing transformations in the job market, including the high expectations of the youngest cohort of employees and a general malaise and uncertainty caused by the global socio-political situation, have highlighted the trend of decreased organizational attachment and greater fluctuations of employee engagement. This has led to higher turnover rates and quiet quitting. Both these phenomena result in significant losses in human capital. When employees leave an organization, they take with them their knowledge, experience, culture, and value system, which may threaten the organization's competitiveness, particularly in the case of high-potential employee turnover. Meanwhile, the underutilization of employee potential observed in the case of quiet quitting, albeit not resulting in actual quitting, can also be represented in terms of losses due to the fact that employees commit to the bare minimum of work required and are emotionally disengaged from their tasks. Quiet quitting, although it is subtle and can be difficult to determine at a glance, may have far-reaching negative consequences for organizations.

Successful management of employee engagement is crucial for minimizing these losses and building organizational resilience. Companies and their managers try to implement countermeasures aimed at enhancing employee engagement.

DOI: 10.4324/9781032715407-1

The scope of such influence may well be multidimensional and should not be limited to technical and organizational, environmental, or economic factors. It has to be noted that employee engagement is a category related to deep-seated attitudes that are embedded in the personality of the individual and, together with an idiosyncratic value system, serves to guide their behavior. Therefore, the level of employee engagement is largely determined by a complex interaction of various psychosocial determinants. Understanding these determinants is of the utmost importance for unlocking full employee potential and creating a highly functional and balanced work environment.

It is worth highlighting that numerous studies on employee engagement have explored a variety of its aspects. However, in the face of current challenges, such as poor employee attachment and their low level of psychological presence at work, it is psychosocial support that appears to play a special role in the stimulation of employee engagement. It draws on the social and psychological resources that foster the experience of well-being and positive mindset in the workplace.

Psychosocial support may comprise a wide range of factors directed toward satisfying the individual needs of employees and conditioning the experience of emotional safety in the organizational environment. These include, among other things, providing employees with a deeper meaning of their work, opportunities for professional development, and an adequate degree of autonomy, as well as the recognition of their achievements and the protection of their work–life balance. A psychosocially responsive environment may promote valuable employee mental states, such as the feeling of being a subject and being acknowledged, the sense of authorship and self-efficacy, and self-actualization and achievement. These may trigger a boost in workplace energy and stimulate employee responsibility for the results of their activity.

By covering a wide range of theoretical approaches and empirical studies, the book aims to represent the multifaceted character of work engagement and shed light on the significance of psychosocial support in its emergence, development, and maintenance (endurance). The book comprises ten chapters focused on selected forms of psychosocial support, crucial for developing highly engaged human capital. Each chapter is intended to provide theoretical knowledge or empirical evidence that can be useful for building a supportive work environment. In order to accomplish this goal, it was vital to include findings derived from several branches of science, including psychology, human resources, organizational behavior, and organizational health. Within the framework of these disciplines, the authors of the respective chapters carried out their analyses of the issues that constitute the field of psychosocial support.

Małgorzata Adamska-Chudzińska and Norbert Andraszak, the authors of Chapter 1, "Work Engagement as a Challenge for Contemporary Management," set out to demonstrate that the basis (theoretical foundation) for developing efficient solutions to the problem of poor employee engagement and frequent turnover can be sought in the concept of work engagement. The pursuit of such solutions is currently a major aspect of employee management and prevention of human capital loss. In order to achieve the objective set, a scoping review was performed using the Scopus and Web of Science databases, as well as secondary sources. The chapter features a comparative analysis of the semantic content of the notion of work engagement against the backdrop of similar constructs, that is, organizational commitment, and job involvement. It has been established that all these constructs refer to the person–job relationship and that they are interrelated; however, within the framework of these interconnections, it does not seem justified to equate these constructs. The concept of work engagement distinguishes itself from the other two terms because of its strong association with the sense of well-being and positive emotions experienced in the workplace. These determine high levels of energy at work. On the basis of the results of comparative analysis, the Work Engagement Determinants model was developed, encompassing factors that generate positive emotions and a sense of well-being in employees, as intermediary determinants of high work engagement. The authors pointed out the fundamental importance of job resources, which should include the qualities that foster a friendly social environment of work, supportive leadership traits, and socio-psychological processes. Stimulating factors were also taken into consideration, among them individual resources and the experience of work–life balance.

In Chapter 2, "Determinants of Employee Well-being," Mariusz Makowski presents the issues related to employee well-being. He observed that the construct largely explains the reasons behind employee turnover and sickness absence. When well-being level falls below a certain point, these unfavorable phenomena become more frequent. High employee well-being, on the other hand, is positively correlated with a series of beneficial aspects of work, including work engagement. In view of the shortage of qualified workers and fluctuations in their engagement, fostering employee well-being is no longer an addition to managerial policy, instead becoming a necessity. The author of the chapter conjectures that in order to successfully improve employee well-being, it is necessary to take into consideration a series of conditions – whether organizational, macroeconomic, cultural, individual – which influence the processes of either fostering or diminishing well-being. The aim of the chapter is to analyze factors that improve or undermine well-being through a critical survey of literature on related concepts. It provides an account of the multitude of connections and interdependencies between employee well-being and a person's value system, their commitment, motivation, agency, and self-awareness. On the basis of Hobfoll's classic conservation of resources theory, an overview of resources was conducted to identify those that may promote well-being. The ways in which an individual may enhance their resources were discussed. Because well-being is a state and a phenomenon subject to examination from an interdisciplinary perspective, the decision has been made to conduct the reflection within the restricted field of industrial and organizational psychology and health psychology. Mutual interpenetration and interrelation of the factors that contribute to well-being were presented, both individual ones and those stemming from the operation of (and in) the organization. The author covered various accounts of the meaning of work, person–job fit, and job crafting.

Chapter 3, "Organizational Culture and Climate That Shape Engagement," by Robert Szydło, Małgorzata Tyrańska, Kamil Wiśniewski, Ireneusz Rynduch, and Magdalena Adamczyk-Kowalczuk, tackles the issue of the influence of organizational culture and climate on employee engagement. It has been observed that there is a strong connection between national and organizational cultures, the former having a far broader scope, of course. The perspective adopted in the chapter is interdisciplinary, as it combines psychological, sociological, and managerial research work. The authors emphasize the importance of both national and organizational culture; however, they pay particular attention to psychological aspects of organizational culture, such as organizational climate, motivation, and employee well-being. The connection of these with employee engagement and job satisfaction was discovered. The empirical research conducted by the authors with the use of a survey questionnaire focuses on understanding how various aspects of national and organizational culture motivate employees to increase their engagement, and what elements of culture are most efficient in this context. The results obtained enabled the scholars to present the perceived influence of national and organizational culture on employee efficiency and facilitated the discussion on practical tools and strategies to help build a sound organizational culture and climate that fosters engagement. The authors emphasize the importance of real activity based on the fundamental values and traits of culture for improving employee engagement and not merely declarative elements, such as the mission and vision statements.

Chapter 4, "Application of the SCARF Model in Building Work Engagement: Supportive Organizational Culture," by Joanna Krzyżak and Jolanta Walas-Trębacz, presents the analysis of the use of the SCARF (Status, Certainty, Autonomy, Relatedness, Fairness) model in the context of developing organizational culture that supports employee engagement. The SCARF model, developed by David Rock, is a key point of reference for studying how various factors influence human behavior in social situations as it provides perspectives on the needs associated with the above elements and their influence on the level of work engagement. The authors aimed to study the connection between the components of the SCARF model and the level of employee engagement among university teachers. Empirical research has been carried out on the basis of an original survey questionnaire. An analysis of the results thus obtained sheds light on the complex relations between satisfying the needs identified by the SCARF model and employee engagement as the crucial element of organizational culture development. Through the lens of the data collected, practical strategies for enhancing the elements of the SCARF model in the academic workplace have been identified. The results of empirical research provided in the study are a testament to the way that elevated status, safeguarded certainty, supported social relationships, and the maintenance of fairness can together enhance employee engagement.

Chapter 5, "Harmony at Work: Work–Life Balance as a Component of Psychosocial Support in Organizations," by Justyna Pawlak, addresses the issue of work–life balance (WLB), which ranks among the key factors that influence work engagement and, at the same time, their well-being. From this point of view, WLB encompasses not only the actual balance between work and leisure time but also the mental, social, and individual aspects that promote harmonious functioning of a person in both professional and private life. The issue of WLB has become particularly relevant in recent years, with the advances in communication technology and remote work tools having significantly impacted the way professional duties are carried out as well as the forms of employee/supervisor contact. On the one hand, these technologies can increase employee flexibility and autonomy; on the other hand, however, they cause a sense of technology overload and blur the work–life boundaries. Meanwhile, the ability to perform tasks and stay in constant contact with colleagues remotely may extend work hours and lead to work–family conflict (WFC), which has a negative impact on family relationships and the mental well-being of employees. On the basis of an analysis of the academic literature on WLB, the chapter offers a discussion of the determinants of the phenomenon, the effects of its absence, and the consequences of the emergence of work–family conflict, and thus also reveals the influence of the potential to maintain WLB on employee engagement. It offers practical guidance for organization managers on how to build such strategies for improving employee work–life balance that may bear on enhancing employee engagement and their general well-being, thus enabling the organization to harmonize its overarching needs with those of its employees.

Chapter 6, "The Influence of Development Opportunities on Work Engagement: The Example of Young Employees," by Alicja Szczygieł, aims to verify whether or not and to what extent the implementation of professional development opportunities in an organization influences Generation Z work engagement. The research was conducted on a group of Generation Z members who participated in training programs offered by their companies. Work engagement was measured using Utrecht Work Engagement Scale (UWES) developed by Schaufeli et al. Additionally, the study used an original survey questionnaire with questions about participation in the training process, including the procedures to identify the development needs and expectations of respondents. The chapter discusses the training process, regarding it as a major contributor to employee development within organizations. The chapter then goes on to focus on the characteristics of Generation Z as employees and their expectations regarding professional development. In the following section, the issues related to a low level of engagement among the youngest cohort of employees were presented.

An analysis of the data obtained during the research confirmed the hypothesis that active participation in the training process that meets the expectations of young workers has a positive impact on their work engagement. These results highlight the significance of adjusting development programs to the needs and expectations of Generation Z, which may contribute greatly to increasing employee loyalty and lowering turnover among them. The study results allow for a deeper understanding of the importance of appropriate selection of training process factors to effectively boost employee engagement within Generation Z, the cohort under study.

Chapter 7, "The Impact of Leadership on Employee Engagement," by Robert Szydło, Małgorzata Tyrańska, Sylwia Wiśniewska, Ireneusz Rynduch, and Magdalena Adamczyk-Kowalczuk, deals with the issues of the influence that leadership has on employee engagement within the organization. The authors take an interdisciplinary perspective, combining psychological and managerial theories, with a particular emphasis on sustainable leadership theory. The first part of the chapter outlines the psychological aspects of leadership, focusing on theories and models that analyze traits, behaviors, and processes related to successful leadership. A trait-based approach posits that certain innate qualities predispose individuals to become leaders. Behavioral theories, meanwhile, focus on leaders' actions and behaviors, emphasizing the importance of leadership styles. Situational theories suggest that the effectiveness of leadership is dependent on the interaction between a leader's personal traits and situational factors. In the context of psychology, the emotional intelligence and authenticity of the leader are also important, as they play a pivotal role in building trust and successful interpersonal relationships. The second part of the chapter analyzes leadership from the point of view of management. Leadership is understood here as the ability to influence employee behaviors. The evolution of leadership theory is presented in terms of its periods, ranging from classic to transactional and transformational approaches. The authors point to the importance of the integration of various leadership styles depending on the situation and organizational context. The third part of the chapter focuses on leadership tools which may help improve employee engagement. The authors stress the value of recognizing achievements, having friendly relationships in the workplace, ongoing development, and ethical behavior as activities that improve work engagement.

Chapter 8, "Emotional Intelligence in Managers and Work Engagement: The Crucial Role of Empathy," by Lech Górniak and Marian Bursztyn, demonstrates the role of emotional intelligence in the process of employee engagement by managers. The emphasis was placed on the importance of empathy, a facet of social competence, as it is one of the main components of emotional intelligence, greatly important for creating positive relationships and collaboration. It has been pointed out that the influence of the leader's empathetic behavior on employees can be strengthened or weakened depending on the level of her or his overall emotional intelligence. The chapter opens with a justification of the need for managers to foster employee engagement, given the challenges facing organizations today. It goes on to discuss the essence and significance of empathy, it being the crucial component of emotional intelligence, particularly in the context of effective employee management. Subsequently, empathetic leadership is characterized alongside the impact that this leadership style has on the level of employee engagement. The final part of the chapter refers to the results of current empirical studies, which indicate a positive influence of empathy shown by managers to employees on increased work engagement among the latter and – consequently – on organizational effectiveness, both as regards the productivity and the climate of cooperation within the company. Additionally, the chapter includes a very practical appendix, which the authors developed in the form of a list of empathetic behaviors and presented as guidelines for managers wishing to show empathy in their relationships with employees.

Chapter 9, "Neurodiverse Persons in Their Workplace: Productive Behaviors and Task Engagement," by Maria Foryś, discusses the issues related to neurodiversity in the workplace. The author asks whether neurodiversity influences the level of employee productive behaviors and engagement. The chapter provides an account of the specificity of neurodiversity in the workplace and also offers definitions of the notions of organizational diversity and neurodiversity, with the latter accounted for as diversity in human brain development and operation with regard to mental functions. It refers to empirical research carried out using the PRO scale, one of the KLIMAT4® battery of scales, aimed at identifying the differences between neurodiverse and non-neurodiverse employees regarding their productive behaviors and task engagement. It has been assumed that (behavioral) task engagement determines the extent to which persons are absorbed in performing the tasks entrusted to them. The results of the study corroborated the initial hypothesis: Neurodiverse persons display a similar level of productive behaviors and engagement to non-neurodiverse persons, both in the case of general level of productive behaviors and the components of such behavior, that is, task engagement, support for colleagues, and pro-organizational behaviors. The author stressed the vital importance of recognizing the strengths of neurodiverse persons, seeking adequate ways to support them, and flexibly adjusting the work environment to their needs. Lastly, a set of factors impairing task performance of neurodiverse persons was presented alongside suggestions of actions that foster human resource management in the context of neurodiversity.

Chapter 10, "Remote Work Engagement: How to Support It?" by Justyna Pawlak and Renata Winkler, closes the contributed volume with a reflection on the factors determining work engagement among remote workers. With the growing popularity of remote work, understanding how organizations can effectively support remote workers is crucial for ensuring a high level of employee engagement and well-being. The chapter, therefore, is focused on developing an in-depth comprehension of organizational practices and strategies to stimulate remote employees and solve managerial challenges presented by this situation.

In order to achieve this goal, a two-stage research procedure was developed. First, a systematic literature review was conducted. It allowed the authors to determine the variables that influence remote employee engagement which were evaluated in the studies performed to date. Subsequently, qualitative research was designed and conducted with the use of in-depth interviews. The results, on the one hand, confirmed the findings of the first stage of research on the determinants of engagement, while on the other, helped identify new areas that are of importance for fostering remote work engagement. Thus, it was possible to develop a list of guidelines and proposals of value for creating strategies to solve management problems associated with stimulating and maintaining remote employee engagement.

In the Conclusion of the book, the editors, Małgorzata Adamska-Chudzińska and Justyna Pawlak, offered a summary of the key conclusions drawn from the deliberations presented in the respective chapters and outlined the areas for further investigation.

The book was co-financed from the subsidy of Krakow University of Economics (UEK) within the WAP 2024 project.

# 1 Work Engagement as a Challenge for Contemporary Management

*Małgorzata Adamska-Chudzińska and Norbert Andraszak*

## Introduction

The belief that work is one of the key values of human life has come to be called into question today. It is especially the young employees who reject the "cult of sacrificing themselves at work and for work" and opt instead to treat work in terms of self-actualization. The observed fluctuations of employee engagement and a weakening bond between workers and their workplace are a testament not only to shifts in attitude to work but also to the current global socio-political situation. Events such as progressive climate change, the COVID-19 pandemic, and the war in Ukraine resulted in a long-term sense of apprehension and uncertainty about living conditions. There is an increased awareness of the fragility of human life, accompanied by the need for a higher quality of all its areas, including the professional one.

Hence, the characterization of contemporary job market entails two points of view. One is shaped by the younger workforce employed by companies in ever greater numbers, and the other is typical of employers abiding by the established principles for organization management. Young employees want to pursue their careers unrestrained by the limitations of a single company, based on their subjective sense of development and the experience of job and life satisfaction (Solarczyk-Ambrozik, 2015). Meanwhile, employers' limited capabilities for meeting these expectations along with certain rigidity and by-the-numbers manner of principles for running a company reveal a major discord between employee aspirations and what employers have to offer.

The resulting decrease in the level of employee engagement and their increased readiness to shape professional activity on their own terms are reflected in the current trends in the job market. After the pandemic, a new movement emerged referred to as the Great Resignation (Serenko, 2023; Cohen, 2021), which saw employees resign from work voluntarily and *en masse*. A great number of reasons to resign can be explained away by the concept of market segmentation (Lambert, 2022), but they fundamentally boil down to the pursuit of greater comfort in balancing professional and private life, friendly atmosphere in the

DOI: 10.4324/9781032715407-2

workplace, and better remuneration. Relatively quickly, the trend came to be replaced by another, called Quiet Quitting (Klotz & Bolino, 2022), which brought to light the decrease in employee engagement and their disaffected neutrality toward organizations even more strongly. The crux of the phenomenon, however, is not related to actually quitting one's job; instead, it consists in performing the required minimum of duties, within the standard working hours only, and avoiding any emotional involvement. It most commonly stems from employees' lacking a sense of purpose in their jobs and friendly relationships in the workplace.

According to the Gallup Report (2023), in the United States and Canada, people not involved in their work, who assume the Quiet Quitting strategy, comprise 52% of all employees, while 17% are actively disengaged (Loud Quitting). Meanwhile, in Europe, these numbers stand at respectively 72% and 15% of employees. In spite of the slight increase in global engagement, the indicators related to uninvolved employees cause much concern. Low employee engagement costs the global economy $8.8 trillion, that is, 9% of the world's GDP (Gallup Report, 2023). These losses are significant enough that solutions be desperately sought. All the more so, because they pertain not only to wasted productivity, missed profits, and clients but also to psychological costs on the part of employees. These are related to the sense of mental discomfort caused by the loss of energy, failure to use one's potential, and the absence of significant results. The two kinds of losses appear to be strongly interrelated.

Counteracting the said losses requires ensuring solutions to problems of employee well-being and, consequently, an improvement in their engagement. Activities undertaken in that regard should become a priority for modern managers. Profound changes to the ways we manage employees appear to be unavoidable. According to employees themselves (Gallup Report, 2023), what they expect is a more friendly work environment: one that provides the sense of well-being, one sensitive to their personality, needs, and achievements. What continues to be a major issue is the need to identify adequate theoretical background as the foundation for effecting the desired changes in the practice of employee management.

The chapter makes an attempt to demonstrate that managerial activity based on the work engagement concept offers the aforesaid opportunity to an extent larger than those grounded in other workplace activity theories. For that purpose, the semantic content of the notion of work engagement was dissected against the backdrop of similar constructs, such as organizational commitment and job involvement. Subsequently, on the basis of the results of the comparative analysis, a Work Engagement Determinants model has been proposed, one that includes factors generating a sense of employee well-being as an intermediary determinant for high levels of proactivity and engagement. In order to carry out the assumed objective, a scoping review has been performed using the Scopus and Web of Science databases, as well as secondary sources. The results enabled the authors to identify a set of key work environment factors essential for fostering the psychological presence of employees in organizations, a characteristic of highly engaged human resources.

## Work Engagement in Light of Related Constructs – Research Methodology

In order to realize our goal of ascertaining whether or not fostering work engagement may serve as the foundation for effective solutions to the poor employee engagement, a scoping review was conducted. The scoping review method is predominantly used when there is vast literature available on the selected topic, with references scattered across various publications and data provided in various forms (Peterson et al., 2017). The method usually centers on specific elements of the research (the population studied, the intervention type, the phenomena identified, etc.). It tends to be assessed as advantageous for practical activity. The characteristic trait of the scoping review method is that it enables scholars to diagnose a given phenomenon (Ćwiklicki, 2020) via the following stages: (a) identification of the research question; (b) identification of the relevant sources; (c) selection of studies; (d) charting of studies; (e) collating the results; (f) result consultation (optional). The stages described define the subsequent steps of the research project carried out.

In the opening phase of the review, before the research question was formulated, an initial survey of the literature on the topic was conducted, which served to recognize the following:

- The literature abounds in a wide range of concepts regarding various ways to foster employee engagement related to the employee–work relationship.
- There are two relatively common constructs in literature, namely, work engagement and organizational commitment, as well as – to a lesser extent – job involvement. These are often confused due to their varying interpretations.
- Researchers often focus on a specific aspect of the employee–work relationship, which further increases the diversity of research approaches and makes their comparison difficult.

In the wake of the research reconnaissance, the following questions were posed:

- How is employee engagement explained by the notions of work engagement, organizational commitment, and job involvement; is the concept of work engagement empirically distinct from other similar constructs?
- What factors help optimize the state of work engagement and are they related to the factors that determine similar constructs?

The second stage involved the identification of literature sources that would enable us to find the relevant data related to the research questions formulated.

Several sources were selected, the first among these being the two electronic databases, that is, Scopus and Web of Science, within which three paper searchers were conducted, one for each of the constructs of engagement. The keywords used were the names of the respective concepts, that is, "work engagement" in the first search, "organizational commitment" in the second, and "job involvement" in the third. The materials obtained were delimited by setting the time period to 2018–2023, publication language to English, and the academic field to management and psychology. The number of hits for each of the respective constructs was, in the Scopus database, 729/325/7, whereas in the Web of Science, it was 473/124/34. The number of papers was then reduced by removing duplicates, thus providing the following combined totals for both databases: 842 items for "work engagement," 368 items for "organizational commitment," and 36 for "job involvement."

The substantive research survey also included secondary sources, particularly data from the study on the constructs related to employee engagement conducted by Hallberg and Schaufeli (2006), as well as a selection of other works. These were complemented by the data from systematic literature surveys regarding "job involvement" conducted by other authors (Brown, 1996; Salessi & Omar, 2018).

The third stage of the project involved selecting the studies that tackle the research questions most aptly. Because of the large number of publications identified in the second stage, the decision was made to pick a choice group of papers for further analysis. The selection process was performed repeatedly. Firstly, the titles and summaries clearly related to the research questions were looked at. Then, it was an analysis of the content of the shortlisted papers that served as the basis for the choice; it was made with a refined set of criteria, that is, the essence and determinants of each of the three constructs of engagement under scrutiny. The doubts as to the usefulness of specific studies, which emerged at that point, were overcome through critical collaboration on qualifying the research material. Ultimately, the authors decided to present the selected papers in three groups, according to the respective constructs. Their content was presented in the following stage of the research procedure. The concepts were also characterized using older studies the authors deemed valuable.

The fourth stage consisted in registering the studies via a narrative record of the variables adopted in the selected studies. In line with the research, as performed thus far, these were examined in three groups, for each of the analyzed constructs of engagement separately. The employed arrangement of the three main issues, that is, work engagement, organizational commitment, and job involvement, enabled us to organize the data and orient them toward distinguishing the essence and factors determining each of the phenomena. The results of this procedure are shown in the following sections of this chapter.

The fifth stage was analytical in nature, and we intended it as a summary of our findings. A comparative analysis of the studied constructs was performed in terms of the aspects selected in view of the aim of this chapter. The most significant results were brought together in Table 1.1. A strong interrelation between employees' work engagement and their well-being as well as psychological presence at work was revealed. Subsequent analytical activities were aimed at organizing the factors determining the state of work engagement. It was reflected in the developed Model 1. The conclusions of this stage were presented in the next section of this chapter.

### *The Essence and Determinants of Work Engagement*

The conceptualization of work engagement (Schaufeli et al., 2002) situates the notion within the field of the psychology of health, in line with the assumption that the main source of energy for work is the employee's experience of well-being and their sense of "operating at their best" in the workplace. The issues of well-being and internal harmony constitute the crucial aspect of the concept of work engagement. It has been confirmed over the years that work engagement is a positive and highly active form of employee well-being (Bakker, 2022). It has also been demonstrated that employee engagement and well-being in the workplace are interrelated (Prakash & Kashyap, 2021), for a mentally healthy employee is fully dedicated to his work and experiences satisfaction (Sypniewska et al., 2023).

Thus, as indicated by scholars (Schaufeli et al., 2002), work engagement is a positive work-related mindset, characterized by vigor, dedication, and absorption. Vigor is reflected in one's high energy level and readiness to expend effort toward workplace activities. Dedication is related to enthusiasm, while absorption means a state of total immersion in one's job. The two former dimensions are regarded as primary, whereas absorption as an additional aspect.

Based on the research performed, a series of factors stimulating work engagement have been identified. These were classified into two groups: situational and individual factors. Scholars point to job resources (situational factors) as the main stimuli leading to work engagement (antecedents); meanwhile, individual factors stimulate work engagement (Van Roekel et al., 2023). Thus, the opportunity for shaping this state lies primarily with situational factors.

The literature survey performed indicated that work engagement can develop as a function of the very same job resources that foster motivation and elicit positive emotions toward the work environment (Hallberg & Schaufeli, 2006, p. 120). This general take was subsequently corroborated by numerous studies by authors interested in an in-detail analysis of the aspects producing work engagement.

Theorists studying the issue of work engagement focus particularly on the qualities of work environment, such as "social support from colleagues, task significance, and autonomy, as well as leadership-related factors like having a good relationship with supervisors and experiencing transformational leadership" (Van Roekel et al., 2023), which result, among other things, in stimulated independence and increased task importance. The list of identified factors indicates that it is social environment and interactions, as well as a (healthy) workplace atmosphere, that prove of major significance for fostering work engagement. Convincing evidence was provided by Bakker (2022), who integrated the copious literature on the interrelations between employees, leaders, colleagues, and partners. The author developed a model of socio-psychological processes, demonstrating that work engagement is the fruit of various processes of this kind. Among them, he listed the following:

- Emotional contagion (colleagues, leaders, and partners may constitute a major source of engagement). Such influence is important for relationships, and it facilitates communication and interpersonal bonding (Hoehl et al., 2021).
- Engagement in teamwork (positive team interactions are edifying and foster a good work atmosphere and proactive behavior of team members). Team boosting behaviors, that is, mood-enhancing, energizing, and unifying activities, are positively correlated with work engagement (Fortuin et al., 2021).
- Managerial influence on employee engagement (increased positive emotional feedback from managers, i.e., their excitement, inspiration, and attentiveness, is related to work engagement). Managers' support and transformational leadership, for instance, stimulating employee autonomy and emphasizing the importance of the task, influence the level of work engagement (Tims et al., 2011; Mukaihata et al., 2020).
- Social forms of proactive behavior (social activity aimed at making work more meaningful). Job crafting and playful work design can meet employee needs in terms of autonomy, competence, and bonding. Workers able to design their own work so that it is more playful/pleasant and competitive pursue their interests and infuse it with meaning (Bakker, 2022). Furthermore, the aspect of agency in creating interesting work also influences senior employee engagement (Kooij et al., 2020).

Studies on work engagement indicate the great significance of the positive emotions experienced by employees. Even though the absence of negative emotions favors positive attitudes to work, it is the experience of positive work-related emotions that plays a much larger role in ensuring work engagement (Majcen et al., 2023; Rusu & Colomeischi, 2020). Handayani et al. (2023) in their research conducted among female lecturers demonstrated that work engagement has a vital connection with the sense of happiness in the workplace. Additionally, it was determined that establishing work–life balance enhances positive emotions experienced in the workplace and work engagement (Handayani et al., 2023; Rusu & Colomeischi, 2020).

As indicated above, besides job resources (situational factors), which are antecedent in nature, work engagement also depends on individual resources, which provide an account of engagement in terms of personality traits. Employees with higher emotional stability, extraversion, and conscientiousness tend to show greater work engagement. Of importance here are also more flexible traits, such as a sense of self-efficacy, optimism, and mindfulness (Van Roekel et al., 2023; Rusu & Colomeischi, 2020). The important thing, however, is the extent to which employees are able to take advantage of their assets – the true strengths of their personalities – in the workplace (Bakker et al., 2018). Proactive employees tend to be more engaged, as they may even influence others by emotionally "infecting" them with their energy (Bakker, 2022).

It should be noted that the analyzed studies justify both the variability and the stability of work engagement. The situational approach has shown that work engagement, traced along the axes of vigor, dedication, and absorption, can change depending on the qualities of work environment. The personal approach, on the other hand, has demonstrated that certain personality traits may predispose employees to be involved in their work (Bakker, 2022). It is therefore important to shape workplace conditions so that they continuously stimulate both types of resources for fostering work engagement.

### *The Essence and Determinants of Organizational Commitment*

The notion of *organizational commitment* (Meyer & Allen, 1997) has its roots in the processes associated with employee attitudes and behavior patterns in the workplace. As indicated by Chang et al. (2021), employee attitude reflects the person's relationship with the organization in the context of whether or not their values align with those of the company, and whether or not the person recognizes the meaning of their work. Other researchers (Abet et al., 2024) further emphasize the significance of the behavioral dimension – as a process that consists in representing a certain pattern of behavior through which employees commit themselves to the operation of the organization. In a bibliometric analysis performed, Marin (2023) acknowledged that considerations on and research into the discussed construct tend to focus on the evaluation and the degree of employee commitment to the organization (affective commitment), the calculation of opportunities and risks associated with remaining with the organization (continuance commitment), and the moral obligation to continue working for the organization (normative commitment). Such an approach confirms the three-component model offered by Meyer and Allen (1991), according to whom attitudes and behaviors can assume various forms, mutually intertwining with and complementing one another.

Kim et al. (2011) emphasize that affective (emotional) commitment is the dominant aspect of organizational commitment, firstly, because it has its origin in employee attitudes toward the organization, and secondly, because organizations are willing to stimulate this type of commitment in relation to the other two, due to its association with employee efficiency and organization financials. Because of the above, it is not infrequent that management or psychology theorists subject to analysis only the discussed component without a comprehensive analysis of organizational commitment.

It should be noted that the processes that stimulate affective commitment are above all associated with the internalization of organizational values (Akin, 2021) and employee identification with the company goals (Lizote et al., 2019). Stazyk and Davis (2021), who studied a group of senior managers in local governments in the United States, discovered that the alignment of values held by employees with the organizational ones is significantly associated with higher levels of organizational commitment. The result of the said correlation is an intrinsic motivation generating in the employee genuine willingness to stay with the organization (Callado et al., 2023).

Studies on affective commitment also underscore the aspect of employee autonomy. On the basis of a research carried out in public hospitals in Pakistan, Zeshan et al. (2023) were able to confirm the moderating influence of the interrelation between the fulfillment of the need for autonomy and mindfulness in the workplace on affective commitment. One's sense of work meaningfulness is also a major factor reducing turnover intention. The studies performed in that field by Murray and Holmes (2021) demonstrated a positive correlation between one's sense of meaningfulness and the feeling of emotional attachment, understood as affective commitment.

Meanwhile, the research on continuance commitment presents this component from the perspective of the balance of costs and losses associated with one's decision to leave the organization. Cohen (2007) points out that there should be distinct indicators to analyze the aspect of calculation and the continuance commitment. In his view, continuance commitment concerns the evaluation of benefits from staying with the organization against the obligation to continue one's participation, which results from the evaluation of the turnover cost. According to Lewicka and Rakowska (2017), among other scholars, the discussed dimension is of an instrumental nature.

There is a complementary component to the concept of organizational commitment, namely that of normative commitment, characterized by a sense of employee loyalty and obligation toward the organization (Vandenberghe et al., 2014; Yao et al., 2019). It is this dimension of organizational commitment that is responsible for the moral obligation to continue working for the organization felt by the employee. Theoretical reflection on that issue (Morrow, 1993) indicates that the aspect of normative commitment should be regarded as the result of cultural and organizational adjustment of the individual to the organization with a particular emphasis on employee loyalty. The distinctive trait of persons with a high level of normative commitment is that they consider remaining in the organization to be their obligation and duty (Jaros, 2017).

The literature analysis conducted in the field of organizational commitment offers a basis to the claim that the respective components of organizational commitment correspond to the various mindsets that can intertwine with and mutually complement one another in a coherent manner. These can assume different forms, such as one's willingness to stay with the organization, one's perception of turnover costs, and the moral obligation to participate in company operations. The intensity of the three states is a reflection of employee's level of organizational commitment.

### ***The Essence and Determinants of Job Involvement***

Our literature survey on the notion of job involvement and the conclusions drawn from the systematic literature review conducted by Salessi and Omar (2019) and Brown (1996) suggest that a majority of researchers frame the construct according to the postulation of Kanungo (1982). The authors defined job involvement as a cognitive or belief state of psychological identification with one's profession (Salessi & Omar, 2019).

Lewicka and Pec (2018) point out not only that job involvement is associated with specific tasks performed by the employee but also that it does not have to bear on their general attitude to work, which means that an individual gets involved in performing their job, which accords with their internal values, beliefs, and the characteristics of the professional situation they identify with.

Moynihan and Pandey (2007) further claim that job involvement serves as a kind of a regulator of a person's level of identification with their work, which they actively participate in and believe that such a regulator's operation is significant for their sense of self-efficacy, self-esteem, and the construction of their self-image. Similar conclusions were presented by Kim (2023). The analysis of empirical data obtained from 398 respondents outlines a pattern in which the sense of self-efficacy is significantly correlated with job involvement and general level of efficiency. Meanwhile, Duffy et al. (2011) demonstrated that individuals who perceive themselves as valuable and important for their organization record higher levels of self-motivation and job involvement.

In other words, job involvement is based on the perception of how a specific job is able to satisfy the most important psychological needs of employees (Diefendorff et al., 2020). Thus, according to this view, job involvement is a personalized relationship between the worker and the work, with the strength of this relationship determining how the existing work conditions are perceived (Scott, 2022). Persons with high intensity of job involvement exhibit dedication to their professional roles and identification therewith (Demir, 2020). They find working to exceed what is expected from them extremely important because they believe efficiency to be, as it were, a leverage to build their self-worth and self-efficacy (Kreitner & Kinichi, 2009).

An important aspect that unifies the sense of self-efficacy with job involvement, according to Yusnita (2021), is that of organizational climate. Based on her analysis of the research findings, the scholar declared that a sense of self-efficacy plays a major intermediary role between organizational climate and job involvement. She further explains that organizational climate stimulates the sense of self-efficacy which in turn contributes to a higher level of job involvement. Other authors (Govender & Parumasur, 2010) place emphasis on the importance of a stimulating work environment, thus confirming that in order to foster job involvement, one needs to satisfy the individual psychological needs of employees.

Concluding, studies on the determinants of job involvement indicate the significance of both individual and situational factors. The former include competences and relatively stable personality traits. The latter, on the other hand, refer predominantly to task meaningfulness, perceptions of professional role, and organizational climate. An analysis of selected data from literature (Salessi & Omar, 2019) showed that researchers today tend to focus rather on the predictive role of situational variables. In this sense, research findings underscore the major influence of organizational climate and culture via employee management practices and organizational values significant in the context of psychological needs of employees and hence via stimulating their internal state of job involvement. This feedback results in employees building their self-worth. They are fully involved in their work: (a) when their job is their main interest in life; (b) when they participate actively in their work; (c) when they see their results as the most significant component of their self-worth or self-esteem; and (d) when they see their results as coherent with their concept of themselves (Saleh & Hosek, 1976).

The research has also revealed that the great significance for employee self-worth ascribed to work performance may in the case of job involvement provide an explanation, at least to some extent, for the low negative employee reactions to psychological contract violations. This aspect was studied by Stoner and Gallagher (2010) in a research on how psychological contract violations committed by employers impact job involvement. The authors researched a group of respondents comprising an appropriately selected cross-section of employees in a mid-size US town. On the basis of the analysis conducted, the researchers concluded that employees with a high level of job involvement are less prone to negative consequences of psychological contract violations. This means that the construct shows no significant correlation with mood deterioration or turnover intention. Furthermore, the authors add that the higher the level of job involvement in employees, the less they are liable to various stress factors at work.

## Results of Comparative Analysis of Work Engagement and Related Constructs

The comparative analysis of the notion of work engagement and related constructs, conducted on the basis of a literature review, cannot be deemed complete due to the vast amount of literature on the subject and the need to limit the scope of the analysis to a selection of papers. It does, however, enable us to make certain significant, albeit preliminary, observations and tackle the research questions posed in the analysis.

- First, all these constructs, that is, work engagement, organizational commitment, and job involvement, are related to the man–work relationship and involve interrelations.
- Second, even though, admittedly, the range of mutual references establishes a set of common or similar aspects in framing the man–work relationship, the actual network of these connections indicates no overlap of the constructs.
- Third, in relation to each construct, it is possible to indicate a distinct and vital approach to work that defines it. Thus, in the case of work engagement, it is a sense of well-being and inner harmony experienced in the workplace and the positive emotions associated therewith. In the case of organizational commitment, meanwhile, there is a strong component of attachment to the organization grounded in the identification of shared goals and the alignment of fundamental values in the employee–organization relationship. As for job involvement, there is a clear connection with intrinsic motivation, considering that results achieved by employees determine their self-esteem.
- Fourth, the above observations also justify a claim that fostering work engagement and organizational commitment depends largely on the organization and situational factors at work. At the same time, the role of organization is different in either case. With regard to work engagement, the organization is the source of well-being and positive emotions, whereas in relation to organizational commitment, the organization with its goals and values is the object of attachment. Job involvement, on the other hand, is marked by individual personal resources of employees because of the correlation between work results and a boost in self-esteem.

The results of the diversification analysis of work engagement and related constructs were subsequently confronted with the findings of research carried out in a similar field by Hallberg and Schaufeli (2006), as well as those offered by Adamska-Chudzińska and Andraszak (2023, p. 64). It enabled us to complement and alleviate the imperfections stemming from the limitations of the method applied and the scope of the analysis. Consequently, it was assumed that there are intercorrelations between the analyzed constructs and that these notions are interconnected, but simultaneously that they are related to other aspects of the man–work relationship. Thus, the semantic content of work engagement, organizational commitment, and job involvement indicates that they are indeed distinct constructs (Hallberg & Schaufeli, 2006). A comprehensive overview of integrated results is provided in Table 1.1.

It has been established that work engagement can be empirically distinguished from related constructs intended to measure employee engagement. The conceptualization of work engagement reveals it to be strongly associated with a sense of well-being and positive emotions experienced in the workplace. These are the

*Table 1.1* Diversity of constructs related to the notion of employee engagement

| *Category of engagement* | *Reference object* | *Source of activity* | *Context of engagement* | *Essence of engagement* | *Key factors* |
|---|---|---|---|---|---|
| Work engagement | Man–work relationship | Well-being and positive emotions in the workplace resulting from the social context | Positive qualities of the work environment, personality traits | Activity resulting from psychological presence in the workplace | Work climate, respect for identity, managerial support, autonomy, task meaning, work–life balance |
| Organizational commitment | Man–work relationship | Attitude of attachment to the organization based on identification with organizational goals and values | Positive goals and values of the work environment, personality traits | Activity resulting from identification with the organization | Accepted goals and values, autonomy, task meaning, pros of staying with the organization, norm of loyalty |
| Job involvement | Man–work relationship | Intrinsic motivation fostered by the value of a particular profession/job for employee's self-esteem | Great significance of professional tasks and their results, personality traits | Activity resulting from self-evaluation in the organizational context | Sense of empowerment, high performance as a token of worth, identification with professional role, organizational climate |

*Source:* Own work based on the literature survey

preconditions for high levels of energy invested in work. This does not rule out being dedicated, enthusiastic, and inspired by one's tasks, proper to the notion of job involvement, or being absorbed and attached to one's organization, distinctive of that of organizational commitment. The variance in shared references does not indicate the identity of constructs. Each measures a different aspect of employee engagement. According to Morrow (1983), work engagement should be analyzed by way of defining precise aspects of that engagement (using precise units), taking into consideration conceptual differences between the constructs.

Work engagement is generated in the domain of health and mental well-being, and as such, it is above all the reflection of an employee's psychological presence in the organization. This aspect is what differentiates it from the other constructs. Work Engagement Determinants model is presented in Figure 1.1. According to

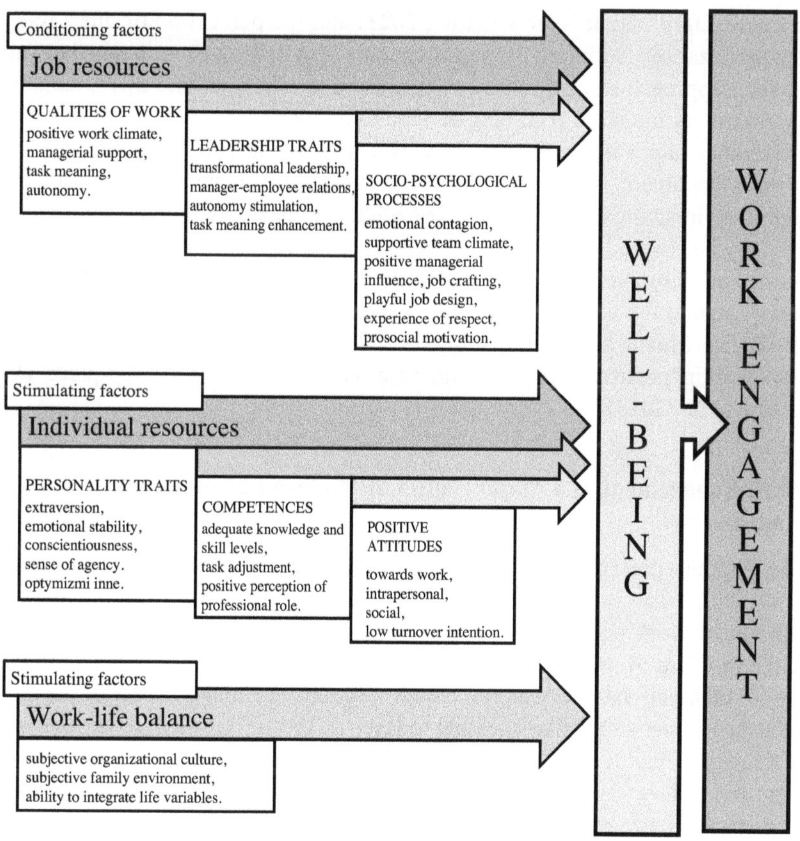


*Figure 1.1* Work Engagement Determinants model

*Source:* Own work based on the literature survey

this model, fundamental significance is attributed to factors behind psychological presence in the workplace, that is, qualities of job resources that produce a friendly social context for preforming work and the sense of well-being as an intermediate state to achieving high levels of engagement. The factors generating it are, above all, supportive relationships within the team, task meaning, autonomy, job crafting, playful job design, the experience of respect, prosocial motivation, and so on.

While characterizing the determinants of work engagement, one should also consider individual resources stimulating well-being as an intermediary state to achieving high levels of engagement. These include the relatively stable and the more flexible employee personality traits that determine levels of proactivity at work (Bakker et al., 2018; Tanaka & Morioka, 2023). What should also be pointed out – as it has been with the earlier concepts of motivation – are the adequacy of employee competence with regard to task requirements (Adamska-Chudzińska & Huculak, 2019; Kristof-Brown et al., 2023) and the perception of one's role in the organization. Additionally, significant are also employee attitudes that valuate their approach to work, to themselves, and to others around them, including their turnover intention (Hallberg & Schaufeli, 2006).

Another factor that enhances employee well-being and, consequently, their work engagement is the experience of work–life balance, not infrequently addressed in studies on this issue. Researchers underscore that the said balance can only be ensured by organizational culture grounded in respect for employee personhood, supportive family environment, and, accordingly, the ability to accommodate the vicissitudes of life (Tanaka & Morioka, 2023; Handayani et al., 2023). Meanwhile, stimulating factors exhibit a positive correlation with empowering positive emotions and creative thinking in the workplace (Van Roekel et al., 2023).

## Work Engagement as a Major Aspect of Modern Personnel Management

The findings presented provide the basis for addressing the objective of our study, which was aimed at demonstrating that managerial activities based on the concept of work engagement offer a platform for fostering efficient solutions to the problem of low employee involvement in contemporary organizations. It should be noted that the search for such solutions is a major aspect of the shifts occurring in personnel management today.

Engaged employees prove highly beneficial for organizations. Work engagement has a direct and positive influence on employee performance as it mediates variables oriented toward learning and development (Qodarian et al., 2019). Engaged employees record high levels of energy directed to work and perseverance in performing it and overcoming difficulties. They take initiative and are open to new ideas and undertakings. Thus, as observed by Reijseger et al. (2017), they strongly influence the efficiency and performance of the entire organization. The authors further demonstrate that this correlation rests on psychological processes experienced by employees and the care for their mental health.

Meanwhile, high indicators (Gallup Report, 2023) of the number of disengaged employees, the fluctuations of employee engagement, and the weakened bond between workers and their organization raise managers' concerns about their increasingly impaired communication with employees and challenges to organizational efficiency and performance. These intensify with the growing complexity and uncertainty of the conditions in which organizations operate and the changes in the approach to employees which indicate higher importance of a friendly work environment that fosters well-being and is sensitive to their identity as persons, needs, and achievements.

The concept of work engagement seems to suggest a valid theoretical basis and direction for the desired solutions to the issues related to declining employee involvement. Nevertheless, it presents modern managers with a major challenge of shaping such conditions of work environment that would allow employees to experience psychological presence and a sense of well-being in the workplace, in the broad sense. The efforts undertaken toward that goal may generate a strategic advantage for the organization. In that regard, one should note the mutual benefits for the employee and the organization. As demonstrated by Turner (2020), employees with good jobs (that generate positive emotions) who are respectfully managed will not only be happier, healthier, and more fulfilled but also be, or therefore, more willing to improve productivity and create better products, services, and innovation. Furthermore, engaged employees work in a way that maximizes their efficiency, which may have a beneficial influence on their health and well-being. These mutual influences are reflected in organizational effectiveness, heightened profitability, and increased value for the stakeholders (Turner, 2020).

In the context of the assumptions behind the work engagement concept, fostering highly engaged human resources in organizations requires allowing for the factors promoting psychological presence in the workplace in the management strategies applied. As demonstrated in the literature review, these are formed predominantly on the basis of positive emotions experienced in relation to job resources, which include qualities of work, leadership traits, and socio-psychological processes. The main factors fostering psychological presence in the workplace are as follows:

- Positive relationships with colleagues and a supportive team climate
- Transformational leadership style and emotional support from the manager
- Autonomous role of the employee in performing tasks
- Genuine significance (meaning) of the tasks performed
- Ability to design one's work
- Prosocial attitudes and the experience of respect

The above factors were identified on the basis of the literature review. By no means do they exhaust the list of important factors for fostering positive emotional dimension in the work environment. Considering, however, that they are among the most often tackled in studies on the subject matter at hand, we can cautiously assume that they do in fact constitute key aspects influencing employees' psychological presence in the organization. This influence also benefits from individual resources of employees and their ability to maintain work–life balance, but these tend to stimulate the positive aspects of job resources. In the survey performed, they were not widely represented.

The findings of the analysis enabled us to confirm the assumption that employee involvement management based on the work engagement concept provides significant opportunities for finding effective solutions to the problem of engagement volatility and low organizational attachment. It should be noted that this study is also prone to certain limitations associated with the fact that quality assessment of the analyzed research has not been made, nor has a detailed account of the research procedure been provided, which are the byproducts of the scoping review method. The need to carry out a selection of the papers for analysis, caused by the vast amount of available literature, on the other hand, indicates that the effort made for the items actually analyzed can be regarded as a partial representation of a sample literature on the matter researched. Furthermore, the factors of the work engagement model presented above have not been framed in terms of their potential dependencies and effects on employees' sense of well-being. These references may serve to set the direction for further research in the analyzed field. It would also be important, in the studies to come, to expand the scope of research with the application of qualitative and quantitative methods that would make it possible to verify and further specify the set of factors fostering an employee's psychological presence in the organization, as presented in this analysis. Thus, the researched phenomenon offers room for further exploration.

## Conclusion

The significance of employee engagement finds its reflection both in academic research and in the insights into managerial practice. The literature review carried out revealed that employee engagement reaches beyond a single point of view (e.g., psychological, sociological, or organizational perspective); therefore, in outlining strategies for employee involvement management, it is vital to connect a given concept with the type of problems that are to be solved on its basis. The study demonstrated that a valid foundation for solving problems related to the fluctuations of employee involvement can be sought for in the concept of work engagement.

The synthesis of research work demonstrated that work engagement is a positive mindset accompanied by the willingness to spend high levels of energy on long-term work. Work engagement is regarded as a multi-component construct that develops in the context of employee relations with the respective components of their work environment. Additionally, personal resources of employees and their ability to balance various aspects of life also have a stimulating effect thereon.

It has been established that the construct of work engagement is a systemic structure that permeates numerous aspects of individual and organizational life. It plays out in the individual emotional experience of every employee. It is formed in the social dimension, that is, it depends on social relationships and the physical work environment in which these relationships develop, fostering the sense of employee well-being. Lastly, it is conditioned by organizational forms of work engagement management, including transformational leadership style and fostering of human-centered work environment. A positive synchronization of all these levels enables employees to experience psychological presence in the workplace, which constitutes the fundamental condition for generating highly engaged human resources.

## References

Abet, Z., Anuar, M. M., Arshad, M. M., & Ismail, I. A. (2024). Factors affecting turnover intention of Nigerian employees: The moderation effect of organizational commitment. *Heliyon*, *10*(1), 4. https://doi.org/10.1016/j.heliyon.2023.e23087

Adamska-Chudzińska, M., & Andraszak, N. (2023). *Podejście sytuacyjne w zarządzaniu zaangażowaniem w organizację*. PWN.

Adamska-Chudzińska, M., & Huculak, M. (2019). Employee-organizational fit as a factor in leveraging human capital for integrated growth. *Social Inequality and Economic Growth*, *58*, 92–104.

Akin, U. (2021). Exploring the relationship between emotional labor and organizational commitment levels of teachers. *Eurasian Journal of Educational Research*, *91*, 61–82. https://doi.org/10.14689/ejer.2021.91.4

Bakker, A. B. (2022). The social psychology of work engagement: State of the field. *Career Development International*, *27*(1), 36–53. https://doi.org/10.1108/CDI-08-2021-0213

Bakker, A. B., Hetland, J., Olsen, O. K., & Espevik, R. (2018). Daily strengths use and employee well-being: The moderating role of personality. *Journal of Occupational and Organizational Psychology*, *92*, 144–168.

Brown, S. P. (1996). A meta-analysis and review of organizational research on job involvement. *Psychological Bulletin*, *120*(2), 235–255. https://doi.org/10.1037/0033-2909.120.2.235

Callado, A., Teixeira, G., & Lucas, P. (2023). Turnover intention and organizational commitment of primary healthcare nurses. *Healthcare*, *11*, 521, 1–12. https://doi.org/10.3390/healthcare11040521

Chang, P. C., Xiaoxiao, G., & Wu, T. (2021). Sense of calling, job crafting, spiritual leadership and work meaningfulness: A moderated mediation model. *Leadership & Organization Development Journal*, *42*(5), 690–704. https://doi.org/10.1108/LODJ-09-2020-0392

Cohen, A. (2007). Commitment before and after: An evaluation and reconceptualization of organizational commitment. *Human Resource Management Review*, *17*(3), 336–354. https://doi.org/10.1016/j.hrmr.2007.05.001

Cohen, A. (2021). How to quit your job in the great post-pandemic resignation boom. *Bloomberg*. https://www.bloomberg.com/news/articles/2021-05-10/quit-your-job-how-to-resign-after-covid-pandemic

Ćwiklicki, M. (2020). Metodyka przeglądu zakresu literatury. In A. Sopińska & A. Modliński (Eds.), *Współczesne zarządzanie – koncepcje i wyzwania* (pp. 53–68). SGH.

Demir, S. (2020). The role of self-efficacy in job satisfaction, organizational commitment, motivation and job involvement. *Eurasian Journal of Educational Research*, *85*, 205–224. https://doi.org/10.14689/ejer.2020.85.10

Diefendorff, B. M., Nolan, M. T., Tseng, S. T., Kenworthy, M. E., & Fiorentino, N. L. (2020). Job involvement. In V. I. Sessa & N. A. Bowling (Red.), *Essentials of job attitudes and other workplace psychological constructs* (pp. 129–155). Routledge.

Duffy, R. D., Manuel, R. S., Borges, N. J., & Bott, E. M. (2011). Calling, vocational development, and well-being: A longitudinal study of medical students. *Journal of Vocational Behavior*, *79*(2), 361–366. https://doi.org/10.1016/j.jvb.2011.03.023

Fortuin, D. J., van Mierlo, H., Bakker, A. B., Petrou, P., & Demerouti, E. (2021). Team boosting behaviours: Development and validation of a new concept and scale. *European Journal of Work and Organizational Psychology*, *30*(4), 600–618. https://doi.org/10.1080/1359432X.2020.1854226

Gallup Report. (2023). *State of the global workplace 2023 report: The voice of the world's employees*. https://www.gallup.com/workplace/349484/state-of-the-global-workplace.aspx#ite-506891

Govender, S., & Parumasur, S. B. (2010). The relationship between employee motivation and job involvement. *South African Journal of Economic and Management Sciences*, *13*(3), 237–253. https://doi.org/10.4102/sajems.v13i3.102

Hallberg, U. E., & Schaufeli, W. B. (2006). "Same same" but different? Can work engagement be discriminated from job involvement and organizational commitment? *European Psychologist*, *11*(2), 119–127. https://doi.org/10.1027/1016-9040.11.2.119

Handayani, N. S., Ancok, D., & Putri, D. K. (2023). Happiness in the workplace of women lecturers based on work-family balance and work engagement. *Russian Psychological Journal*, *20*(2), 94–105. https://doi.org/10.21702/rpj.2023.2.6

Hoehl, S., Fairhurst, M., & Schirmer, A. (2021). Interactional synchrony: Signals, mechanisms and benefits. *Social Cognitive and Affective Neuroscience*, *16*, 5–18.

Jaros, S. (2017). A critique of normative commitment in management research. *Management Research Review*, *40*(5), 517–537. https://doi.org/10.1108/MRR-08-2016-0200

Kanungo, R. N. (1982). Measurement of job and work involvement. *Journal of Applied Psychology*, *67*(3), 341–349. https://doi.org/10.1037/0021-9010.67.3.341

Kim, B. C., Lee, G., Murrmann, S. K., & George, T. R. (2011). Motivational effects of empowerment on employees' organizational commitment: A mediating role of management trustworthiness. *Cornell Hospitality Quarterly*, *53*(1), 10–19. https://doi.org/10.1177/1938965511426

Kim, J. S. (2023). Effect of psychological meaningfulness on job involvement, proactive behavior, and performance: Focusing on the mediating effect of self-efficacy. *Sustainability*, *15*(13), 1–14. https://doi.org/10.3390/su151310208

Klotz, A. C., & Bolino, M. C. (2022). When quiet quitting is worse than the real thing. *Harvard Business Review: Managing Employees*. https://hbr.org/2022/09/when-quiet-quitting-is-worse-than-the-real-thing

Kooij, D., Nijssen, H., Bal, P. M., & van der Kruijssen, D. (2020). Crafting an interesting job: Stimulating an active role of older workers in enhancing their daily work engagement and job performance. *Work, Aging and Retirement*, *6*(3), 165–174. https://doi.org/10.1093/workar/waaa001

Kreitner, R., & Kinichi, A. (2009). *Organizational behaviour* (9th ed.). Mc Graw-Hill International Edition.
Kristof-Brown, A., Schneider, B., & Su, R. (2023). Person-organization fit theory and research: Conundrums, conclusions, and calls to action. *Personnel Psychology*, *76*(2), 375–412. https://doi.org/10.1111/peps.12581
Lambert, T. (2022). The great resignation, unemployment, and underemployment in the US: A study of labor market segmentation. *MPRA*, 114067. https://mpra.ub.uni-muenchen.de/114067/
Lewicka, D., & Pec, M. (2018). The impact of human resources management on job involvement: The mediating role of vertical trust. *Folia Oeconomica Stetinensia*, *18*(2). https://doi.org/10.2478/foli-2018-0017
Lewicka, D., & Rakowska, A. (2017). Calculative and affective commitment – The case study of the best polish employer "gaz transmission operator". *Argumenta Oeconomica*, *2*(39), 213–237. https://doi.org/10.15611/aoe.2017.2.09
Lizote, S. A., Alves, C. S. R., & Cavalheiro, C. C. (2019). Perceived organizational factor, internal marketing and organizational commitment in university teachers. *Revista Pensamento Contemporâneo em Administração*, *13*(2), 91. https://doi.org/10.12712/rpca.v13i2.28209
Majcen, J., Tonković Grabovac, M., & Černja Rajter, I. (2023). Recovery experiences and work engagement: The role of emotions at work. *Psihologija*, *56*(3), 305–322. https://doi.org/10.2298/PSI210721017M
Marin, R. (2023). Organizational commitment: A bibliometric analysis. *Proceedings of the International Conference on Business Excellence*, *17*(1), 1227–1239. https://doi.org/10.2478/picbe-2023-0110
Meyer, J. P., & Allen, N. J. (1991). A three-component conceptualization of organizational commitment. *Human Resource Management Review*, *1*(1), 61–89. https://doi.org/10.1016/1053-4822(91)90011-Z
Meyer, J. P., & Allen, N. J. (1997). *Commitment in the workplace: Theory, research, and application*. Sage.
Morrow, P. C. (1983). Concept redundancy in organizational research: The case work of commitment. *The Academy of Management Review*, *8*(3), 486–500. https://doi.org/10.2307/257837
Morrow, P. C. (1993). *The theory and measurement of work commitment*. JAI Press Inc.
Moynihan, D. P., & Pandey, S. J. (2007). Finding workable levers over work motivation: Comparing job satisfaction, job involvement, and organizational commitment. *Administration & Society*, *39*(7), 803–832. https://doi.org/10.1177/009539970730554
Mukaihata, T., Fujimoto, H., & Greiner, C. (2020). Factors influencing work engagement among psychiatric nurses in Japan. *Journal of Nursing Management*, *28*(2), 306–316. https://doi.org/10.1111/jonm.12923
Murray, W. C., & Holmes, M. R. (2021). Impacts of employee empowerment and organizational commitment on workforce sustainability. *Sustainability*, *13*(6), 1–14. https://doi.org/10.3390/su13063163
Peterson, J., Pearce, P. F., Ferguson, L. A., & Langford, C. A. (2017). Understanding scoping reviews: Definition, purpose, and process. *Journal of the American Association of Nurse Practitioners*, *29*(1), 12–16. https://doi.org/10.1002/2327-6924.12380
Prakash, P., & Kashyap, B. (2021). Relationship between employees' workplace well-being and work engagement. *Elementary Education Online*, *20*(2), 2300–2306.
Qodarian Akbar, M., & Mauluddin, M. (2019). Effect of work engagement, job satisfaction, and organizational to employee performance. *International Journal of Recent Technology and Engineering*, *8*(2), 815–822. https://doi.org/10.35940/ijrte.B1164.0782S419

Reijseger, G., Peeters, M. C. W., Taris, T. W., & Schaufeli, W. B. (2017). From motivation to activation: Why engaged workers are better performers. *Journal of Business and Psychology*, *32*(2), 117–130. https://doi.org/10.1007/s10869-016-9435-z

Rusu, P. P., & Colomeischi, A. A. (2020). Positivity ratio and well-being among teachers: The mediating role of work engagement. *Frontiers in Psychology*, *11*, 1608. https://doi.org/10.3389/fpsyg.2020.01608

Saleh, S. D., & Hosek, J. (1976). Job involvement: Concepts and measurements. *Business Academy of Management Journal*, *19*(2), 213–224. https://doi.org/10.5465/255773

Salessi, S., & Omar, A. (2018). Dark triad of personality, job satisfaction and organizational cynicism: A structural model. *Universitas Psychologica*, *17*, 21–32.

Salessi, S., & Omar, A. (2019). Job involvement in current research: Update and state of the art. *Psychologist Papers*, *40*(1), 46–56. https://doi.org/10.23923/pap.psicol2019.2882

Schaufeli, W. B., Salanova, M., Gonzàlez-Romä, V., & Bakker, A. B. (2002). The measurement of engagement and job burnout: A two-sample confirmatory factor analytic approach. *Journal of Happiness Studies*, *3*, 71–93.

Scott, K. S. (2022). Making sense of work: Finding meaning in work narratives. *Journal of Management & Organization*, *28*(5), 1057–1077. https://doi.org/10.1017/jmo.2019.43

Serenko, A. (2023). The great resignation: The great knowledge exodus or theon set of the great knowledge revolution? *Journal of Knowledge Management*, *27*, 1042–1055.

Solarczyk-Ambrozik, E. (2015). Nowe trendy w teoriach rozwoju karier – implikacje dla poradnictwa kariery. *Studia Edukacyjne*, *35*.

Stazyk, E. C., & Davis, R. S. (2021). Birds of a feather: How manager-subordinate disagreement on goal clarity influences value congruence and organizational commitment. *International Review of Administrative Sciences*, *87*(1), 39–59. https://doi.org/10.1177/0020852319827082

Stoner, J. S., & Gallagher, V. C. (2010). Who cares? The role of job involvement in psychological contract violation. *Journal of Managerial Psychology*, *40*(6), 1490–1514. https://doi.org/10.1111/j.1559-1816.2010.00626.x

Sypniewska, B., Baran, M., & Kłos, M. (2023). Work engagement and employee satisfaction in the practice of sustainable human resource management – Based on the study of Polish employees. *International Entrepreneurship and Management Journal*, *19*, 1069–1100.

Tanaka, K., & Morioka, I. (2023). Factors related to work engagement in occupational health nurses: From both aspects of work environmental and individual factors. *Nihon eiseigaku zasshi. Japanese Journal of Hygiene*, *78*. https://doi.org/10.1265/jjh.22004

Tims, M., Bakker, A. B., & Xanthopoulou, D. (2011). Do transformational leaders enhance their followers' daily work engagement? *The Leadership Quarterly*, *22*, 121–131.

Turner, P. (2020). Engagement driven strategic HRM. In V. I. Sessa & N. A. Bowling (Eds.), *Employee engagement in contemporary organizations*. Palgrave Macmillan. https://doi.org/10.1007/978-3-030-36387-1_9

Van Roekel, H., Wigger, E. F. J., Veldkamp, B. P., & Bakker, A. B. (2023). What is work engagement? A text mining approach using employees' self-narratives. *Applied Psychology*, 1–32. https://doi.org/10.1111/apps.12501

Vandenberghe, C., Mignonac, K., & Manville, C. (2014). When normative commitment leads to lower well-being and reduced performance. *Human Relations*, *68*(5), 843–870. https://doi.org/10.1177/001872671454706

Yao, T., Qiu, Q., & Wei, Y. (2019). Retaining hotel employees as internal customers: Effect of organizational commitment on attitudinal and behavioral loyalty of employees. *International Journal of Hospitality Management*, *76*(Part A), 1–8. https://doi.org/10.1016/j.ijhm.2018.03.018

Yusnita, N. (2021). Does self-efficacy play an intervening role? Studying between organizational climate and job involvement. *Journal of Humanities and Social Studies*, *5*(1), 44–49. https://doi.org/10.33751/jhss.v5i1.3207

Zeshan, M., de La Villarmois, O., Rasool, S., & Niazi, A. R. K. (2023). The perfect moment is this one. The effect of mindfulness on employees: A perspective from self-determination theory. *International Journal of Organizational Analysis*, *31*(7), 12. https://doi.org/10.1108/IJOA-07-2022-3346

# 2 Determinants of Employee Well-being

*Mariusz Makowski*

## Introduction

The issues related to employee well-being have gained prominence both among management practitioners and scholars over the last dozen or so years. It was noted that this construct largely accounts for the reasons of employee turnover and sickness absence (Wright & Bonett, 2007). When the level of well-being in an organization is too low, these negative phenomena escalate. There is a positive correlation, on the other hand, between high levels of well-being and a series of positive dimensions of work, such as high-quality employee relationships, work efficiency, work engagement, satisfaction with the tasks performed, and organizational attachment (Kamdron, 2005; Ford et al., 2011). In view of the shortage of qualified employees, fostering employee well-being – no longer a matter of auxiliary effort but of necessity – requires staff education on the topic and constant monitoring of its levels. In order to effectively increase employee well-being, it is necessary to both precisely define what it means for an employee and recognize a set of organizational, macroeconomic, cultural, and individual conditions that influence the processes of well-being development or deterioration.

The objective of this chapter is to analyze the factors that foster and those that decrease employee well-being by way of performing a critical review of selected concepts. Effort has been made to present a multiplicity of connections and interdependencies that link well-being with the person's system of values, engagement, motivation, personhood, and self-awareness. On the basis of Hobfoll's classic conservation of resources theory, a review of assets that may influence the level of well-being was conducted. The fact that well-being is a state and a phenomenon subject to interdisciplinary perspective led to the decision that the considerations here be limited to industrial and organizational psychology, as well as health psychology. The notion of well-being is a complex and ambiguous one; it is understood differently depending on the research discipline. Within I-O psychology, it is the central construct that conditions a series of job qualities that are positive for both the employee and the organization, such as

DOI: 10.4324/9781032715407-3

employee engagement and loyalty, productivity, health, and growth. Meanwhile, in management sciences, well-being is regarded as a desired, albeit not a prerequisite, state experienced by the employee. The text below presents data and argumentation in support of the psychological point of view. Additionally, it shows the mutual interpenetration and interdependence of the factors that determine well-being, both those of subjective origin and those resulting from the activity and operation of (and in) the organization. The first part of the chapter provides an outline of questions related to the definition of well-being and an account of the types of resources according to Hobfoll's conservation of resources theory. The latter part of the text discusses the various understandings of work meaning, person–job fit, and the potential of job crafting.

## The Meaning of Well-being

The plurality of ways to define well-being ranges between two main perspectives. The first of these is value-oriented. Within it, scholars speak of a hedonic or a eudaimonic point of view (see Czerw, 2017). Crucial for the other is the vantage point on the issue – whether we evaluate well-being as objective or whether we adopt an individual's assessment of their well-being as the basis for our conclusions (see Diener, 1984; Moore & Keyes, 2003). Hedonic well-being is based on the fulfillment of two categories: the experience of job satisfaction and positive emotional balance. In other words, to attain a high level of well-being, an employee needs to frequently experience job satisfaction ("my output is of high quality"; "I am pleased with the results of my work"; "I feel an important member and am proud of my team"; "this profession suits me well"), as well as feel significantly more positive than negative emotions. Offering attractive salary may be a vital element to foster this type of well-being ("I'm good at what I do and I'm paid well for it"). Eudaimonic approach broadens the requirements for achieving well-being by including the components of meaning and value of one's work. Here, work (its character and results) is regarded as a major life choice, as it can support a person's self-actualization, is beneficial for their broader social environment, is worthwhile for the person, and serves as an important source of their meaning of life. Well-being in its eudaimonic understanding does not rule out the possibility of satisfying one's hedonic needs; however, these are conditional and secondary to the sense of meaning and the fulfillment of personal values.

Well-being, though far from being an unambiguous construct, may be measured by its consequences. It has been noted that it is positively correlated with productivity, particularly in its long-term measurements (Harter et al., 2003). Moreover, when the level of well-being is high, teams record smaller number of conflicts, increased effective work time, strengthened employee loyalty, improved group relationships, and greater employee innovation and organizational attachment (Ford et al., 2011). Well-being fosters engagement, understood both as being fully invested in work activities, having high levels of energy and satisfaction, and as organizational commitment. On the grounds of psychology, this can be explained by referring to resource management. When employees have significant resources at their disposal, such as a sense of attachment and psychological safety in the workplace, they are likely to regard their work as meaningful and useful and, thus, valuable. They can see their work as well-managed and know that if they commit a mistake, they will receive support and guidance on how to avoid it in the future. It is then that they are able to dedicate themselves to their work completely, employing all their creative powers and providing significant value added for the enterprise. And conversely, when an employee has meager, limited resources, or when their resources are constantly drained (e.g., by terrible feedback system, inadequate work management, double standards from superiors), their orientation is not as much toward development as toward continuance (survival).

## Resources and Well-being

When looking at personal resources as the pillar of well-being, the application of Hobfoll's conservation of resources theory (Hobfoll, 2006) becomes a viable course of action. At the heart of this concept lies the thesis that people strive to achieve, retain, and protect what they find valuable. They tend to attach great importance to investing their resources, protecting them from being depleted or exchanged to others, to which Hobfoll refers globally as "resource economy." The key tenet of the conservation of resources theory, as far as operating under stress is concerned – and such is the reality of human work, is that people experience a loss or lack of a resource far more than the benefit of acquiring a new one. With modest personal resources, therefore, they are inclined to adopt a passive defensive strategy: "protect at all cost." Resources are not given once and for all; a continuous process of operation requires pursuing and gaining new assets, protecting the existing ones, and replacing those that have been lost. Having resources facilitates acquiring more. Hobfoll put together a list of 74 detailed resources, organized according to the following four categories:

- Personal resources (personality traits, sense of self-worth, attributional style, skills)
- Object resources (money, accommodation, work tools)
- Condition resources (employment, medical condition, relationship status, stage of life)
- Energy resources (vitality, knowledge, experience, motivation)

One could argue that having plentiful and diverse resources ensures employee well-being. It does follow from the picture of this situation that the person has increased the likelihood of having their needs met. Nevertheless, Bakker and

Demerouti in their job demands-resources model (2007) express the belief that well-being is a function of the relationship between employee's resources and job demands. In the context of the subject matter of this chapter, it seems interesting which employee resource categories belong to the organizational domain (with the organization either providing or developing those), and which fall in the personal domain (employees discover those within themselves, develop them intentionally, and draw on them).

As for personal resources, they may well seem to constitute a field totally dependent on the individual. This, in fact, is the case with such resources as the sense of self-worth (high, low), personality traits (e.g., extraversion, neuroticism), or attributional style (optimistic, pessimistic). These factors are relatively stable and, as demonstrated in numerous studies, significantly influence an individual's well-being and their sense of happiness. A high level of neuroticism and a pessimistic attributional style impair mental well-being (see Scheier et al., 2001; Chico-Libran, 2006). This determinant of employee well-being tends to be underestimated, particularly from the point of view of people managing large teams. Such managers are prone to overestimating the efficacy of programs implemented in order to improve the organizational climate; and they likewise overemphasize the importance of the employee benefit packages provided. One could say that in the aforementioned subset of personal resources, organizational activity reaches its limit. Employee skills can be regarded with slightly more optimism. These can be diagnosed and developed through various means, such as training sessions, mentoring, and ambitious goal setting. Employee development is possible in a team where workers feel supported and able to improve their skills and competences, which will result in their achieving a better person–job fit.

Object resources fall very much within the organizational domain. The remuneration for the job performed constitutes a very relevant component of employee well-being. It is, indeed, downright critical for employee groups who are motivated to perform their job by money ("it doesn't matter what, what matters is how much"). A salary that is too low in relation to demands leads to frustration and causes a sense of injustice, a feeling of being treated unfairly by the organization. An employee experiencing such states must find it ever more difficult to maintain the expected productivity level. In his theory of motivation, Herzberg (1968) referred to this domain of "material subsistence" as hygiene factors. According to him, with these needs unmet, it is difficult for an employee to do anything but the bare minimum (at work), that is, any and all developmental components are inactive. A similar view was shared by another author of a theory of motivation and needs, Maslow (1954), who stated that man needs to first satisfy the lower needs (food, safety, accommodation) in order for the higher needs to emerge, including the need of relationships, respect, and self-actualization. In our social functioning, we are driven by social comparisons, which play a major regulative role in it ("upward comparisons," "downward comparisons"). In this context, it is important for us to know both how much other people earn (more, less, as much), and what the salary of someone employed in the same position is. A negative comparison triggers a state known as relative deprivation. This means that a person does not experience frustration if everyone in their environment (the field of their social perception) suffers equally or is deprived of a certain good. However, when one notices that someone in the same situation has it better, say, because they benefit from a certain privilege or earn more even though they perform exactly the same job, that is when frustration arises. This is a consequential social issue on the verge of cultural and political context. It can be exemplified by the social conflicts around the pay gap between men and women, and the socio-legal dilemmas whether or not to implement pay transparency laws. Besides the amount, adequacy, and market reality of employee salary, it is also important that it is regular, timely paid, and the worker is eligible for a pay rise. A clear and solid bonus system and financial promotions regime are essential for providing an employee with object resources, which in turn ensures their well-being. Other object resources, such as workplace and work tools, belong to the organizational domain. Here is the room for implementing novel ergonomic solutions and innovation. We are still dealing here with the influence that an organization has on employee well-being; it is, however, an influence that is conditional. Expanded office space in another part of town may make sense if employees are also guaranteed a comfortable commute; the purchase of more state-of-the art equipment will be regarded as a benefit by employees provided that they are trained in its full and safe operation.

Condition resources are the subjective determinant of well-being. It can be contended that a person's attitude to their job is the crucial variable here. This is a case of eudaimonic well-being. Of crucial importance at this juncture is whether or not the employee recognizes the value of employment itself. The experience of gratitude is the modulator of this instance of condition resources, meaning that the more keenly the employee is aware of the fact that they acquire certain goods solely by virtue of their employment, the greater the value of this particular condition resource is for them. In positive psychology, gratitude is one of the major constructs; it is understood both as a mental state and as a personal trait (Watkins, 2013). Hence, it can constitute an emotional experience, a reaction to a specific event or insight, but it can also be a person's relatively stable attitude toward what they experience. It is defined as "the appreciation of what is valuable . . . for oneself" (Sansone & Sansone, 2010). The importance of individual perception has been emphasized here because it is *par excellence* a subjective contributor to well-being. In this instant, man is responsible for his well-being through his mental activity. There is room for choice here as to what the person does and does not want to see, what she or he wishes to value and what to disregard. The ability to be grateful benefits both the employee and the organization. At an individual level, gratitude leads to an increase in the number of prosocial acts and the strengthening of team relationships (Cameron & Spreitzer, 2012);

furthermore, it increases positive emotions toward one's profession (Emmons & Stern, 2013). From the organizational point of view, employee gratitude is positively correlated with their productivity (Fehr et al., 2017).

### *The Meaningfulness of Work*

What makes people realize the value of their work? According to scholars studying I-O psychology and work management (Pratt & Ashforth, 2003; Steger & Dik, 2010), it is perceiving the work that one performs as meaningful. They believe the need for meaning to be the crucial of employee needs, with its satisfaction impacting a series of dimensions and parameters of, and attitudes toward, work activities. They indirectly refer to the legacy and paradigm of humanistic psychology, which places at its center man's self-awareness, the intentionality of developmental activities, subjectivity, responsibility for one's fate, and the constant search for meaning (e.g., Frankl, 1962; Maslow, 1954).

In their model of work meaningfulness, Pratt and Ashforth (2003) identify three domains:

- Meaningfulness in work
- Meaningfulness at work
- Transcendence, meaningfulness of work

The authors believe that in order to relate to each of the above, employees need to answer the questions: "What do I do?" "Where do I belong?" "Who am I?" "What am I here for?"

The meaningfulness in work is related to the person–job fit, that is, the extent to which the person's individual resources, talents, skills, and experience align with the activities, tasks, and objectives typically assigned to their position in the organization. A good person–job fit requires adequacy, that is, both the employee's competencies and knowledge have to be sufficient, whereas the task they are assigned needs to be challenging and, conversely, cannot be too easy, trivial, way below their skill level. Moreover, employees have to be offered an appropriate range of autonomy and variety of activities and need to have many rewarding and valuable relationships in the workplace, both with their colleagues, superiors, and clients (Kahn, 1990).

The meaningfulness at work is related to the person–organization fit, that is, the extent to which a person is suitable for a specific organizational culture, with its values, rituals, norms, and goals. Employees experience a high sense of meaning when they feel recognized, respected, trusted, and treated fairly by the organization. An employee with a high sense of this type of meaningfulness feels at home in the company and identifies her- or himself with the organization, which is often reflected in the language they use when speaking about themselves, their higher-ups, and colleagues in the company using the first person plural – "we."

The meaningfulness at work is also fostered by a psychological contract that is balanced and adhered to (see Makin et al., 2000), that is, implicit expectations both on the part of the employee and of the organization (employer). At this point, Pratt and Ashforth (2003) further emphasize the importance of leadership within the organization. If it is transformational in nature – that is, if it comprises such interactions as modeling, authority, mentoring, coaching, stimulating ambition, and promoting a vision for growth – it thereby better facilitates the person–organization fit (see Avolio & Bass, 1991).

The meaningfulness of work (transcendence) is related most closely to the sense of professional identity, meaning the "self" that is largely based on one's professional occupation and activities associated therewith in the social sphere. The notion of "transcendence" refers here to going beyond one's personal goals toward social ones. In the context of work, we could identify it as a synonym of "service," "vocation," or "mission." The meaningfulness of work overlaps with a person's core values and the perception they have of their profession. This type of meaningfulness eludes precise definition to a greater degree than the ones discussed above. It can be conceived of as meaning: 1) a connection with something greater than oneself, movement beyond one's self through being committed to something; 2) the integration of the various aspects of one's self, such as personal traits and aptitudes, into a coherent system; 3) the state of self-development consisting in the actualization of one's potential and aspirations, stepping out of the *status quo* and one's limitations toward something new and greater than oneself (Pratt & Ashforth, 2003). As demonstrated in a study by Bailey and Madden (2016), the type of occupation is of no consequence in this context; the meaningfulness of work was experienced by persons in such diverse professions as refuse collectors, art restorers, and academic teachers. The authors of the model emphasize the "sensitivity" of the meaningfulness of work (as transcendence). It is somewhat akin to a calling, and it still is not completely clear whether or not meaning-enhancing activities and person–organization fit have a direct bearing on the meaningfulness of work. Furthermore, employees can define their sense of meaning *elsewhere*, based not on their work, but, say, on the family, religion, hobby, which – by the way – is their inalienable right. Thus, it is a highly subjective phenomenon; to quote Pratt and Ashforth (2003, p. 325), who rephrased a well-known saying: "Meaning is in the eye of the beholder."

Other condition resources, such as one's medical state, close emotional relationships, and the stage of life, fall within the sphere of individual responsibility. Although here, too, organizational culture and climate create an interdependence. An employee takes up an occupation in a specific health state, which may undergo a negative change when they are exposed to the toxic atmosphere in the company, when job demands exceed contractual arrangements, when the business violates health and safety regulations, when one is forced to carry out work tasks in harmful conditions, and so on. On the other hand, an employee aware of these threats may undertake protective and remedial measures.

Successful personal life (close relationships, friendships, family), a major pillar of well-being, requires deliberate care and time. Work overload may affect work–life balance to the detriment of the latter. Also in that regard, however, organizational culture that honors this balance proves to be of primary importance for maintaining well-being.[1] It should be added that an often-overlooked facet of this issue is the actual quality of leisure time. The problem lies in whether what employees do after work fosters their health, resource growth, and development, or whether that sphere of their lives is rife with stressors, draining their energy and reducing their well-being and/or happiness. Having a partner or a family has a beneficial influence on a person's well-being; numerous studies have demonstrated that successful long-term relationships increase life expectancy and improve life satisfaction, particularly in men (Manzoli et al., 2007; Wilcox & Wolfinger, 2024). On the other hand, staying in unsatisfactory and toxic relationships or going through the process of divorce takes a dire toll on the mentality of the persons involved. One could venture that it hardly matters that an organization undertakes to strictly and comprehensively protect work–life balance, and its employees enjoy much time off to take care of themselves if, having finished their work for the day, they enter a world in which they can hardly rest, regenerate, or revitalize themselves, with their everyday reality being that of a constant struggle for mental survival. Concluding, it is not the actual balance that is of vital importance, but the *quality* of the time used for personal purposes, and the meaning attributed to it. At the same time, it should be noted, as did Diener et al. (1999), that objective aspects of life, such as marriage, age, gender, life events, and income, only to a minor extent contribute to individual well-being. According to Lyubomirsky (2001), we can develop a much greater predictive value as to human well-being/happiness by analyzing how a person "construes" their world, what meaning they attribute to individual experiences.

This leads us to the final group of resources, one that Hobfoll (2006) calls energy resources. These include vitality, which is a set of biological parameters (determined genetically – one's temperament, medical immunity, regenerative capacity, stress resistance). Additionally, these have a partial positive correlation with young age and can be intentionally maintained through healthy lifestyle practices. It is worth noting that employee vitality may be a significant determinant of their well-being. This conclusion stems from a series of studies on happiness, a notion that overlaps significantly with that of well-being (see Seligman, 2011). We know that the level of happiness experienced by people is genetically determined. For many years now, a Dutch scholar, Ruut Veenhoven (2024), has compiled subsequent editions of the Gross National Happiness Index, based on a methodology to measure *subjective* appreciation of life. The latter indication should not be overlooked as there are also rankings made on the basis of objective indicators for a specific population, such as life expectancy, GDP, level of civic freedom/human rights protection, and access to state support. Unfounded comparisons of happiness levels measured according to different methodologies and definitions of the studied concept may lead to incorrect conclusions. In line with Czapiński's (2017) so-called "onion" theory of happiness, regardless of beneficial and pleasant or unfavorable and unpleasant life experiences, happiness level – albeit fluctuating in accordance with the type of events encountered – tends to quickly return to a constant base level that is characteristic for the person. That level is moderated by a component known as the will to live, with subjective well-being and partial satisfactions also contributing thereto.

***Experience and Motivation***

The group of energy resources further includes knowledge, experience, and motivation. The first two are classified within the typology of personal resources developed by Adamiec and Kożusznik (2000, as cited in Kożusznik, 2007, p. 62) as additive resources, that is, such that grow throughout professional career. The authors offer a tripartite division of personal resources into those that are stable, growing, and decreasing throughout the lifetime. Formal education is an instance of the first type, knowledge and experience of the second, and the time available of the third. Another criterion is that of renewability and the manner of depletion (whether through use or disuse). Here, work tools and life energy are among resources that deplete through use, whereas intellectual and physical ability depletes through disuse. A resource that can be expected to grow may seem as a valid predictor of well-being; however, certain additional conditions have to be met. Professional knowledge requires continuous updating and practical verification; otherwise, it turns into pseudo knowledge, as is evident in the practice of medicine. Outdated treatment methods, obsolescent etiopathogenesis, unreliable diagnostic procedures – all of these can lead to iatrogenesis, that is, professional malpractice against the current state of knowledge, which has negative repercussions for both the patient and the physician. Meanwhile, it would be erroneous to account for experience exclusively in quantitative terms with a complete disregard for its qualitative content.

Professional experience can not only foster well-being of employees but also limit and undermine it. In this context, a valuable experience means one of which a positive balance has been established. This occurs through recognizing the logical connections between the different phases of one's career, understanding the meaning of various, at times difficult, experiences, and perceiving connections between past successes and the hope for future ones (see Lyubomirsky & Tucker, 1998). A limiting or demotivating experience is one that is valued negatively. A sense of lost time, wrong choices, disappointment, bitterness, injustice – all these emotional states are characteristic of a personal experience that is perceived as a burden (inner stressor) rather than a resource. This is clear in the case of people experiencing professional burnout. In her classic account of burnout, Maslach (1982) described it as physical and emotional exhaustion, depersonalization (treating other people in an impersonal, reserved, instrumental, cynical way), and an employee's subjective feeling of professional worthlessness (negative evaluation of one's skills, accompanied by a sense being a failure career wise). For people in various stages of burnout, their professional experience becomes an impediment to their well-being; nonetheless, it is possible to change such a situation by working on redefining the person's past, usually over the course of psychotherapy. It needs to be stressed that it is not the case that an accumulation of negative experiences has to always reduce the value of the resource in question. Numerous studies on resilience have demonstrated that it is through failures, losses, traumas, and crises – when they are worked through – that growth, thriving in personal resources, is achieved. This is referred to as post-traumatic growth (PTG). According to Ogińska-Bulik and Juczyński (2012), the main component of PTG is the cognitive and emotional effort expended in order to reevaluate one's past experiences and give them meaning that will enable one to discover new values in life and accept a new self-image.

An employee's work experience contributes to their professional identity; over time, however, it becomes a major organizational resource. This resource will help achieve the goals of the organization provided it is recognized and put to most effective use. The issue was approached by Blanchard (2007; Hersey & Blanchard, 1969) in his situational leadership model. He is of the opinion that employees with extensive experience should be managed in a distinct manner. He calls them "autonomous experts" and suggests that managers should delegate tasks to them. The level of supportive and directive behaviors (the two main dimensions of managerial activities according to Blanchard) should be low. The superior should grant such an employee the greatest possible level of trust, leaving it to them to make decisions regarding everyday operation and motivation to further improve their work performance (Blanchard, 2007, p. 99). He believes experienced workers to be able to support themselves (or find adequate support from their social resources), while if they do need instructions, to seek these in literature or in conversation with other professionals. Following the sequence "employee autonomy as perceived by the superior – employee's maturity – decision to delegate tasks – work autonomy" results in the most effective performance by experienced employees. In other words, activities undertaken by the organization to foster the adaptation and implementation of situational leadership lead to correct identification of employee potential. As discovered by scholars over the last several decades of studying employee behaviors in the workplace, the sphere of autonomy in performing tasks is one of the crucial factors in building such states as job satisfaction, work value, meaningfulness of work, experiencing positive emotions in the workplace, and intrinsic motivation, which ultimately contribute to employee well-being (Hackman & Oldham, 1979; Ryan & Deci, 1985; Ryff, 1989; Schein, 1992). Furthermore, it has been noted that the correlation between the level of autonomy and employee well-being is positive and linear (Clausen et al., 2021).

The final item on the list of energy resources is motivation, that is, a need-based set of mental and physiological processes that determine the background for behaviors and their changes. The division of motivation into extrinsic and intrinsic is a classic approach to the problem in psychology. It can be argued that what is important for well-being is not the actual type of motivation but its intensity and strength. This will hold true in the short term. It is well-known that extrinsic motivation (delayed gratification) faces many limitations. Over time, the reward potential decreases because of hedonic adaptation, whereas the increase in salary and other forms of compensation reaches the limit of economic feasibility for the employer. There tends to be a temporal delay between work activities and the reward which ranges from a few to over a dozen hours (praise from the superior) to a month (salary payment). The research by Mischel (2015) showed that people differ significantly in their tolerance for delayed gratification. The limit to the extrinsic motivation potential also lies in the fact that we may at times be rewarded for activities that are at odds with our sense of justice, honesty, and dignity. Acting on such a motivation in turn generates the additional psychological cost of a cognitive and emotional burden (resolution of cognitive dissonance, intensification of defense mechanisms, such as denial, repression, rationalization, isolation, projection, increased sense of guilt, anxiety, shame, and self-disappointment). Intrinsic motivation, also called autotelic motivation, as described by Ryan and Deci's self-determination theory (1985), seems more promising in the context of fostering well-being. They indicate the importance of three spheres of needs in individuals: autonomy, competence, and relatedness. Seeking to satisfy these needs generates intrinsic motivation. Autonomy is related to a person's need to be free, make independent choices, opt for certain modes of action, and eschew others. People want to have a choice in what they do and how they do it. The feeling of having a choice and being able to control an aspect of reality (occupation) boosts this type of motivation. Meanwhile, competence pertains to one's objective ability to perform certain tasks as well as one's perceived competence: "This is what I'm cut out for," "I know my way around these things." Lastly, relatedness concerns the meaning a person attributes to their activities, the subjective value these may have, and their meaningfulness. As you can see, there is much room for organizational contribution. It was already noted in the 1970s by Oldham and Hackman, who developed the job characteristics model (1979). They identified universal job characteristics that make work worthwhile for employees:

- Task significance: The work has noticeable and significant impact on others. It is perceived as worth the effort, meaningful.
- Task identity: Pieces of work are performed from the beginning to the end or in such a way that employees have access to the tangible results of their contribution.
- Skill variety: Work is designed in such a manner as to take advantage of the various talents, competencies, and abilities of employees.

- Autonomy: A degree of freedom granted to employees allows them to determine their tasks and find the means to tackle them. Employees are provided with the opportunity to manage their time and equipment, which encourages innovation.
- Feedback: Employees have access to the results of their work, and they receive feedback from multiple sources within the organization. Thus, they gain an instrument not only for regulating their effectiveness and efficiency but also for correcting their mistakes.

The results of work that is designed in line with the above guidelines are reflected in the so-called "critical psychological states in employees," namely: 1) the sense that one's work is relevant, meaningful, and important; 2) the experience of personal responsibility for job performance; 3) the ability to regulate the parameters of one's work (effectiveness, efficiency) on the basis of the feedback received. High levels of the above job characteristics result in job satisfaction, intrinsic motivation, and high quality of work, also referred to by Oldham and Hackman as "desired psychological states." It is worth adding that working with intrinsic motivation enables employees to achieve the state of flow, which is a very rewarding physical and psychological state associated with the experience of happiness (Csikszentmihalyi, 1996).

**Well-being and Person–Job Fit**

Thus far, our considerations have focused on the resources of an individual. Another perspective to describe the determinants of well-being can be the level of person–job fit. There are two main types[2] of work-related compatibilities that are usually identified: person–organization fit and person–job fit. The former determines the extent to which a person is suitable for a specific organizational culture, the expectations set by the organization, and the person's adjustment to the role they are assigned (Kristof, 1996). Person–organization fit involves a similarity – regarding the set of descriptive traits – between the two entities, as well as an overlap in the needs of both parties, understood in terms of psychological contract. Muchinsky and Monahan (1987) further specify two aspects of congruence: supplementary and complementary models of fit. Supplementary fit refers to the similarity of value systems, employee goals and aspirations based upon it, and those represented by the employer (organization). Complementary fit is related to the aspect of congruence between what the employee brings to the organization and what the organization expects (demands) from them. In the case of person–job fit, we recognize the congruence between an employee's skills and competencies and the demands of the workplace (profession, position). Also of importance is the extent to which the job is able to help the persons realize their aspirations (Edwards, 1991). Although the types of congruence overlap with one another in their characteristics and may appear identical, there is a significant distinction between them. The most important in relation to the organization seems to be *where* and *with whom* I work. In the case of person–job fit, the accent shifts toward *what* I do and *how* I do it (and what the consequences are for me, rather than what the importance for the organization is). Sometimes, it so happens that workers are well suited to their jobs but poorly suited to their organizations, for they feel uncomfortable, say, with the climate in the workplace, the policy of the board, leadership style, and so on. And vice versa, employees with high person–organization fit may experience lower person–job fit due to diminished work engagement, lack of adequate competences, no sense of meaningfulness of their individual work, and progressive burnout.

Person–job fit constitutes a significant predictor of employee well-being. Lack of such fit will lead to problems with motivation, counterproductive employee behaviors (Khan et al., 2022), and the experience of boredom in the workplace (Fisher, 2018). This raises the question of whose side is responsible for ensuring this kind of match. To what extent does the responsibility belong to the employee, and to what to the organization? It is, in fact, split between the parties. For instance, during the recruitment process, which Pratt and Ashforth (2003) consider to be the key organizational activity that lays the ground for fostering the meaningfulness of work, the team may successfully employ a person suitable for the vacant post. This would mean that the organization took adequate measures to draft a well-qualified employee to fill the position. What happens, however, if a candidate has presented unreliable information in their CV, and their purported competences are no more than their ambitions? Or if an employee, having been onboarded, decides that the workplace conditions do not meet their expectations, that he imagined these differently, or that the position is unsatisfactory compared with their previous job? Pratt and Ashforth (2003) point to the three pillars of person–job fit, which are rooted in the person's self-awareness, and their self-reflection on their situation, goal, and relevance in the workplace. The person needs to find their own answers to such questions as: Who am I? What am I for? What do I do? There is a series of interrelations between them, and the order of asking them is important too. The first question is about the person's identity and value system; hence, it is foundational. Without self-knowledge of who we are, identifying our needs can be difficult. When we are aware of our genuine needs, the actions that we take gain in meaning. They become deliberate, intentional, purposeful, and significant. What we do is the natural consequence of our knowledge of ourselves and our priorities in life.

## Job Crafting

Besides the questions that are essential for establishing a sense of meaningfulness of work, "What am I for?" and "What do I do?" another to be asked is the rather brief: "How?" Even though it takes the last place in the discussed sequence and appears to play a merely "operational" role, its importance is far greater. We are aware of that thanks to over two decades of research into job design. The pioneers of job crafting research, Wrzesniewski and Dutton (2001), define it as: activities undertaken independently by employees and aimed at adjusting the work to their needs and preferences. The scholars believe that there are three needs behind any such activities: the need for personal control, the need for a positive self-image, and the need for positive relationships with others. Job crafting may occur in three fields, as differentiated by Wrzesniewski and Dutton (2001):

- Task crafting
- Relational crafting
- Cognitive crafting

Task crafting means modifying work tasks both in terms of the method and the scope. Even though the task – resulting from the norms or assigned by the superior – remains the same, what changes is the approach to realizing it through the creative effort undertaken by employees, based on their preferences. One could say that they "do it their way." The transition results in enriched work tasks and an employee's increased sense of self-efficacy.

Relational crafting is associated with working on satisfactory relationships in the workplace. It comprises activities aimed at building a network of contacts (relational capital) in the organization and efforts to improve existing relationships with colleagues (trust, reciprocity, support). It also involves seeking and discovering what others are like outside their professional roles.

Cognitive crafting refers directly to the meaningfulness of work. Using thought, imagination, reflection, and self-awareness, an employee is able to see with fresh eyes what their work is and what consequences it has for her- or himself and for their broader social environment. This kind of job crafting is based on the search for meaning, the discovery of connections between the individual and the collective, and the contribution of one's individual work to the common good. This amounts to the redefinition of one's work. The importance here lies in the ability to connect one's value system with what the object of everyday work activities is along with their short- and long-term results.

According to Tims and Bakker[3] (2010), job crafting combines two spheres, the adjustment of work to one's resources of knowledge, skills, and competences, and the adjustment of work performance to one's personal needs and preferences. Based on samples of 122 investigations on organizational and individual results of job crafting, Rudolph et al. (2017) carried out an impressive meta-analysis covering over 35 thousand employees. It resulted in the conclusion that job crafting is strongly correlated with work engagement and proactive personality traits. Tims and Bakker (2010) pointed out a significant connection between job crafting and motivation. Redesigning and modifying work have a positive influence on job satisfaction (Tims et al., 2013), particularly when relationship crafting and employee self-learning are involved. Furthermore, as discovered in a study by Tims et al. (2016), job crafting activities enhance the sense of meaning in employees.

Job crafting may be a major pillar of employee well-being as long as the organization where they work offers systemic and managerial opportunities for its emergence. In organizational cultures dominated by authoritarianism, traditionalism, social distance, no tolerance for mistakes, and primitive conservatism, employee-driven grassroots undertakings may be substantially limited and not infrequently punished. Management aware of organizational benefits created by job crafting will support it. A limitation of a different kind may emerge on the part of the individual. It has been observed that there is a connection between the openness to job crafting and proactive personality (Rudolph et al., 2017; see Bateman & Crant, 1993), and the latter, as such, is relatively stable. This leads to the conclusion that not all employees regard job crafting as attractive or even accessible.

## Conclusion

Employee well-being is a complex phenomenon. Depending on the "paradigm" assumed, it can be understood in various ways. It may be the narrower hedonic perspective or the broader eudaimonic one, the subjective or the objective point of view. Some authors developed original concepts of well-being (Warr, 1987; Ryff, 1989), and others study and describe phenomena within this field of I-O psychology referring to states and processes indirectly linked to well-being, such as job satisfaction, work engagement, proactivity, and the meaningfulness of work (Schaufeli & Bakker, 2003; Lips-Wiersma & Morris, 2009; Bateman & Crant, 1993; Lysova et al., 2019). The connection between well-being and other organizationally desirable job characteristics is bidirectional. This means that achieving a state of well-being has a positive impact on engagement, motivation, creativity, and the ability to cooperate, while frequent experience of job satisfaction, being praised by superiors, and achieving the state of flow at work facilitate employee well-being. The determinants of well-being are numerous and varied. Some fall within the traits of an individual (set of personality traits, level of proactivity, innate potential for happiness, frame of mind, level of intrinsic motivation, dynamics of the need for self-actualization), others belong to the person–environment interaction of one's life and work (person–organization fit, person–job fit, job crafting, work design), while the remaining ones depend on organizational characteristics (organizational culture and climate, leadership quality, psychological safety at work). As we have attempted to demonstrate here, organizational determinants and the individual ones are "interdependent." Employee qualities and traits have to be recognized and fostered in the workplace so that employee well-being is high and stable. Many efforts undertaken by employees with the aim of achieving well-being are shattered when they encounter a work environment that is deaf to these needs. It is necessary on the part of the organization, as Pratt and Ashforth (2003) emphasize, that attempts be made at skillful employee recruitment and selection, while afterward at "socialization," that is, fostering and maintaining well-being in order to achieve good person–organization fit. Concluding, the greatest likelihood of employee well-being occurs when the needs experienced by a person in this field are adjusted to her or his work environment, the organization-environment, which for its part monitors, recognizes, and attaches importance to these needs and creates conditions for their realization in the workplace.

## Notes

1. For more on work–life balance and employee well-being, the reader should consult Chapter 5 of this contributed volume, written by Justyna Pawlak.
2. These are the types of adjustments that are most frequently referred to in I-O psychology and managerial psychology. A broader category encompassing the two compatibilities mentioned above is that of person–environment fit. Person–team fit is also represented in literature.
3. Tims and Bakker base their construct of job crafting on a different model than that developed by Wrzesniewski and Dutton; they use the job demands-resources (JD-R) model instead. See Bakker and Demerouti (2007).

## References

Adamiec, M., & Kożusznik, B. (2000). *Zarządzanie zasobami ludzkimi. Aktor, kreator, inspirator*. Wydawnictwo Akademickie.

Avolio, B. J., & Bass, B. M. (1991). *The full range leadership development programs basic and advanced manuals*. Bass, Avolio Associates.

Bailey, C., & Madden, A. (2016). What makes work meaningful – Or meaningless. *MIT Sloan Management Review*, *57*(4), 53–61.

Bakker, A. B., & Demerouti, E. (2007). The job demands-resources model: State of the art. *Journal of Managerial Psychology*, *22*(3), 309–328.

Bateman, T. S., & Crant, J. M. (1993). The proactive component of organizational behavior: A measure and correlates. *Journal of Organizational Behavior*, *14*(2), 103–118.

Blanchard, K. (2007). *Przywództwo wyższego stopnia. Blanchard o przywództwie i tworzeniu efektywnych organizacji*. Wydawnictwo Naukowe PWN.

Cameron, K. S., & Spreitzer, G. M. (2012). What is positive in positive organizational scholarship. In K. S. Cameron, & G. M. Spreitzer (Eds.), *The Oxford handbook of positive organizational scholarship* (pp. 1–16). Oxford University Press.

Chico-Libran, E. (2006). Personality dimensions and subjective well-being. *Spanish Journal of Psychology*, *9*(1), 38–44.

Clausen, T., Pedersen, L., Andersen, M., Theorell, T., & Madsen, I. E. H. (2021). Job autonomy and psychological well-being: A linear or a non-linear association? *European Journal of Work and Organizational Psychology*, *31*, 3.

Csikszentmihalyi, M. (1996). *Przepływ. Jak poprawić jakość życia*. Wydawnictwo Studio Emka.

Czapiński, J. (2017). Psychologia szczęścia. In *Kto, kiedy, dlaczego kocha życie i co z tego wynika, czyli nowa odsłona teorii cebulowej*. Wydawnictwo Naukowe Scholar.

Czerw, A. (2017). *Psychologiczny model dobrostanu w pracy. Wartość i sens pracy.* Wydawnictwo Naukowe PWN.
Deci, E. L., & Ryan, R. M. (1985). The general causality orientations scale: Self-determination in personality. *Journal of Research in Personality*, *19*(2), 109–134.
Diener, E. (1984). Subjective well-being. *Psychological Bulletin*, *95*, 542–575.
Diener, E., Suh, E. M., Lucas, R. E., & Smith, H. L. (1999). Subjective well-being: Three decades of progress. *Psychological Bulletin*, *125*, 276–302.
Edwards, J. R. (1991). Person-job fit: A conceptual integration, literature review, and methodological critique. In C. L. Cooper & I. T. Robertson (Eds.), *International review of industrial and organizational psychology* (Vol. 6, pp. 283–357). Wiley & Sons.
Emmons, R. A., & Stern, R. (2013). Gratitude as a psychotherapeutic intervention. *Journal of Clinical Psychology*, *69*, 846–855.
Fehr, R., Fulmer, A., Awtrey, E., & Miller, J. A. (2017). The grateful workplace: A multilevel model of gratitude in organizations. *Academy of Management Review*, *42*, 361–381.
Fisher, C. D. (2018). *Boredom at work: What, why, and what then?* In D. Lindebaum, D. Geddes, & P. J. Jordan (Eds.), *Social functions of emotion and talking about emotion at work*. Edward Elgar Publishing.
Ford, M. T., Cerasoli, C. P., Higgins, J. A., & Decesare, A. L. (2011). Relationships between psychological, physical, and behavioural health and work performance: A review and meta-analysis. *Work & Stress*, *25*(3), 185–204.
Frankl, V. (1962). *Man's search for meaning*. Beacon Press.
Hackman, J. R., & Oldham, G. R. (1979). *Work redesign*. Addison-Wesley.
Harter, J. K., Schmidt, F. L., & Keyes, C. L. M. (2003). Well-being in the workplace and its relationship to business outcomes: A review of the Gallup studies. In C. L. M. Keyes & J. Haidt (Eds.), *Flourishing: Positive psychology and the life well-lived*. American Psychological Association.
Hersey, P., & Blanchard, K. H. (1969). Life cycle theory of leadership. *Training and Development Journal*, *23*.
Herzberg, F. (1968). One more time how do you motivate employees. *Harvard Business Review*, *81*(1), 87–96.
Hobfoll, S. (2006). *Stres, kultura i społeczność: psychologia i filozofia stresu*. Gdańskie Wydawnictwo Psychologiczne.
Kahn, W. A. (1990). Psychological conditions of personal engagement and disengagement at work. *The Academy of Management Journal*, *33*(4), 692–724.
Kamdron, T. (2005). Work motivation and job satisfaction of Estonian higher officials. *International Journal of Public Administration*, *28*, 1211–1240.
Khan, J., Ali, A., Saeed, I., Vega-Muñoz, A., & Contreras-Barraza, N. (2022). Person–job misfit: Perceived overqualification and counterproductive work behavior. *Frontiers in Psychology*, *13*, 936900.
Kożusznik, B. (2007). *Zachowania człowieka w organizacji*. Polskie Wydawnictwo Ekonomiczne.
Kristof, A. L. (1996). Person-organization fit: An integrative review of its conceptualizations, measurement, and implications. *Personnel Psychology*, *49*(1), 1–49.
Lips-Wiersma, M., & Morris, L. (2009). Discriminating between 'meaningful work' and the 'management of meaning'. *Journal of Business Ethics*, *88*(3), 491–511.
Lysova, E. I., Allan, B. A., Dik, B. J., Duffy, R. D., & Steger, M. F. (2019). Fostering meaningful work in organizations: A multi-level review and integration. *Journal of Vocational Behavior*, *110*(Part B), 374–389.
Lyubomirsky, S. (2001). Why are some people happier than others?: The role of cognitive and motivational processes in well-being. *American Psychologist*, *56*, 239–249.

Lyubomirsky, S., & Tucker, K. L. (1998). Implications of individual differences in subjective happiness for perceiving, interpreting, and thinking about life events. *Motivation and Emotion, 22*, 155–186.

Makin, P., Cooper, C., & Cox, C. (2000). *Organizacje a kontrakt psychologiczny. Zarządzanie ludźmi w pracy*. Wydawnictwo Naukowe PWN.

Manzoli, L., Villari, P., Pirone, G. M., & Boccia, A. (2007). Marital status and mortality in the elderly: A systematic review and meta-analysis. *Social Science & Medicine, 64*(1), 77–94.

Maslach, C. (1982). *Burnout: The cost of caring*. Prentice-Hall.

Maslow, A. (1954). *Motivation and personality*. Harper.

Mischel, W. (2015). *Test marshmallow. O pożytkach płynących z samokontroli*. Wydawnictwo Smak słowa.

Moore, K. A., & Keyes, C. L. M. (2003). A brief history of well-being in children and adults. In M. Bornstein, L. Davidson, C. L. M. Keyes, & K. A. Moore (Eds.), *Well being: Positive development across the life course* (pp. 1–11). Lawrence Erlbaum Associates.

Muchinsky, P. M., & Monahan, C. J. (1987). What is person environment congruence? Supplementary versus complementary models of fit. *Journal of Vocational Behavior, 31*(3), 268–277.

Ogińska-Bulik, N., & Juczyński, Z. (2012). Prężność jako wyznacznik pozytywnych i negatywnych konsekwencji doświadczonej sytuacji traumatycznej. *Polskie Forum Psychologiczne, 17*, 395–410.

Pratt, M. G., & Ashforth, B. E. (2003). Fostering meaningfulness in working and at work. In K. S. Cameron, J. Dutton, & R. Quinn (Eds.), *Positive organizational scholarship* (pp. 309–327). Berrett-Koehler.

Rudolph, C. W., Katz, I. M., Lavigne, K. N., & Zacher, H. (2017). Job crafting: A meta-analysis of relationships with individual differences, job characteristics, and work outcomes. *Journal of Vocational Behavior, 102*, 112–138.

Ryff, C. D. (1989). Happiness is everything, or is it? Explorations on the meaning of psychological well-being. *Journal of Personality and Social Psychology, 57*(6), 1069–1081.

Sansone, R. A., & Sansone, L. A. (2010). Gratitude and well being: The benefits of appreciation. *Psychiatry, 7*, 18–22.

Schaufeli, W., & Bakker, A. (2003). *UWES Utrecht work engagement scale: Preliminary manual [version 1]*. Occupational Health Psychology Unit, Utrecht University.

Scheier, M. F., Carver, C. S., & Bridges, M. W. (2001). Optimism, pessimism, and psychological well-being. In E. C. Chang (Ed.), *Optimism & pessimism: Implications for theory, research, and practice*. American Psychological Association.

Schein, E. (1992). *Organizational culture and leadership*. Jossey-Bass Publishers.

Seligman, M. E. P. (2011). *Flourish: A visionary new understanding of happiness and well-being*. Free Press.

Steger, M. F., & Dik, B. J. (2010). Work as meaning: Individual and organizational benefits of engaging in meaningful work. In P. A. Linley, S. Harrington, & N. Garcea (Eds.), *Oxford handbook of positive psychology and work* (pp. 131–142). Oxford University Press.

Tims, M., & Bakker, A. B. (2010). Job crafting: Towards a new model of individual job redesign. *South African Journal of Industrial Psychology, 36*, 1–9.

Tims, M., Bakker, A. B., & Derks, D. (2013). The impact of job crafting on job demands, job resources, and well-being. *Journal of Occupational Health Psychology, 18*(2), 230–240.

Tims, M., Derks, D., & Bakker, A. B. (2016). Job crafting and its relationships with person–job fit and meaningfulness: A three-wave study. *Journal of Vocational Behavior, 92*, 44–53.

Veenhoven, R. (2024). Average happiness in 149 nations 2000–2009. *World Database of Happiness. Rank Report Average Happiness*. Retrieved April 16, 2024, from https://worlddatabaseofhappiness.eur.nl/wp-content/uploads/2020/07/AVERAGE-HAPPINESS-IN-149-NATIONS-2000-2009.pdf

Warr, P. (1987). *Work, unemployment, and mental health*. Oxford University Press.

Watkins, P. C. (2013). *Gratitude and the good life: Toward a psychology of appreciation*. Springer Science & Business Media.

Wilcox, W. B., & Wolfinger, N. H. (2024). *Men & marriage: Debunking the ball and chain myth*. Institute for Family Studies. Retrieved February 12, 2024, from https://ifstudies.org/wp-content/uploads/2017/02/IFSMenandMarriageResearchBrief2.pdf

Wright, T. A., & Bonett, D. G. (2007). Job satisfaction and psychological well-being as non-additive predictors of workplace turnover. *Journal of Management*, *33*(2), 141–160.

Wrzesniewski, A., & Dutton, J. E. (2001). Crafting a job: Revisioning employees as active crafters of their work. *Academy of Management Review*, *26*(2), 178–201.

# 3 Organizational Culture and Climate That Shape Engagement

*Robert Szydło, Małgorzata Tyrańska, Kamil Wiśniewski, Ireneusz Rynduch and Magdalena Adamczyk-Kowalczuk*

## Introduction

National culture, characterized by shared beliefs, values, and norms within a society, provides a foundational framework that significantly influences individual behaviors and perceptions in the workplace. Cultural dimensions such as collectivism vs. individualism, power distance, uncertainty avoidance, and masculinity vs. femininity, as proposed by Hofstede and further refined by other scholars, offer valuable insights into how societal cultures shape employee attitudes and behaviors toward work engagement.

Moreover, within the microcosm of organizations, distinct organizational cultures further model employee experience. Organizational culture encapsulates the shared values, beliefs, and norms within a specific workplace environment, profoundly impacting employee behaviors, motivations, and levels of engagement. Whether characterized by a strong emphasis on innovation and risk-taking or a more hierarchical and process-driven approach, organizational culture serves as a potent force in shaping employee perceptions of their roles, fostering a sense of belonging, and ultimately influencing their commitment to organizational objectives.

The research was designed as an explorative investigation. The main aim is to identify critical cultural elements that enhance employee engagement. The main research question was formulated as follows: what elements of culture impact employee engagement?

There were also six supplementary questions:

- Is age correlated with certain cultural elements?
- Is work experience correlated with certain cultural elements?
- Can gender influence the perception of the engagement level of cultural elements?
- Is occupation important in perceiving cultural elements as engaging?
- Is company size important in how cultural elements are perceived?
- Can the organization type impact the perception of cultural elements?

DOI: 10.4324/9781032715407-4

To elicit answers to the above questions, a Computerized Self-Administered Questionnaire (CSAQ) was created, to be followed by descriptive and mathematical statistics. The publication presents the result of the Project no 068/ZZS/2024/POT financed from the subsidy granted to the Krakow University of Economics.

## Overview of National and Organizational Cultures

The impact of culture, both national and that of a company (organizational), on employee engagement can be an intriguing area for research and effective management as it would be highly beneficial to explore how the culture of a nation/organization influences the level and characteristics of employee engagement. Such knowledge can contribute to the success or failure of today's organizational leaders, as they often engage in projects within multicultural teams. The concept of culture has long been a part of scientific research in various fields, such as anthropology, philosophy, psychology, and the management sciences. It is also associated with legal considerations, individualism, and collectivism. However, there is no universal definition of culture (Steenkamp, 2001). It will, therefore, be discussed in the context of the division into national and organizational cultures and how these may impact employee engagement.

One of the most popular approaches to characterize national culture was proposed by Hofstede (1984). He defined culture as the collective programming of the mind, the result of growing up in a particular country which influences an individual's behavior, their cherished values, and competencies. Significant differences between national cultures primarily manifest in value systems (Hofstede et al., 2000). Hofstede identified the following dimensions of national cultures (Hofstede, 2011): power distance, collectivism and individualism, femininity and masculinity, uncertainty avoidance, as well as long-term and short-term orientation.

Power distance is the emotional space between subordinates and superiors. In countries with a low power distance, subordinates freely communicate with superiors and express their needs and dissatisfaction. In contrast, in countries with a high power distance, this rarely occurs or is perceived negatively due to the dominance of managers over subordinates. For example, the USA and the UK are low power distance countries, while high power distance scores are typical of Asian countries (Subocz, 2012).

Collectivism and individualism determine the perception of an individual's good in relation to the benefit for the entire society. African and Asian societies are predominantly collectivistic, while Western cultures, such as Europe, the USA, and Canada, are inclined toward individualism (Chmielecki, 2020). The dimension of masculinity and femininity relates to identifying behaviors and traits specific to each gender in a particular nation (Hofstede, 2011).

Uncertainty avoidance denotes the willingness of a nation and its members to submit themselves to laws, restrictions, rules, and control regulations to minimize the potential danger. Citizens in countries with high uncertainty avoidance rarely engage in social movements and politics because they are generally distrustful, whereas in cultures with a low degree of uncertainty avoidance, the situation is reversed (Vollero et al., 2020).

Long-term orientation nations focus on development, future, investment projects, innovations, savings, perseverance, and prudence. Attitudes that focus on past and present events are embraced in cultures with short-term orientation (Chun et al., 2021).

The issue of organizational culture, much like that of national culture, is a complex one. There are numerous definitions of organizational culture. It can be assumed, however, that the term has its origins dating back to the development of the management field, and human relations, in particular (Shulyn & Yazdanifard, 2013), and that it refers to cooperation aimed at advancing the company's mission (Kobylińska & Majewski, 2023). The examination of organizational cultures has come up with characteristics that modern managers, especially those who work with multicultural teams, should be familiar with (Piwowar-Sulej, 2012; Szymańska, 2012), namely, holism, reflection of the organization's history, connection with anthropology, human significance, resistance to change, quick response and adaptability to market situations, promotion of creativity, entrepreneurship, and innovativeness. Organizational culture possesses universal components that allow for an understanding of its essence, but these elements vary for each organization depending on the issues it deals with (Table 3.1).

*Table 3.1* Elements characterizing organizational culture

| *Elements* | *Characteristic* |
|---|---|
| Symbols | Elements facilitating the identification of an individual with the organization, such as office appearance, logo, corporate privileges, dress code, and indicators of one's position in the organization |
| Communication | Components of language that members of a specific organization, such as company-specific terminology, mainly understand |
| Rituals | Repetitive actions, gestures, and situations characteristic of a particular organization, for example, how the company or its employees celebrate successes |
| Myths | Indication what is and isn't accepted in a particular organizational culture. Including various stories, retold and modified histories from the company's past |
| Taboos | All aspects of organizational life that should not be discussed, such as employees' private lives, and preferences, politics, and salary details |

*Source:* Own compilation based on Wojtowicz (2004, pp. 159–161)

One of the most popular definitions of organizational culture was offered by Schein (2010). It provides an account of how individuals and groups create a specific culture through their assumptions, norms, and values, as well as artifacts. The so-called Schein pyramid, while focusing primarily on the degrees of "visibility," materialization, and company-wide awareness of the elements of organizational culture (Kopczewski et al., 2012; Kobylińska & Majewski, 2023), comprises the three aforementioned levels; they are as follows:

- The artifacts level (at the top of the pyramid): external, visible elements such as symbols, behaviors, and physical objects that shape organizational culture, for example, dress code and logos.
- The level of espoused values and norms (in the middle of the pyramid): partially visible, encompassing norms and values imposed by the company, necessary to achieve organizational goals, such as business honesty and interpersonal behavior.
- The level of underlying assumptions (at the base of the pyramid): deeply rooted concepts within the organization, unnoticed by most, influencing the priorities and values within the work environment.

Both national and organizational cultures influence individuals within them (Szydło & Grześ-Bukłaho, 2020), thus impacting the level of employee engagement (Pepra-Mensah & Kyeremeh, 2018; Rattrie et al., 2020). Individuals are primarily shaped by their national culture, which imprints upon them its set of values, attitudes, ways of valuing work, and the role of individuals in society (Dartey-Baah, 2011; Nazarian et al., 2013). Organizations, which develop their own culture, face the challenge of adapting to it their employees (Wallace et al., 1999; Pandey & Chitranshi, 2023). This is not an easy task, considering that managers have to be aware of the cultural differences among the people they manage (Zen et al., 2023). Their leadership style has to be modified to best reflect the needs of their subordinates and the arguments used – be valued by team members of various cultural backgrounds (Szara & Klukow, 2022; Kożak-Siara & Olak, 2022). In the case of multicultural teams, that is, those that comprise people of more than one nationality, efficient management becomes even more challenging. Managers need to understand the values espoused by the members of each culture and be able to coordinate their work, including potential conflict management interventions as these may soon arise in such teams (Gadomska-Lila et al., 2011; Haile & Jabang, 2019; Pauliene et al., 2019).

## Psychological Aspects of Company Culture

Organizational culture encompasses the shared values, beliefs, attitudes, and behaviors that characterize an organization and its employees. From the point of view of psychology, company culture influences various aspects of employees' experiences, interactions, and overall well-being, resulting in their engagement (Silverthorne, 2005). One of the critical psychological aspects of the organization's culture is a sense of belonging. When individuals feel valued, respected, and accepted within the organization, they are more likely to identify with the company's mission and goals. Such a sense of belonging can contribute to higher levels of engagement, motivation, and loyalty among employees, as research shows that the experience of belonging developed in the workplace has as much significance for employees' emotions, cognition, and sense of self, as for their performance (Waller, 2020). Furthermore, a positive culture that encourages open communication, collaboration, and innovation can enhance employee motivation and commitment to their work (Pathiranage, 2019).

Effective communication and transparency are essential for a healthy company culture. Transparent communication builds trust and credibility while fostering a sense of inclusion and organizational cohesion. Conversely, a lack of transparency or miscommunication can erode trust, fuel rumors, and create a hostile work environment (Jiang & Luo, 2018). All the aspects discussed are closely connected to psychological safety, which refers to the belief that one can express oneself without the fear of negative consequences. In a supportive company culture, employees feel psychologically safe to voice their opinions, share ideas, and take calculated risks. This fosters creativity, problem-solving, and a culture of continuous improvement (Gong et al., 2012).

It is for this reason that leadership plays a critical role in shaping company culture. The leadership style adopted by executives and managers influences employee morale, job satisfaction, and the overall organizational climate. Transformational leaders, who inspire and empower their teams, tend to foster a positive and inclusive culture.

Company culture influences attitudes toward work–life balance and employee well-being. A culture that prioritizes flexibility, autonomy, and work–life balance promotes employee health, reduces burnout, and improves job satisfaction. Conversely, a culture that glorifies overwork or discourages taking time off can lead to stress and dissatisfaction (Santos et al., 2012). Company culture has profound psychological implications for the employee's experience, attitudes, and organizational behavior. By fostering a positive and supportive culture, companies can enhance employee well-being, trust, engagement, and overall organizational performance. Indeed, employees who feel appreciated and recognized for their contributions are more likely to experience job satisfaction and loyalty (Matzler & Renzl, 2006).

## Organizational Cultures That Build Employee Engagement – A Contemporary View

Organizational culture manifests in the values and beliefs, in the adopted assumptions, in the language and symbols, and in the types of conduct espoused by the members of an organization. These are specific features of the institution that distinguish it from others. Each organization creates a specific culture that comprises symbols, myths, rituals, values, and norms. These shape the atmosphere, relationships between employees and management, and connections with external customers (Chuda & Wyrwicka, 2013).

According to Kania (2007), modern management, researchers, analysts, and consultants have identified culture as the source of success or failure in pursuing increasingly complex goals (missions, strategies, tasks, and roles). It unifies, consolidates, stabilizes, reduces uncertainty, promotes a shared vision of goals, and facilitates finding solutions to problems. It provides a strong foundation for the organization's strategic planning.

Organizational culture justifies the existence of an organization from a historical, ethical, emotional, and practical standpoint, indicating where and why the organization currently is and where it is heading. Organizational culture is of great importance for mobilizing the team, building employee commitment, and successfully accomplishing its organizational goals. Organizational culture influences how people and groups, customers, and stakeholders interact with each other. If the organization aims to care for the customer and offer the highest quality service, the culture should promote empathy, responsibility, and professionalism On the other hand, a lack of alignment (conflict) between organizational culture and goals may lead to difficulties in achieving the latter. If an organization strives to be a leader in sustainable development, but its organizational culture lacks in promoting ecology and social responsibility, these goals may prove impossible to achieve.

The artifacts level is the most overt layer of organizational culture. Generally speaking, an artifact is the work of the human mind and hands, as opposed to products of nature. The artifacts of organizational culture are the visible and concrete elements in an organization that reflect its values and activity (Kostera et al., 2000). Cultural artifacts mean all the phenomena that can be seen, heard, and felt when encountering a group with an unfamiliar culture (Karwasz, 2023). Based on such artifacts, we may infer what its organization is like, what it sees as essential, and what values it follows.

We can classify artifacts into three groups (Schein, 1993). Linguistic artifacts refer to specific words, phrases, abbreviations, and terms used in an organization. These linguistic elements are an essential aspect of organizational culture because they reflect the ways of thinking, values, and communication strategies within that organization. Physical artifacts are things or objects that can be seen and touched in the workplace. These are part of organizational culture because they reflect its values, norms, and traditions. Workplace dress is a good example of that. Lastly, behavioral artifacts are the specific behaviors, actions, and practices visible in everyday work in a given company or organization.

Customers read organizational culture through artifacts that communicate the most critical values for the organization. The development of a competitive advantage based on organizational culture depends on the effectiveness of this form of communication (Aniszewska, 2004).

Although easy to spot for researchers, artifacts are not necessarily evident for the people participating in an organizational culture. It should be borne in mind that artifacts constitute the outside layer of the culture core, which may lead to misinterpretation, especially on the part of novice observers. Hence, the organization's culture can be compared to an "iceberg" for, at first glance, you can only see a about seventh of its entirety in the form of a tip above the water surface, while its most significant part hides below. Artifacts reflect a given culture's dominant norms and values, which are not easy to recognize but can be when violated. However, these norms and values are shaped by the more profound and challenging to detect foundations of a culture. To discover those, one needs a more extensive stay with a given community and a more detailed observation of its members (Strychalska-Rudzewicz & Sobol, 2023).

Organizational climate is one of the critical constructs for organizational behavior. It is a difficult concept to define, as it is most often outlined as the subjective feeling in an organization that affects its employees (Shaheen et al., 2022). In general, organizational climate is employees' assessment of the organizational environment that influences their behavior (Gray, 2001). It is the distinctive ethos or aura within an organization at a given time that reflects how its members perceive, experience, and respond to the organizational context (Rollinson, 2005). Besides, organizational climate is framed as employees' shared perception of the organizational environment – specific organizational events, practices, and procedures, and the competing values model (Patterson et al., 2005).

Another thing is that there needs to be greater conceptual clarity between the concepts of organizational culture and climate. Some researchers believe organizational culture to be an alternative to organizational climate or vice versa, but there is a distinction between the two and there are contexts in which one cannot be substituted for the other (Mikuła, 2000). Organizational climate reflects the characteristics of an organization's internal environment through concepts that individuals adapt to the realities within. Organizational culture, in contrast, comprises all the beliefs, expectations, values, behaviors, and norms contributing to advancing the organization's goals (El-Majali, 2016).

There are studies in the literature on the subject that point to the vital role of organizational climate in improving employee engagement. The research on the topic has been able to establish its relationship with job satisfaction (Song, 1992), employee and organizational performance, employee engagement (Febriansyah et al., 2018), and well-being (Viitala et al., 2015; Shaheen et al., 2022).

The source literature features accounts of well-being developed within either the hedonistic (subjective) or eudaimonic (objective) approaches. According to the hedonistic definition, well-being is tantamount to experiencing positive emotions and low negative affectivity, with the relevant criterion being a subjective sense of satisfaction (Argyle, 2001). From the eudaimonic perspective, on the other hand, well-being is viewed by considering how people realize their potential. Thus, it can be assessed objectively, for instance, by observing how someone copes with challenges (Ryff, 2014). Significantly, well-being allows individuals or societies to develop and prosper (Ruggeri et al., 2020).

Well-being is composed of five elements that affect the level of perceived job satisfaction. These are referred to by the acronym PERMA (Kern et al., 2015; Seligman, 2018), meaning respectively: P – *positive emotions* – for example, enjoyment, appreciation, comfort, inspiration, hope, and curiosity, the experience of which increases satisfaction, enhances creativity, and helps build a good atmosphere at work; E – *engagement* – understood as a favorable perception of reality, the state resulting from devoting oneself to a task which one is competent to perform and which in itself motivates one to action, and its completion brings satisfaction; R – *relationships* – being with people, working together; M – *meaning* – a sense of meaningful action, associated with the knowledge that one is needed and that the activities we perform are purposeful; A – *accomplishment/achievement* – achievements and their appreciation, that is, the state in which one has specific goals and achieving them allows one to develop.

Research results indicate that there is a relationship between work engagement and well-being (Schaufeli et al., 2008; Gupta & Shaheen, 2018). Achievements that result from engagement generate positive feelings among employees (Gupta & Shaheen, 2018). Through engagement, employees experience more positive and achieve successes that build and maintain their well-being (Bakker & Schaufeli, 2008).

Employee well-being is positively influenced by a culture that values employee support, cooperation, and trust (Chumg et al., 2016). Likewise, empowerment, delegation, focus on cooperation, and task diversity positively correlate with employee well-being (Lichtenthaler & Fischbach, 2018). A lower hierarchy level in an organization increases job satisfaction too (Lok & Crawford, 2004). What is more, a leader who allows autonomy, delegates authority (Chumg et al., 2016), sets goals, and motivates and treats employees individually contributes to an increase in employees' meaningfulness of work, which in turn translates into their well-being (Mockałło, 2011). It is worth noting that an organizational culture that supports well-being of its employees provides their work with a sense of autonomy and meaning and fosters a friendly atmosphere of mutual support and cooperation, that is, a culture that has characteristics of a clan or adhocracy (Białas et al., 2023).

## Materials and Methods

The procedure adopted in the research is presented here in the following stages: data collection tool and the operationalization of variables, data collection procedure, data analysis tools, and a brief description of the research sample.

The initial questionnaire was developed using the Computerized Self-Administered Questionnaire (CSAQ) format. In this questionnaire, the respondents can provide their answers directly. A proper use of this instrument solves the problem of non-response error because the application does not allow the user to access the next question block until mandatory questions have been answered.

The questionnaire is informed by three cultural theories:

- Hofstede's national culture theory – based on a semantic differential scale from 1 to 7
- Organizational culture by Wojtowicz – based on Likert scale from 1 to 5
- Schein's organizational culture model – based on Likert scale from 1 to 5

The questionnaire is also informed by the following independent variables:

- Age – coded by research participants according to their age
- Work experience – total length of service in months for every position held until the research
- Gender – participants had the choice between man, female, and others
- Occupation – labor market status identified as student, working student, employee
- Company size – according to the general scale: micro (1–9 employees), small (10–49 employees), medium (50–249 employees), and large (more than 250 employees)
- Organization type operationalized as: public sector, NGO, private sector – local company, private sector – regional company, private sector – global company

In order for these questions to be answered, in February 2024, a total of 108 students and employees were inquired about various elements of culture using a purpose-created data collection questionnaire. The data collection tool was presented to the target group through several channels, to wit: social media profiles and groups, e-mails to companies – especially the HR departments, direct messages to employees, as well as through data collection during university lectures. The research was anonymous; respondents could resign from participating in the study at any stage.

The statistical methods introduced in the research procedure are as follows:

- Shapiro–Wilk test – distribution normality
- Kruskal–Wallis *H* test – for comparing more than two independent samples
- Mann–Whitney *U* test – for comparing two independent samples
- Spearman's Rho – for a correlation check
- Friedman's ANOVA
- General descriptive statistics

All the research and calculations were prepared using the SPSS 27 software.

The research sample comprised 27 men (25%) and 81 women (75%). The majority of them, 44 (40.7%), were working students, 38 (35.2%) were students only, and 26 people (24.1%) were employed but did not study. A group of 50 respondents (46.3%) were working in small and medium organizations, 33 persons (30.6%) in big, and 25 (23.1%) in micro organizations. According to the type of organizations, the vast majority of respondents, 83 (76.9%), were working in private sector (27 respondents in global companies, 22 in regional ones, 32 in local, and 2 in family owned small businesses). Only 6 respondents (5.6%) were working in NGOs, while 19 (17.6%) found employment in the public sector. The average age (in years) was $M = 24.71$, SD = 7.515, whereas the average work experience (in months) was $M = 42.98$, SD = 67.163. These statistics are a testament to the fact that the researchers were able to ensure a diverse research sample.

None of the variables used had a normal distribution; in the Shapiro–Wilk test, $p < 0.001$ for each case. A non-parametric test will be used in the Results section.

## Results

In order to enhance the clarity of the statistical analysis results, the section is structured according to the research questions. The research question refers to the perceived impact of culture, understood and described by various theories, on employee engagement.

**Research question 1.** What elements of culture impact employee engagement?

A set of tests and analyses were performed to find answers to this question. In order to introduce the general assessment, descriptive statistics are provided. These will be followed by Friedman's ANOVA test that allows to check the statistically significant differences between the various areas national and organizational culture. The results of a descriptive statistics analysis are compiled in Table 3.2.

As the theories referred to here embrace different understandings of both the national and organizational dimensions of culture, it proved impracticable to offer a combined analysis. Therefore, the findings will be presented within the framework of each approach respectively.

### *Hofstede's National Culture Theory*

The scale of possible answers was set as a seven-point differential scale. The results indicate that employees feel more engaged during the following conditions:

- The company operates on a strategic level and has long-term goals. There is a need for long-term relationships with partners and an opportunity to be a part

*Table 3.2* Descriptive statistics for the respective culture theories

| | *Mean* | *Mode* | *Standard deviation* | *Variance* | *Min* | *Max* | *Percentiles* | | |
|---|---|---|---|---|---|---|---|---|---|
| | | | | | | | *25* | *50* | *75* |
| Dimensions of Hofstede's national culture theory | | | | | | | | | |
| Long-term orientation | 4.99 | 6 | 1.495 | 2.234 | 1 | 7 | 4.00 | 5.00 | 6.00 |
| Femininity and masculinity | 4.04 | 4 | 1.570 | 2.466 | 1 | 7 | 3.00 | 4.00 | 5.00 |
| Indulgence | 3.72 | 4 | 1.540 | 2.371 | 1 | 7 | 2.00 | 4.00 | 5.00 |
| Individualism | 3.22 | 2 | 1.687 | 2.847 | 1 | 7 | 2.00 | 3.00 | 5.00 |
| Uncertainty avoidance | 3.14 | 2 | 1.721 | 2.962 | 1 | 7 | 2.00 | 3.00 | 5.00 |
| Power distance | 2.47 | 2 | 1.463 | 2.139 | 1 | 6 | 1.00 | 2.00 | 3.00 |
| Dimensions of the organizational culture theory by Wojtowicz | | | | | | | | | |
| Human significance | 4.68 | 5 | .653 | .427 | 1 | 5 | 4.00 | 5.00 | 5.00 |
| Promoting creativity | 4.45 | 5 | .715 | .512 | 1 | 5 | 4.00 | 5.00 | 5.00 |
| Adaptability | 4.24 | 4 | .784 | .614 | 1 | 5 | 4.00 | 4.00 | 5.00 |
| Resistant to change | 4.00 | 4 | .995 | .991 | 1 | 5 | 3.00 | 4.00 | 5.00 |
| Holistic approach | 3.82 | 4 | .863 | .744 | 1 | 5 | 3.00 | 4.00 | 4.00 |
| Reflection of the organization's history | 3.04 | 3 | 1.093 | 1.195 | 1 | 5 | 2.00 | 3.00 | 4.00 |
| Connection with anthropology | 2.81 | 3 | 1.036 | 1.074 | 1 | 5 | 2.00 | 3.00 | 3.00 |
| Dimensions of Schein's organizational culture model | | | | | | | | | |
| Values and norms | 4.04 | 4 | .916 | .840 | 1 | 5 | 4.00 | 4.00 | 5.00 |
| Assumptions level | 3.85 | 4 | .863 | .744 | 1 | 5 | 3.00 | 4.00 | 4.00 |
| Rituals | 3.61 | 4 | 1.084 | 1.174 | 1 | 5 | 3.00 | 4.00 | 4.00 |
| Symbols | 3.36 | 4 | 1.115 | 1.242 | 1 | 5 | 3.00 | 4.00 | 4.00 |
| Communication | 3.26 | 4 | 1.195 | 1.427 | 1 | 5 | 2.00 | 4.00 | 4.00 |
| Taboos | 3.06 | 4 | 1.130 | 1.276 | 1 | 5 | 2.00 | 3.00 | 4.00 |
| Artifacts | 3.06 | 4 | 1.130 | 1.276 | 1 | 5 | 2.00 | 3.00 | 4.00 |
| Myths | 2.90 | 3 | 1.127 | 1.270 | 1 | 5 | 2.00 | 3.00 | 4.00 |

*Source:* Own study

of the organization's success – due to a higher level of long-term orientation ($M = 4.99$, SD = 1.495, Mdn = 5).

- There is a balance maintained between culture of emotions and care for co-workers against that of persistence, agency, and material success – due to a moderate level of the femininity–masculinity dimension ($M = 4.04$, SD = 1.57, Mdn = 4).
- There is a balance between caution and cynicism, between controlling one's needs for the overall success against impulsiveness, instant gratification, due to a moderate level of indulgence ($M = 3.72$, SD = 1.540, Mdn = 4).
- Work is relatively collaborative, successes are shared, while collective achievements of the team/company are celebrated over those of individual employees – due to a rather low level of individualism ($M = 3.22$, SD = 1.687, Mdn = 3).

- The company creates a culture of openness to change and facilitates a rapid detection of new trends and risk-taking – due to a rather low level of uncertainty avoidance ($M = 3.14$, SD = 1.721, Mdn = 3).
- The company succeeds in implementing direct communication and embraces partnership-like, free relationships – due to a low power distance score ($M = 2.47$, SD = 1.463, Mdn = 3).

***Dimensions of the Organizational Culture Theory by Wojtowicz***

Out of the seven distinct dimensions of organizational culture, as defined by Wojtowicz, mean scores recorded for three were above 4.0, which indicates factors influencing employee engagement. These are: human significance, with $M = 4.68$, SD = 0.653, Mdn = 5; promoting creativity, with $M = 4.45$, SD = 0.715, Mdn = 5; and adaptability, with $M = 4.24$, SD =.784, Mdn = 4. The lowest score was recorded for the connection with anthropology category, with $M = 2.81$, SD = 1.036, Mdn = 3. It may indicate that it has hardly any impact on employee engagement.

The second step of the analysis involved exploring the differences between the various dimensions. Friedman's ANOVA revealed differences between the perceived impact of the respective organizational practices on employee engagement: $\chi^2(6) = 292.811, p < 0.001$. The Wilcoxon test revealed differences between most of the factors. The results are presented graphically in Figure 3.1.

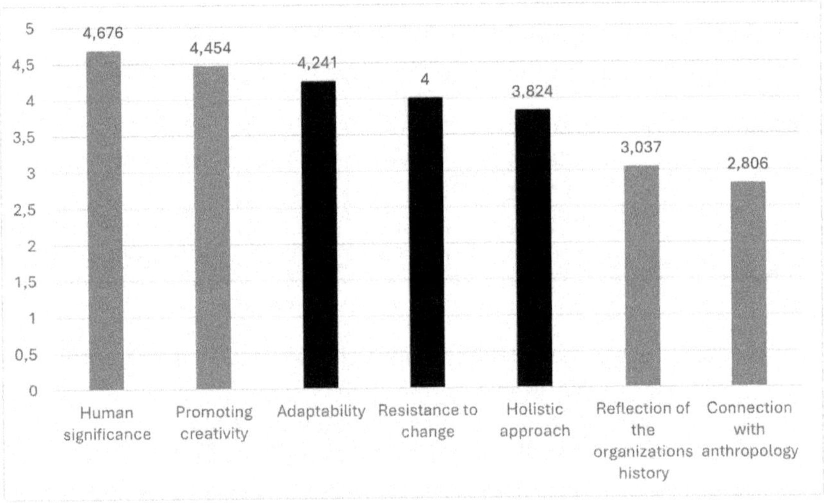


*Figure 3.1* Differences between perceived impact of organizational culture qualities on employee engagement – Wojtowicz theory

*Source:* Own study

Three groups were identified during the analysis. The factors of human significance and promoting creativity scored the highest. Adaptability, resistance to change, and holistic approach scored lower, and there were no statistically significant differences between them. The two lowest scoring dimensions were reflection of the organization's history and the connection with anthropology.

### *Dimensions of Schein's Organizational Culture Model*

It is important to emphasize that out of the eight dimensions accounted for by the theory, a score above 4.0 with $M = 4.04$, SD = 0.916, and Mdn = 4 was only recorded for one, namely, values and norms. Six other dimensions scored between $M = 3.06$ and $M = 3.85$, while the dimension of myths even fell below 3.0 (with $M = 2.90$, SD = 1.127, and Mdn = 3).

Friedman's ANOVA revealed differences between the perceived impact of the respective organizational practices on employee engagement: $\chi^2(7) = 127.538$, $p < 0.001$. The Wilcoxon test revealed some differences between most of the factors. The minuteness of the differences between the respective dimensions, however, made it impracticable to present them graphically.

### *Supplementary Questions*

**Supplementary question 1.** Is age correlated with certain cultural elements?

The Spearman's rho test was used to answer supplementary question 1. The analysis revealed:

- A very weak negative correlation $\rho = -0.241, p = 0.012, N = 108$ between age and power distance;
- A very weak positive correlation $\rho = 0.209, p = 0.030, N = 108$ between age and holistic approach;
- A very weak negative correlation $\rho = -0.198, p = 0.040, N = 108$ between age and promoting creativity;
- A very weak negative correlation $\rho = -0.197, p = 0.041, N = 108$ between age and rituals.

**Supplementary question 2.** Is work experience correlated with certain cultural elements?

The Spearman's rho test was used to answer supplementary question 2. The analysis revealed a single statistically significant correlation, namely, a very weak positive correlation $\rho = 0.09, p = 0.049, N = 108$ between work experience and holistic approach.

**Supplementary question 3.** Can gender influence the perception of the engagement level of cultural elements?

The Mann–Whitney *U* test was used to answer supplementary question 3. The analysis revealed a statistically significant gender difference with regard to the dimension of indulgence: $U(N_{men} = 27, N_{women} = 81) = 700.0$, $z = -2.846$, $p = 0.004$. Men (Mdn = 5) tend to prefer a more spontaneous and challenging work culture with more instant gratification than women do (Mdn = 3).

**Supplementary question 4.** Is occupation important in perceiving cultural elements as engaging?

The Kruskal–Wallis *H* test was used to answer supplementary question 4. The analysis did not reveal any statistically significant differences between various occupations in the perceived impact of culture on employee engagement. The asymptotic significance for each of the tests was equal or greater than 0.005.

**Supplementary question 5.** Is company size important in how cultural elements are perceived?

The Kruskal–Wallis *H* test was used to answer supplementary question 5. The analysis revealed statistically significant differences in:

- Power distance $H_{(3,n = 108)} = 8.40$, $p = 0.038$. The pairwise comparisons with Bonferroni correction showed a statistically significant difference between medium-sized (Mdn = 3) and large (Mdn = 2) organizations.
- Myths $H(_{3,n = 108)} = 8.479$, $p = 0.037$. The pairwise comparisons with Bonferroni correction showed no statistically significant differences for the respective company sizes.

**Supplementary question 6.** Can the organization type impact the perception of cultural elements?

The Kruskal–Wallis *H* test was used to answer supplementary question 6. The analysis revealed statistically significant differences in:

- Adaptability $H_{(5,n=108)} = 12.264$, $p = 0.031$. The pairwise comparisons with Bonferroni correction showed a statistically significant difference between local/family (Mdn = 3) and global (Mdn = 2) organizations.
- Communication $H_{(5,n=108)} = 11.378$, $p = 0.044$. The pairwise comparisons with Bonferroni correction showed no statistically significant differences between organizational types.

## Discussion and Conclusions

The above study is prone to certain limitations, the most important of which is the sample size. As it is rather small, the research results can only be treated as a pilot study.

From the perspective of students, working students, and employees, both national and organizational culture has a vital role in building employee engagement. Ensuring direct communication, free of formalities and bureaucratic barriers, is essential to keeping younger employees engaged. At the outset of their careers, they are willing to work in teams, but as their work experience grows, they become more competitive. According to Deal and Kennedy (1984), symbols, rituals, and narratives are all forms of expressions conveying the notion that leaders ought to seek opportunities to bolster the desired type of culture. Our research has shown, however, that when it comes to organizational culture, symbols may not play a significant role in shaping the engagement of employees. The focus should rather be shifted to rituals and internal language/communication; it is also essential to foster values, norms, and assumptions. Contrariwise, the respondents' assessment of the importance of artifacts was notably lower. This may stem from the fact that even though most companies nowadays develop their mission, vision, and values statements, these tend to be perceived as fake by employees. They expect bold actions, not mere declarations. As indicated by Steers and Shim (2013), leaders exert their influence on culture predominantly via their strategies, practices, values, leadership style, and example. The conduct of leaders, their approach to achieving goals, the principles they uphold, and their readiness to implement personal changes combine to serve as a guiding example for others to emulate (Gehman et al., 2013).

Among the various elements that influence the perception of organizational cultures as instruments for building employee engagement, only age, work experience, and occupation have a profound importance. Gender has no bearing on the issue, and neither do company size or industry type. This substantiates our claim that organizational culture as an engagement-building instrument is universal and may be pursued by various types of organizations.

Numerous studies have demonstrated that negative cultures are likely to adversely affect various other aspects, such as productivity, morale, drive, collaboration, customer relations, service quality, organizational development, and loyalty (Yeniyurt & Townsend, 2003; Morelli & Wang, 2020). Concluding our research, here are some implications it may have for businesses:

- Adopt a low power distance and direct communication – as most global companies nowadays do. This may be particularly advisable for the public sector.
- Balance individualism and team orientation – it is smart to create opportunities and tasks not only for individuals but also for the various teams within the organization.
- Implement rituals and use the internal language – the two visible elements of organizational cultures can be great identity-building tools for both organizations and employees. These will help to develop the organizations in the anthropological dimension.

The above suggestions refer to both national and organizational cultures. As using internal language and introducing rituals to the company seem a fairly straightforward task, what about the national culture theories then? The intensity of our contemporary style of work, performed mostly for international conglomerates, might help us transition to treating these as "nations" and build their cultures based on employee demands.

## References

Aniszewska, G. (2004). Rola kultury organizacyjnej w zarządzaniu, *Przegląd Organizacji*, *1*, 10.

Argyle, M. (2001). *The psychology of happiness*. Taylor & Francis Ltd.

Bakker, A. B., & Schaufeli, W. B. (2008). Positive organizational behavior: Engaged employees in flourishing organizations. *Journal of Organizational Behavior*, *29*(2), 147–154. https://doi.org/10.1002/job.515

Białas, S., Molek-Winiarska, D., & Pelc, A. (2023). Kultura organizacyjna sprzyjająca poprawie dobrostanu pracowników. *Zarządzanie Zasobami Ludzkimi*, *1*, 73–93. https://doi.org/10.5604/01.3001.0016.2926

Chmielecki, M. (2020). *Hofstede – wymiary kultury*. https://www.projektprzywodztwo.com/komunikacja-miedzykulturowa/hofstede-wymiary-kultury

Chuda, A., & Wyrwicka, M. (2013). Diagnoza kultury organizacyjnej przedsiębiorstwa produkcyjnego. *Zeszyty Naukowe Politechniki Poznańskiej. Organizacja i Zarządzanie*, *59*, 6.

Chumg, H. F., Seaton, J., Cooke, L., & Ding, W. Y. (2016). Factors affecting employees' knowledge-sharing behavior in the virtual organization from the perspectives of well-being and organizational behavior. *Computers in Human Behavior*, *64*(C), 432–448. https://doi.org/10.1016/j.chb.2016.07.011

Chun, D., Zhang, Z., Cohen, E., Florea, L., & Genc, O. F. (2021). Long-term orientation and the passage of time: Is it time to revisit Hofstede's cultural dimensions? *International Journal of Cross-Cultural Management*, *21*(2), 353–371.

Dartey-Baah, K. (2011). The impact of national cultures on corporate cultures in organizations. *Academic Leadership: The Online Journal*, *9*(1), 47.

Deal, T., & Kennedy, A. (1984). *Corporate cultures: The rites and rituals of corporate life*. Basic Books.

El-Majali, B. A. W. (2016). Organizational culture and its relationship with the organizational climate in the youth higher council from the perspective of council staff. *Journal of Education and Practice*, *7*(8), 39–51.

Febriansyah, H., Pringgabayu, D., Hidayanti, N., & Febrianti, F. C. (2018). Enhancing employee engagement through the organizational climate (a study of the School of Business and Management). *The Journal of Business and Retail Management Research*, *12*(3), 104–112. https://doi.org/10.24052/JBRMR/V12IS03/ART-09

Gadomska-Lila, K., Rudawska, A., & Moszoro, B. (2011). Rola lidera w zespołach wielokulturowych. *Przedsiębiorczość i Zarządzanie*, *12*(4), 7–20.

Gehman, J., Trevino, L., & Garud, R. (2013). Values work: A process study of the emergence and performance of organizational values practices. *The Academy of Management Journal*, *56*, 84–112. https://doi.org/10.5465/amj.2010.0628

Gong, Y., Cheung, S. Y., Wang, M., & Huang, J. C. (2012). Unfolding the proactive process for creativity: Integrating the employee proactivity, information exchange, and psychological safety perspectives. *Journal of Management*, *38*(5), 1611–1633.

Gray, R. J. (2001). Organizational climate and project success. *International Journal of Project Management*, *19*(2), 103–109. https://doi.org/10.1016/S0263-7863(99)00060–5

Gupta, M., & Shaheen, M. (2018). Does work engagement enhance general well-being and control at work? Mediating role of psychological capital. *Evidence-Based HRM*, *6*(3), 272–286. https://doi.org/10.1108/EBHRM-05-2017-0027

Haile, S., & Jabang, E. (2019). *The meeting of cultures: Effective leadership in multicultural organisations* [Linnaeus University Dissertation]. https://urn.kb.se/resolve?urn=urn:nbn:se:lnu:diva-85138

Hofstede, G. (1984). *Culture's consequences: International differences in work-related values*. Sage.

Hofstede, G. (2011). Dimensionalizing cultures: The Hofstede model in context. *Online Readings in Psychology and Culture*, *2*(1), 8.

Hofstede, G., Hofstede, G. J., & Minkov, M. (2000). *Kultury i organizacje*. PWE.

Jiang, H., & Luo, Y. (2018). Crafting employee trust: From authenticity, transparency to engagement. *Journal of Communication Management*, *22*(2), 138–160.

Kania, S. (2007). Kulturowe wyznaczniki efektywności organizacji. In S. Banaszak & K. Doktór (red.), *Socjologiczne i psychologiczne problemy organizacji i zarządzania*. Wydawnictwo Wyższej Szkoły Komunikacji i Zarządzania.

Karwasz, M. J. (2023). Propozycja narzędzia badawczego do pomiaru artefaktów kulturowych: Kwestionariusz MCA. *Forum Oświatowe*, *30*.

Kern, M. L., Waters, L. E., Adler, A., & White, M. A. (2015). A multidimensional approach to measuring student well-being: Application of the PERMA framework. *The Journal of Positive Psychology*, *10*(3), 262–271. https://doi.org/10.1080/17439760.2014.936962

Kobylińska, U., & Majewski, P. (2023). Kulturowe aspekty partycypacji–ujęcie teoretyczne. *Zarządzanie Zasobami Ludzkimi*, *150*(1), 94–111.

Kopczewski, M., Pączek, B., & Tobolski, M. (2012). Istota kultury organizacyjnej w zarządzaniu przedsiębiorstwem produkcyjnym. In *Innowacje w zarządzaniu i inżynierii produkcji* (pp. 929–938). Oficyna Wydawnicza Polskiego Towarzystwa Zarządzania Produkcją.

Kostera, M., Kownacki, S., & Szumski, A. (2000). Zachowania organizacyjne: Motywacja, przywództwo, kultura organizacyjna. In A. K. Koźmiński & W. Piotrowski (red.), *Zarządzanie. Teoria i praktyka*. PWN.

Kożak-Siara, T., & Olak, A. (2022). Przewaga konkurencyjna współczesnego przedsiębiorstwa. *Współczesne Problemy Zarządzania*, *10*(1 (20)), 67–84.

Lichtenthaler, P. W., & Fischbach, A. (2018). Leadership, job crafting, and employee health and performance. *Leadership & Organization Development Journal*, *39*(5), 620–632. https://doi.org/10.1108/LODJ-07-2017-0191

Lok, P., & Crawford, J. (2004). The effect of organisational culture and leadership style on job satisfaction and organisational commitment: A cross-national comparison. *Journal of Management Development*, *23*(4), 321–338. https://doi.org/10.1108/02621710410529785

Matzler, K., & Renzl, B. (2006). The relationship between interpersonal trust, employee satisfaction, and employee loyalty. *Total Quality Management and Business Excellence*, *17*(10), 1261–1271.

Mikuła, B. (2000). Klimat organizacyjny a kultura organizacyjna – próba systematyzacji pojęć. *Zeszyty Naukowe Małopolskiej Wyższej Szkoły Ekonomicznej w Tarnowie*, *3*, 33–40. https://doi.org/10.25944/znmwse.2000.03.3340

Mockałło, Z. (2011). Styl przywództwa a dobrostan psychiczny pracowników. *Bezpieczeństwo Pracy: Nauka i Praktyka*, *1*, 10–13.

Morelli, M., & Wang, M. (2020). Impacts of organizational culture. *International Journal of Managerial Studies and Research*, *8*(7), 95–99.

Nazarian, A., Irani, Z., & Ali, M. (2013). The relationship between national and organisational culture: The case of Iranian private sector organizations. *Journal of Economics, Business and Management*, *1*(1), 11–16.

Pandey, R., & Chitranshi, J. (2023). *The impact of organisational culture on employees' behaviour in research and development organisation* [Conference session]. AIP Conference Proceedings (Vol. 2523, No. 1). AIP Publishing.

Pathiranage, J. (2019). Organizational culture and business performance: An empirical study. *International Journal of Economics and Management*, *24*(2), 264–278.

Patterson, M., West, M. A., Shackleton, V. J., Dawson, J. F., Lawthom, R., Maitlis, S., Robinson, D. L., & Wallace, A. M. (2005). Validating the organizational climate measure: Links to managerial practices, productivity, and innovation. *Journal of Organizational Behavior*, *26*(4), 379–408. https://doi.org/10.1002/job.312

Pauliene, R., Diskiene, D., & Matuzeviciute, E. (2019). Complex approach on multicultural teams management & leadership. *Journal of Educational and Social Research*, *9*(2), 8.

Pepra-Mensah, J., & Kyeremeh, E. A. (2018). Organisational culture: A catalyst for employee engagement in the Ghanaian public sector. *Global Journal of Human Resource Management*, *6*(3), 11–28.

Piwowar-Sulej, K. (2012). Cechy kultury organizacyjnej a metodyki prowadzenia projektów. *Edukacja Ekonomistów i Menedżerów*, *26*(4), 39–51.

Rattrie, L. T., Kittler, M. G., & Paul, K. I. (2020). Culture, burnout, and engagement: A meta-analysis on national cultural values as moderators in JD-R theory. *Applied Psychology*, *69*(1), 176–220.

Rollinson, D. (2005). *Organizational behavior and analysis: An integrative approach*. Pearson Education.

Ruggeri, K., Garcia-Garzon, E., Maguire, Á., Matz, S., & Huppert, F. A. (2020). Well-being is more than happiness and life satisfaction: A multidimensional analysis of 21 countries. *Health and Quality of Life Outcomes*, *18*(1), 192. https://doi.org/10.1186/s12955-020-01423-y

Ryff, C. D. (2014). Psychological well-being revisited: Advances in the science and practice of eudaimonia. *Psychotherapy and Psychosomatics*, *83*(1), 10–28. https://doi.org/10.1159/000353263

Santos, A., Hayward, T., & Ramos, H. M. (2012). Organizational culture, work, and personal goals as predictors of employee well-being. *Journal of Organizational Culture, Communication and Conflict*, *16*(1), 25–48.

Schaufeli, W. B., Taris, T. W., & Van Rhenen, W. (2008). Workaholism, burnout, and work engagement: Three of a kind or three different kinds of employee well-being? *Applied Psychology*, *57*(2), 173–203. https://doi.org/10.1111/j.1464-0597.2007.00285.x

Schein, E. H. (1993). Legitimating clinical research in the study of organizational culture. *Journal of Counseling & Development*, *71*, 703–708.

Schein, E. H. (2010). *Organizational culture and leadership* (Vol. 2). John Wiley & Sons.

Seligman, M. (2018). PERMA and the building blocks of well-being. *The Journal of Positive Psychology*, *13*(4), 333–335. https://doi.org/10.1080/17439760.2018.1437466

Shaheen, R., Bano, S., & Ahmed, J. (2022). Organizational climate is a way to increase the employees' well-being in the presence of social undermining. *Indian Journal of Economics and Business*, *21*(1), 305–320.

Shulyn, T., & Yazdanifard, R. (2013). *The review of changes in organizational behavior, human relations, and performance through interpersonal communication in new millennium*. www.researchgate.net/publication/258048827

Silverthorne, C. P. (2005). *Organizational psychology in cross cultural perspective.* New York University Press.

Song, U. (1992). *The impact of organizational climate on the relationship between job characteristics and job satisfaction: An empirical assessment of public sector managers* [Dissertations and Theses, Paper 1324]. https://doi.org/10.15760/etd.1323

Steenkamp, J. B. E. (2001). The role of national culture in international marketing research. *International Marketing Review*, *18*(1), 30–44.

Steers, R., & Shim, W. (2013). Strong leaders, strong cultures: Global management lessons from Toyota and Hyundai. *Organizational Dynamics*, *42*, 217–227. https://doi.org/10.1016/j.orgdyn.2013.06.007

Strychalska-Rudzewicz, A., & Sobol, D. (2023). *Kultura innowacji a innowacyjność przedsiębiorstw: Uwarunkowania i pomiar*. Instytut Badań Gospodarczych.

Subocz, D. (2012). Geert Hofstede–praktyczne zastosowanie wymiarów kultur narodowych. *Annales Universitatis Mariae Curie-Skłodowska*, *25*(1–2), 41–52.

Szara, M., & Klukow, J. (2022). Przywództwo jako element kultury organizacyjnej zespołów pielęgniarskich. In *Inwestowanie w pielęgniarstwo i poszanowanie praw pielęgniarek–kontrowersje i wyzwania* (p. 85). Państwowa Wyższa Szkoła Zawodowa w Głogowie.

Szydło, J., & Grześ-Bukłaho, J. (2020). Relations between national and organisational culture – Case study. *Sustainability*, *12*(4), 1522.

Szymańska, K. (2012). Kultura organizacyjna–czynnik rozwoju współpracy MSP ze sferą nauki i administracją publiczną. *Studia i Prace Kolegium Zarządzania i Finansów*, *116*, 174–183.

Viitala, R., Tanskanen, J., & Säntti, R. (2015). The connection between organizational climate and well-being at work. *International Journal of Organizational Analysis*, *23*(4), 606–620. https://doi.org/10.1108/IJOA-10-2013-0716

Vollero, A., Siano, A., Palazzo, M., & Amabile, S. (2020). Hoftsede's cultural dimensions and corporate social responsibility in online communication: Are they independent constructs? *Corporate Social Responsibility and Environmental Management*, *27*(1), 53–64.

Wallace, J., Hunt, J., & Richards, C. (1999). The relationship between organisational culture, organisational climate, and managerial values. *International Journal of Public Sector Management*, *12*(7), 548–564.

Waller, L. (2020). Fostering a sense of belonging in the workplace: Enhancing well-being and a positive and coherent sense of self. In *The Palgrave handbook of workplace well-being* (pp. 1–27). Palgrave Macmillan.

Wojtowicz, A. (2004). Istota i modele kultury organizacyjnej-przegląd koncepcji. *Zeszyty Naukowe Małopolskiej Wyższej Szkoły Ekonomicznej w Tarnowie*, *5*, 159–171.

Yeniyurt, S., & Townsend, J. D. (2003). Does culture explain acceptance of new products in a country? An empirical investigation. *International Marketing Review*, *20*(4), 377–396. https://doi.org/10.1108/02651330310485153

Zen, A., Yanti, S., Hutomo, M. R., Kraugusteeliana, K., & Arisutama, H. Y. (2023). The role of leadership in managing organisational culture change in the context of information technology implementation. *Jurnal Minfo Polgan*, *12*(1), 1247–1255.

# 4 Application of the SCARF Model in Building Work Engagement

## Supportive Organizational Culture

*Joanna Krzyżak and Jolanta Walas-Trębacz*

### Introduction

In a period of rapid organizational change and increased expectations for productivity and employee engagement, striving to discover innovative models to foster a positive organizational culture has become a crucial endeavor. Among various theoretical frameworks developed to increase the dynamics of the work environment, the SCARF model, introduced by Rock (2008), stands out as a particularly promising approach. The model, with its roots in the social cognitive and affective neuroscience, allows for an understanding of factors that significantly impact the interactions and engagement of individuals in their work environment. The SCARF model identifies the five basic needs (i.e., the social domains of: status, certainty, autonomy, relatedness, and fairness), which are believed to motivate or inhibit human social behaviors, especially in the organizational environment.

The implementation of the SCARF model in creating organizational culture opens novel research prospects, above all in the field of academic institutions, where culture is decisive for the work engagement and performance of teachers. Academic communities, with their unique combination of autonomy, competition, and collaboration, are likely to render the research of this model both important and relevant today. The implementation of the SCARF model into the organizational culture of a university is of paramount importance for psychosocial support for the academic staff. The understanding and active use of the domains defined in the model may significantly contribute to the satisfaction of employee needs. This study is aimed to demonstrate how the SCARF model can shape organizational culture that recognizes and uses its dimensions to improve employee engagement among the university staff members.

This chapter will present the four theoretical bases of the SCARF model, tracing its origins back to the social cognitive theory (Bandura, 1997; Lee et al., 2012), and its further refinements in the field of neuroscience (Cherchia & Singer, 2017; Beugré, 2018; Zak, 2018; Newman & Purnell, 2023; Gkintoni et al., 2023), in order to provide a comprehensive framework for developing

DOI: 10.4324/9781032715407-5

the research instrument, conducting the study, and performing an analysis of its results. In investigating the five domains of the model (i.e., status, certainty, autonomy, relatedness, and fairness) in the context of academic institutions, our study is aimed to identify the potential mechanisms located within these domains that impact the engagement, motivation, and general job satisfaction of university teachers. The empirical research conducted employs a mixed approach, combining the analysis of quantitative data obtained from a wide-scale study of academic staff at universities throughout Poland with their various observations expressed during the research (as answers to the open-ended questions in the survey), in order to create a complete picture of the use and influence of the SCARF model. By identifying the key aspects bearing on employee engagement, the study provides valuable guidelines for developing personnel policy in universities. It shows how a strategy for promoting an organizational culture that is supportive, integrative, and fair can lead to an improvement in employee engagement among university teachers. The latter, facing the challenges of contemporary higher education with its emphasis on excellence in teaching, research, and social involvement, make valuable observations about their work that support their development and adaptation processes.

## Theoretical Basis and Domains of the SCARF Model

The model of social cognitive and affective neuroscience, developed by Rock in 2008, offered an innovative solution for understanding and managing social interactions. It is based on the principles of social cognitive neuroscience, which underscores the neurological foundation of social behaviors and interactions. It provides a comprehensive framework for understanding how individuals perceive and react to social situations. It integrates theories from the fields of psychology, neuroscience, and organizational behavior (Rock, 2008). The SCARF model is a concept that accounts for five key areas that influence how people react to social situations. The SCARF acronym stands for the following five domains: Status, Certainty, Autonomy, Relatedness, and Fairness (Rock, 2008).

The development of the SCARF model can be traced to the early works within the social cognitive theory, particularly the research by Bandura (1977), who emphasized the role of observational learning, a sense of self-efficacy, and reciprocal determinism in behavior. Then, there were other foundational advances in neuroscience, especially in understanding the brain's "reward system," which provided biological basis for social cognitive theories (Lee et al., 2012). The origins of the SCARF model can be attributed to the interdisciplinary field of cognitive neuroscience, which attempts to understand how biological processes shape our social behavior and cognition (Becker & Cropanzano, 2010; Cherchia & Singer, 2017; Beugré, 2018).

The psychological roots of the SCARF model are also embedded in theories of human motivation and social behavior, such as Maslow's hierarchy of needs

(1943), and Alderfer's ERG theory (1969). These highlighted the importance of social needs and thus paved the way for an understanding of the social dimensions of motivation and behavior in the organizational environment. The research in the field of social neuroscience conducted by Lieberman and Eisenberger (2009) made the crucial contribution to the development of the SCARF model as they were able to demonstrate how social threats and rewards processed in the brain, particularly in such regions as the amygdala, the prefrontal cortex, and the ventral striatum (Kringelbach & Berridge, 2009), activate neuronal circuits similar to those triggered by physical pain and pleasure. These discoveries confirmed the assumption behind the model, namely, that social experiences may influence the brain in much the same way that physical pain and pleasure do (Masten et al., 2010).

The SCARF model, therefore, is a testament to the successful cooperation between neuroscience and psychology. Rock's contribution consists in the integration of these various research threads into a coherent model encompassing the five key domains that influence human behavior in social contexts. He believes that getting to know and understanding these issues may enhance the effectiveness of leadership and improve the organizational culture by adjusting management practices to natural social motivations "hard-wired" into the human brain (Rock, 2008). Presented below are synthetic accounts of the key domains (dimensions) of the SCARF model and their influence on the social interactions and behaviors that constitute the basis for creating organizational culture oriented toward employee motivation and engagement.

The domain of *status* refers to an individual's relative importance in social interactions and their relative importance for others. This concept is firmly rooted in the theory of social comparison processes (Festinger, 1954), which suggests that people evaluate their abilities and opinions by comparing themselves to others. In social and organizational environments, the perception of status has an impact not only on interpersonal interactions but also on the decision-making processes. Persons of high status tend to have a higher self-esteem (Maslow, 1943) and higher sense of organizational attachment (Anderson et al., 2006); they may exert a greater influence and are listened to more intently (Owens & Sutton, 2001), receive more acceptance and support from others (Tortoriello et al., 2011), and may also be able to persuade others to work and increase their engagement (Magee & Galinsky, 2008; Sekiguchi et al., 2017). And conversely, a perceived decline in status may result in a sense of threat and diminished engagement (Berg et al., 2013). A study conducted by Jordan et al. (2011) revealed that the perception of social status in the workplace has a significant influence on employee engagement and productivity (Deng et al., 2019; Eka & Anik, 2020). Employees with higher perceived social status displayed higher job satisfaction; they were more engaged and productive (Liu et al., 2021). The latter finding highlights the significance of managing the perception of status for fostering a positive team dynamic.

The brain's desire for predictability and structure, meanwhile, is the reason behind the need for *certainty*. This accords with the theory of cognitive dissonance (Festinger, 1957), which discusses how the discrepancy between beliefs, behaviors, and information produces a feeling of mental discomfort. Thus, certainty involves the ability to predict future outcomes. In uncertain environments, individuals experience stress because unpredictability can be psychologically taxing. In their research, van den Bos and Lind (2002) demonstrated that providing certainty in the workplace, especially when implementing changes, helps reduce employee resistance. The results they obtained suggest that communicating clearly defined plans and expectations alleviates the fear of the unknown, which in turn fosters acceptance of change and adaptation. Furthermore, certainty with regard to an individual need to predict future events is strictly connected to Vroom's expectancy theory of motivation (1964). It posits that individuals are motivated when they believe that their efforts will lead to the desired outcome. The need for certainty also concurs with Herzberg's two-factor theory (1959), in which work safety is an important hygiene factor, one that may significantly influence job satisfaction (Chao et al., 2021). The lack of certainty may cause stress and disengagement (Chen et al., 2022), whereas the presence of certainty is likely to foster a sense of safety (Edmondson & Lei, 2014), enabling employees to focus on intrinsic motivators and improve their level of work engagement.

Next domain of the SCARF model, that of *autonomy*, is closely related to the self-determination theory (SDT), developed by Ryan and Deci (1985, 2020), which highlights autonomy as a basic psychological need that influences a person's behavior and well-being (Vansteenkiste & Ryan, 2013), and a significant determinant of motivational processes (Gagné & Deci, 2005; Gagné & Bhave, 2011; Li et al., 2018). According to this theory, fulfilling the need for autonomy fosters intrinsic motivation, resulting in a higher level of engagement and well-being (Ryan & Deci, 2000; Deci & Ryan, 2009). This idea is also reflected in Pink's Motivation 3.0 theory (2009), in which autonomy – besides mastery and purpose – is essential for fueling intrinsic motivation and effectiveness. In the workplace, autonomy is associated with job satisfaction (Van den Broeck et al., 2010) and engagement (Choong et al., 2014; Alhassan et al., 2022). When employees feel that they can influence their work, make their own choices, and implement changes to their job tasks (Hughes & Lewis, 2020), they are more creative (Sia & Appu, 2015), are more willing to be engaged, and improve their work performance (Bindl & Parker, 2011). However, too much autonomy without appropriate support may lead to a feeling of being isolated and overwhelmed. Therefore, balancing autonomy with adequate guidance is crucial in organizational environment (Boccoli et al., 2023).

The domain of *relatedness* within the SCARF model is focused on the meaning of social connections and interactions, including those in the working environment. The domain of relatedness is associated with attachment theory (Bowlby, 1969) and the need for social bonds and relationships (Bakker &

Oerlemans, 2019; Zeijen et al., 2020). It places emphasis on the importance of belonging and interpersonal bonds for social cognition (Ryan & Deci, 2020). Both in the social and organizational contexts, relationships are a basic human need (Baard et al., 2004). Workplace relationships are founded on mutual interchange; such social interactions may be powerful motivators that influence engaging in work and entering in interactions with a broader community and stakeholders (Orazbayeva et al., 2021). Positive relationships with colleagues and a sense of belonging to the group can improve collaboration, communication, and team work (Van den Broeck et al., 2008; Rajhans, 2012). Organizations that foster culture of integration and participation are likely to boost employee morale and reduce turnover. Promoting a sense of organizational community and belonging inspires cooperation and loyalty, which in turn improves employee engagement (McGrath et al., 2017).

The final domain, that of *fairness*, refers to the concepts of fairness and equity, drawing on Adams' equity theory (1963, 1965), which posits that individuals in their interactions and relationships are motivated by justice. Justice refers to a sense of having honest contacts and exchange with others. In a research conducted by Colquitt et al. (2001), organizational justice (i.e., perceived justice in decision-making and employee relations) was strongly associated with employee engagement, job satisfaction, and organizational commitment. The authors argue that practices that promote equity and justice may constitute a major element of human resource management. Unfair treatment may lead to animosity, conflicts, demotivation, and a lack of employee engagement (Cohen-Charash & Spector, 2001; Blakely et al., 2005).

The above rundown of the domains of the SCARF model is evidence of it being not only a mere theoretical concept but also a practical tool for improving interpersonal dynamics, raising the level of motivation and employee engagement, as well as that of organizational effectiveness. Each domain of the model – status, certainty, autonomy, relatedness, and fairness – plays a critical role in shaping the employee experience in the workplace and their level of work engagement.

Since its inception, the SCARF model has gained widespread recognition because of its practical usability in various fields, including leadership development (Rock, 2011; Donde & Williams, 2012), organizational change (Derler, 2019; Zak, 2018; Campbell et al., 2022), medicine (Diabat et al., 2022), as well as education (Li & Foung, 2019; Javadizadeh et al., 2022; Newman & Purnell, 2023; Gkintoni et al., 2023), and its significance only continues to grow (Rock & Cox, 2012; Waldman et al., 2019).

It should also be noted that the SCARF model provides a convenient tool for understanding social dynamics in the workplace, but there are also some limitations to its practical application. Acknowledging these limitations is crucial for a successful use of the model in various work-related contexts.

For the purpose of conducting empirical research to identify the influence that each of the five SCARF domains has on employee engagement among university teachers, we adopted one of the conceptions of employee engagement that is frequently used and described in literature, namely, that of work engagement developed by Schaufeli et al. (2002). According to their conception, employee engagement is a positive and satisfying state of mind, characterized by vigor, dedication, and absorption at work. Vigor refers to displaying high levels of energy and mental resilience in the workplace, which enable employees to persevere despite the challenges they face. Dedication to work involves a sense of meaning, enthusiasm, inspiration, and pride in one's occupation. Absorption is defined as a state of deep concentration and immersion in work, which makes time seem to pass extremely quickly.

## Research Methodology

The aim of the empirical research component is to identify the extent of the influence of satisfying the five social needs as defined by the SCARF model on the level of employee engagement among university teachers in their work environment. The study is to facilitate the verification of the following hypothesis: strategies or practices implemented by higher education institutions (HEI) that successfully address these needs contribute to enhancing academic employee engagement. In line with the assumptions behind the SCARF model, the research is based on the belief that meeting these fundamental social needs influences motivation, emotional well-being, and general work engagement, which has a direct bearing on the academic community.

The conceptual framework suggested to illustrate the influence of needs' satisfaction on employee engagement among university teachers, based on the SCARF model, was presented in Figure 4.1.

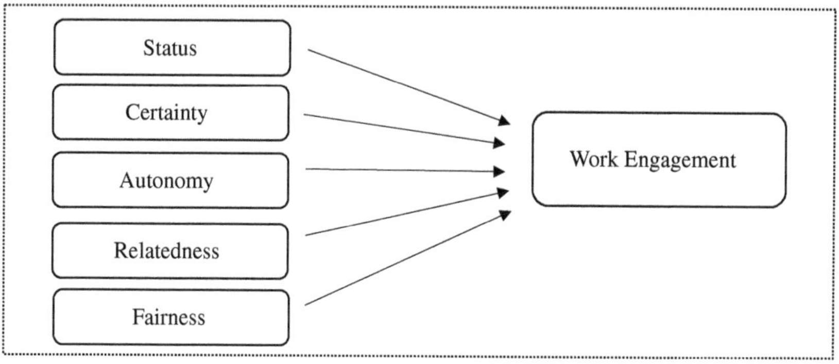


*Figure 4.1* Model of the influence of satisfying the (SCARF) needs on work engagement among academic teachers

*Source:* Own elaboration

The above model has the following structure:

***Independent Variables***

The model identifies five independent variables corresponding to the domains of the SCARF model:

- Status – recognition of a person's value and contribution
- Certainty – as to future events and expectations
- Autonomy – freedom in making choices and control over one's work
- Relatedness – quality of social relations and a sense of belonging
- Fairness – perception of equal treatment and justice

***Dependent Variable***

The basic dependent variable in the model is work engagement among university teachers measured in terms of vigor, dedication, and absorption.

***Paths***

The model posits direct paths connecting each of the five needs to work engagement and suggests that satisfaction in each domain independently contributes to the increase in the level of work engagement.

Thus, the visual account of the research model incorporates hypothetical connections between satisfying specific needs (defined by the SCARF model) and work engagement among university teachers. It provides a structural framework for empirical research aimed at clarifying how the satisfaction of these needs may serve as a mechanism for enhancing employee engagement in academia.

It has been decided to use questionnaire survey as the main research method for the study. This choice was dictated by the method's capability to aggregate data of a high degree of variability and representativeness. The survey method enabled the authors to reach a broad group of academic teachers working in various universities (in Poland), representing diverse disciplines and roles, to ensure the results are representative and take into consideration various perspectives and experiences within these institutions. The questionnaire used in the study was divided into two parts: part A measuring needs satisfaction according to the SCARF model (original approach), and part B focused on measuring employee engagement (the UWES© questionnaire, developed by Schaufeli & Bakker). Both parts use Likert seven-point scale for answers. Additionally, the questionnaire has a demographic information section.

The selected method made it possible to gather data on subjective experiences associated with each of the domains in the SCARF model, thus providing an insight into how these factors contribute to or impair the development of a supportive and engaging organizational culture.

The survey questionnaire comprises both closed-ended and open-ended questions. Such an approach allows for a comprehensive exploration of the application of the SCARF model to organizational culture. The responses to close-ended questions yielded quantitative indicators of the influence of the SCARF model on work engagement among university teachers. The responses to the close-ended questions, meanwhile, facilitated an in-depth understanding of the causes and mechanisms behind the observed outcomes. The complementarity of the data helped conduct a thorough analysis, enabling the authors to assess the importance and the potential for implementing the SCARF model in the academic work environment.

In order to ensure the credibility of the study, the process of development and validation of the 19 questions of part A of the questionnaire, intended to measure the satisfaction of the needs in line with the SCARF model, was carried out in the following four stages:

- A literature review was conducted on the SCARF model, which enabled the authors to identify the key constructs and variables as well as formulate valid questions.
- The questions were validated through a focus group study, whose feedback led to the introduction of changes in the questions, making them more clear and relevant.
- The questionnaire developed was subject to further evaluation by experts in the fields of psychology and research methodology, which allowed for further refinement of the questions regarding their relevance and congruence with the constructs of the SCARF model.
- In the final stage of validation, reliability tests on a representative sample of the target population were conducted, along with a statistical analysis aimed at assessing the questionnaire reliability. For each construct in part A of the questionnaire, Cronbach's alpha was calculated, which demonstrated that the coherence of questions was at an acceptable level ($\alpha = 0.936$), with the value of 0.7 and higher considered satisfactory.

Part B of the questionnaire consisted of 17 questions intended to evaluate the level of the respondent's work engagement in three dimensions: vigor, dedication, and absorption. The study also used the Utrecht work engagement scale (UWES) developed by Schaufeli et al. (2006).

The process of data collection in the research centered on academic lecturers in Polish higher education institutions was conducted online (with the Computer-Assisted Web Interview – CAWI), using a platform that is both secure and easy to use (Google Form), which was aimed at ensuring a broad participation and representativeness of the research group. In order to guarantee data integrity and adhere to ethical standards, the survey was anonymous and confidential, which contributed to eliciting honest answers from respondents. The procedure for conducting the study was approved by the University Ethics Committee for Scientific Research, confirming its compliance with the standards of ethical research (decision no. KEBN/71/0044/D29/2023). The research was conducted between November 2023 and February 2024, with the use of regression analysis for causal links and descriptive statistics for data characteristics. Initial analysis was performed in Excel, whereas advanced statistical analysis was performed with the Statistica 13.3 software.

In order to achieve the research goal, a purposive sampling method was used, which entails deliberate selection of study participants. The selection criteria were closely related to the research assumptions and were crucial for accomplishing the research goal. Purposive sampling proved useful in the study as it allowed for detailed insights into specific aspects of the research topic.

The analyzed sample comprised 416 respondents, who varied in terms of their demography, profession, and academic experience. The group is balanced as far as gender is concerned, namely, women comprise 50.5% and men 47.1% of respondents. A small fraction (2.4%) did not provide information on their gender. Regarding age, the study participants represented various demographic groups: The majority belong to the age bracket of 41–50 years (35.5%); the next age group, 51–60 years, comprises 28.4% of the sample; the least numerous are people below 29 years of age – they account for only 4.2% of respondents.

As regards their positions, the biggest group is that of postdocs, representing 48.3% of respondents. The second largest group is that of associate professors – 26.4%; assistant professors comprise 16.8% of the sample, whereas lecturers and full professors represent smaller groups of 2.4% and 5.5%, respectively. In the context of experience in academic teaching, the most represented group is that of persons with 21–30 years of experience, who comprise 36.3% of the sample. Then, there are those with 11–20 years' experience (21.2%), whereas the least numerous group is that of persons with less than 5 years' experience (10.8%). As for the various employee groups, the majority of respondents are employed as researchers-lecturers (81.5%); meanwhile, 17.8% are teaching employees, and 0.7% belong to the group of research associates. Lastly, with regard to the type of institution, an overwhelming majority of respondents is associated with public universities (94.2%), while the remaining ones with private universities (5.8%).

## Influence of the Satisfaction of the SCARF Needs on Employee Engagement Among University Teachers – Research Results

The authors start the presentation of the research results by discussing their key findings that shed light on the study issues and facilitate a deeper understanding of it. Table 4.1 provides the descriptive statistics for the six variables: Status, Certainty, Autonomy, Relatedness, Fairness, and Engagement, each of which comprises 416 valid observations. The analysis provides a penetrating review of these variables, focusing on central tendencies (mean, median), variability

*Table 4.1* Descriptive statistics for the variables (for valid $N = 416$)

| *Variable* | *Mean* | *Confidence −95.000%* | *Confidence 95.000%* | *Median* | *Min* | *Max* | *Q1* | *Q3* | *SD* |
|---|---|---|---|---|---|---|---|---|---|
| **Status** | 3.85 | 3.701972 | 4.004759 | 4 | 1 | 7 | 3 | 5 | 1.57 |
| **Certainty** | 4.41 | 4.275032 | 4.547084 | 5 | 1 | 7 | 3 | 5 | 1.41 |
| **Autonomy** | 5.30 | 5.177551 | 5.418603 | 5 | 1 | 7 | 5 | 6 | 1.25 |
| **Relatedness** | 5.23 | 5.115541 | 5.336382 | 5 | 1 | 7 | 5 | 6 | 1.15 |
| **Fairness** | 4.28 | 4.127948 | 4.424937 | 4 | 1 | 7 | 3 | 5 | 1.54 |
| **Engagement** | 4.02 | 3.918002 | 4.120460 | 4 | 0 | 6 | 3 | 5 | 1.05 |

Legend: SD – standard deviation, Q1 – lower quartile, Q3 – upper quartile

*Source:* Own work based on the results of the empirical research

*Table 4.2* Relations between the needs defined by the SCARF model and employee engagement

| *Variable* | *β Parameter* | $R^2$ |
|---|---|---|
| **Status** | 0.362438 | 0.13136097 |
| **Certainty** | 0.296982 | 0.08819818 |
| **Autonomy** | 0.263455 | 0.06940838 |
| **Relatedness** | 0.398851 | 0.15908186 |
| **Fairness** | 0.313851 | 0.09850214 |

Legend: $p$ – statistical significance; $\beta$ – simple linear regression coefficient; $R^2$ – coefficient of determination

$N = 416$; $p < 0.000001$

*Source:* Own work based on the results of the empirical research

(standard deviation, minimum, maximum, the first quartile – Q1, and the third quartile – Q3), and confidence intervals at the level of 95%.

The highest mean was recorded for the domains of autonomy and relatedness, whereas the lowest was recorded for the status domain (see Table 4.1). The highest standard deviation was recorded in the domains of status and fairness, which suggests moderate variability and a symmetric distribution around the mean value; meanwhile, the lowest standard deviation was found for the domains of relatedness and autonomy.

The next part of the study presents the results of the analysis of the influence of SCARF domains (status, certainty, autonomy, relatedness, and fairness as independent variables) on employee engagement, using a simple analysis of linear regression (see Table 4.2).

The results revealed significant positive correlations between all the variables, highlighting the importance of each SCARF element for enhancing employee engagement.

Among the domains of the SCARF model, the most marked influence on employee engagement is that of relatedness and status, as indicated by the simple regression coefficient and the coefficient of determination. Fairness also has a major influence on employee engagement, which highlights the role of fair treatment in fostering engagement among teachers. Autonomy and certainty, on the other hand, are valid predictors of employee engagement, albeit to a lesser degree than the above domains.

Thus, the research results made it possible to confirm the initial research hypothesis regarding the satisfaction of the needs specified in the SCARF model and their influence on the level of employee engagement among university teachers in their work environment.

## Discussion and Inferences

Within the academic environment, satisfying the needs of university teachers becomes the key factor influencing not only their job satisfaction and an increase in their motivation (Daumiller et al., 2020) but also their effectiveness in contributing to the realization of the educational and research mission of the institution.

As pointed out by Rock (2008), the domains of the SCARF model are of crucial importance for shaping human behavior in social contexts, including work environment. The results of the presented study are in line with Rock's theory and further expand it by having empirically explored the influence of these elements on work engagement of 416 respondents.

The research revealed a significant positive correlation between status and work engagement, which indicates that the latter increases along with the growth in the perceived status. This accords with the findings of Deci and Ryan (2009), who claim that recognition and self-worth in the workplace are an integral part of fostering motivation and engagement, a fact that highlights the importance of status as a psychological need (Deng et al., 2019).

The variable of certainty showed a positive influence on employee engagement. This corroborates the belief that certainty reduces stress and anxiety, facilitating focus on productive tasks (Hirsh et al., 2012). By reducing ambiguity and ensuring predictable work environment, organizations can increase employee engagement (Hwang & Lee, 2015).

Autonomy had a positive impact on work engagement. Gagné and Deci (2005) place emphasis on autonomy as a critical factor for intrinsic motivation and suggest that enabling employees to make choices can improve their levels of engagement. Greater autonomy fosters a sense of personal involvement and responsibility for one's work, which leads to intrinsic motivation (Tang et al., 2020; Itzchakov et al., 2022) and job satisfaction (Worth & Van den Brande, 2020), and encourages workers to take initiative (Lartey, 2021).

The highest regression coefficient among the SCARF domains is that of relatedness, the most significant predictor of work engagement. This observation refers to a study by Kahn (1990), who underscored the role of interpersonal relationships and a supportive work environment in promoting personal engagement of employees.

The emphasis on relationships implies that friendly atmosphere in which employees feel supported and connected may greatly improve their work engagement (Van den Broeck et al., 2008; McGrath et al., 2017; Owens et al., 2016).

Fairness was also shown to impact employee engagement in a major way, which agrees with the theory of justice developed by Colquitt et al. (2001), which posits that the perception of justice and equity are closely related to employee behavior, including engagement (Blakely et al., 2005).

The analysis of the data obtained from the answers to open questions, comprising part A of the survey, allowed for a more in-depth understanding of the respondents' opinions on their needs' satisfaction. Their input was interpreted in relation to the domains of the SCARF model and presented in Table 4.3.

The respondents' opinions on the needs satisfaction among university teachers pertain mainly to the expectation of recognition, stability, autonomy, supportive relationships, and justice. Meeting these needs requires a holistic approach aimed at cultivating an environment where teachers feel appreciated, safe, empowered, integrated, and treated fairly. Such efforts are not only vital for the well-being and job satisfaction of academic lecturers but also indispensable for fostering an academic environment ready to innovate, collaborate, and excel.

The research presented above emphatically confirms the value of the SCARF model for work engagement and helps identify the methods to significantly improve the satisfaction of these social needs. Empirical evidence suggests that interventions aimed to enhance the recognition of status, ensuring certainty as to future events and expectations, enabling greater autonomy, fostering positive social relationships, and promoting justice can combine to enhance work engagement among academic staff. Ensuing studies and collected data should allow for an analysis of these relations in various contexts and cultures to further generalize the results.

However, the research conducted has some limitations, including the following:

- The respondents were a quite specific group due to a greater command of their work time than other professional groups.
- The results obtained cannot be generalized to other demographic groups or sectors without further in-depth research.
- The method used (questionnaire) may be prone to biased responses.

In order to mitigate these constraints, scholars performing future research should consider including a broader and more diverse group of participants, using mixed research methods (quantitative analysis and qualitative approaches, e.g., interviews, case studies), which may enrich our understanding of the influence that the SCARF model may have in various contexts. Moreover, longitudinal research could provide an insight into the causality and dynamics of needs' satisfaction and work engagement over time.

*Table 4.3* Interpretation of the respondents' opinion on their levels of needs' satisfaction

1. **Status**
   The university teachers surveyed expect an improvement in work conditions and a compensation system that would reflect their contribution. They stress the importance of better management practices and recognizing their achievements; they also call for changes in the organizational culture and in the dynamics of cooperation with university authorities. This feedback highlights the urgent need for institutions to reevaluate the way they assess the professional status and value of academic staff; it also suggests that a lack of recognition and appreciation can drastically reduce motivation and engagement.
2. **Certainty**
   The dominant theme in the responses is that of the pursuit of greater stability and certainty in the academic environment. The respondents are in favor of better communication, clearer criteria for evaluating performance and awarding promotions, as well as a harmonious work–life balance. Concerns due to constantly changing regulations, administrative burden, and ambiguous requirements with respect to publications and promotions further exacerbate the sense of uncertainty, indicating a crucial need for universities to create a more predictable and supportive environment for their academic staff.
3. **Autonomy**
   The responses given to the survey clearly indicate that university employees hope to be granted more autonomy in their professional activity. This involves the freedom to make decisions regarding academic research, teaching, and managing their schedules, a work environment free from bureaucratic limitations. The call for autonomy extends to the choice of research topics, methodology, collaborators, working hours, and teaching methods, underscoring the fundamental expectation that the position of academic staff be strengthened, which would enable them to implement innovation and excel in their respective fields.
4. **Relatedness**
   The respondents expressed their need for improved support, communication, and sense of integration within the academic community. They point to the challenges caused by systemic pressure, perceived injustice, and divergent approaches to work, advocating a cultural change toward respect, dialogue, and a more collegial atmosphere. These findings suggest that an improvement in relational aspects and support mechanisms in universities can contribute to a more coherent and productive academic environment.
5. **Fairness**
   As for this aspect, the academic teachers under study point to the differences in teaching loads, wages, promotion processes, and access to resources. They make a strong call for greater clarity, equal treatment, and means ensuring a more balanced work–life dynamic. These apprehensions reflect a broader demand for institutional policy and practice that would support the principles of fairness and equity, thus alleviating the experienced insufficiency of rights of lecturers.

*Source:* Own work based on the opinions obtained from respondents

## Conclusion and Recommendations

In light of the identified needs and expectations of academic staff, as underscored in the discussion of the research results within the SCARF framework, it is necessary for higher education institutions to implement a strategic approach to reforming the organizational culture and enhancing work engagement among academic staff. The authors offer a number of recommendations intended to adjust it to the basic domains of the SCARF model to foster environments that not only recognize but also actively support the multifaceted needs of academic teachers.

First of all, in terms of improving recognition, efforts should be made to create professional and career development programs, especially by adopting clear and transparent paths of career advancement that would acknowledge a broad spectrum of academic contribution, including teaching, research, and social involvement of lecturers. Also to be implemented are mentoring programs to support professional development and recognition for teachers.

It is extremely important to develop and implement clear formal systems for recognizing and rewarding academic achievements, innovation, and contributions to university's operation in a broader community. This could entail granting awards, organizing public events in recognition of such merits, and incorporating these achievements into university communication: all that could be instrumental for raising the perceived status among colleagues and within a wider academic community.

As for the provision of certainty about future events and expectations, it is vital to establish clear and easily accessible communication channels through which university teachers could be provided with the latest information on the changes introduced to the policies and administrative procedures, as well as the development of the institution. Such activities, ensuring the transparency of decision-making processes, can dramatically reduce the level of uncertainty. Furthermore, it is important to strive to create more predictable models for financing research and teaching goals, which would help minimize the uncertainty resulting from budgetary instability. To this end, clear criteria for resource distribution should be established to allow equal access to the necessary academic support, which would contribute even more to the predictability and stability of the academic environment.

Meanwhile, regarding autonomy, it is vital to adopt principles that would allow university teachers more flexibility in selecting their research projects, teaching methods, and creating their schedules. Promoting innovation and experimentation in academia, such initiatives bolster the sense of independence. Additionally, it is important to implement simple, straightforward, and rapid decision-making procedures, a more decentralized management structure, enabling the respective departments and their members to decide independently regarding their administrative and academic tasks. This in turn should contribute to the increase in the sense of autonomy and greater commitment to the development of the institution, thus additionally strengthening its position and boosting the effectiveness of university's activities.

The effort to build a supportive academic community requires holding periodic events and initiatives promoting interactions and collaboration among lecturers from different departments. Such activities are aimed at enhancing the sense of attachment and mutual help through establishing a support network for new and current employees. Moreover, it is essential to develop and inform about clear and efficient channels for solving complaints and conflicts that arise within the academic community. Promoting the culture of respect, understanding, and constructive dialogue is indispensable for creating a friendly work environment, which has a major influence on the improvement in work engagement and job satisfaction.

Ensuring honesty and equality in the academic environment calls for an implementation and regular reviewing of policies that guarantee a fair division of teaching and administrative duties, and equitable access to development opportunities and research resources. The transparency of these processes is of utmost importance in order to reinforce a sense of justice among university teachers. It is also crucial to establish a set of coherent and fair criteria for academic staff evaluation, promotion, and the tenure decision. These processes have to be transparent, enable mutual assessment, and provide constructive feedback, which may contribute to fostering the professional development of each and every member of the academic community. Not only do such undertakings strengthen trust and motivation among employees, but they also help build organizational structure based on mutual respect and honesty.

For the implementation of the above guidelines, a joint effort has to be undertaken by university authorities, administrative staff, and the academic community. There is a need for constant commitment to evaluation and adaptation in order to make sure that the policies and practices implemented not only respond to the current demands of the academic staff but also adapt flexibly to the changing landscape of higher education. By adjusting the organizational culture to the principles of the SCARF model, universities can establish an environment that maximizes employee engagement, productivity, and job satisfaction among the academic staff, ultimately making a contribution to the success of the institution and the realization of its broad academic mission.

The SCARF model offers valuable guidance for shaping organizational culture that fosters employee engagement by way of satisfying their social needs. Focusing on the needs thus identified and simultaneously providing psychosocial support, organizations are able to not only better manage workplace relationships and interactions but also create an environment in which employees feel emotionally and socially cared for. Not only does such a strategy help improve their morale and productivity, but it also strengthens the mental resilience capabilities of employees, a crucial asset in the dynamically changing world of work.

## References

Adams, J. S. (1963). Toward an understanding of inequity. *Journal of Abnormal and Social Psychology*, *67*(5), 422–436. https://doi.org/10.1037/h0040968

Adams, J. S. (1965). Inequity in social exchange. *Advances in Experimental Social Psychology*, *2*, 267–299. https://doi.org/10.1016/S0065-2601(08)60108-2

Alderfer, C. P. (1969). An empirical test of a new theory of human needs. *Organizational Behavior and Human Performance*, *4*(2), 142–175. https://doi.org/10.1016/0030-5073(69)90004-X

Alhassan, Y. M., Akparep, J. Y., & Ngmenkpieo, F. (2022). Employee autonomy and employee creativity: The mediating role of intrinsic motivation. *Open Journal of Leadership*, *11*, 356–369. https://doi.org/10.4236/ojl.2022.114019

Anderson, C., Srivastava, S., Beer, J. S., Spataro, S. E., & Chatman, J. A. (2006). Knowing your place: Self-perceptions of status in face-to-face groups. *Journal of Personality and Social Psychology*, *91*(6), 1094–1110. https://doi.org/10.1037/0022- 3514.91.6.109438

Baard, P. P., Deci, E. L., & Ryan, R. M. (2004). Intrinsic need satisfaction: A motivational basis of performance and well-being in two work settings. *Journal of Applied Social Psychology*, *34*, 2045–2068. https://doi.org/10.1111/j.1559-1816.2004.tb02690.x

Bakker, A. B., & Oerlemans, W. G. M. (2019). Daily job crafting and momentary work engagement: A self-determination and self-regulation perspective. *Journal of Vocational Behavior*, *112*, 417–430. https://doi.org/10.1016/j.jvb.2018.12.005

Bandura, A. (1977). *Social learning theory*. Prentice Hall.

Bandura, A. (1997). *Self-efficacy: The exercise of control*. W. H. Freeman and Company.

Becker, W. J., & Cropanzano, R. (2010). Organizational neuroscience: The promise and prospects of an emerging field. *Journal of Organizational Behavior*, *31*(7), 1055–1059. http://dx.doi.org/10.1002/job.668

Berg, J. M., Dutton, J. E., & Wrześniewski, A. (2013). Job crafting and meaningful work. In B. J. Dik, Z. S. Byrne, & M. F. Steger (Eds.), *Purpose and meaning in the workplace* (pp. 81–104). American Psychological Association.

Beugré, C. (2018). *The neuroscience of organizational behavior*. Edward Elgar Publishing.

Bindl, U. K., & Parker, S. K. (2011). Proactive work behavior: Forward-thinking and change oriented action in organizations. In S. Zedeck (Ed.), *APA handbook of industrial and organizational psychology* (Vol. 2, pp. 567–598). American Psychological Association.

Blakely, G., Andrews, M., & Moorman, R. (2005). The moderating effects of equity sensitivity on the relationship between organizational justice and organizational citizenship behavior. *Journal of Business Psychology*, *20*(2), 259–273. http://dx.doi.org/10.1007/s10869-005-8263-3

Boccoli, G., Gastaldi, L., & Corso, M. (2023). The evolution of employee engagement: Towards a social and contextual construct for balancing individual performance and wellbeing dynamically. *International Journal of Management Reviews*, *25*, 75–98. https://doi.org/10.1111/ijmr.12304

Bowlby, J. (1969). *Attachment and loss. 1. Attachment*. Basic Books.

Campbell, S. J., Walsh, K., Prior, S. J., Doherty, D., Bramble, M., Marlow, A., & Maxwell, H. (2022). Examining the engagement of health services staff in change management: Modifying the SCARF assessment model. *International Practice Development Journal*, *12*(1), 1–13. https://doi.org/10.19043/ipdj.121.005

Chao, R. F., Zhang, L., & Yang, Y.-C. (2021). How the psychological safety of employees influences job performance in the insurance industry? The mediation role of organizational communication and organizational learning. *The International Journal of Organizational Innovation*, *14*(1), July, 130–144. https://www.ijoi-online.org

Chen, B., Wang, L., Li, B., & Liu, W. (2022). Work stress, mental health, and employee performance. *Frontiers in Psychology*, *13*, 1006580. https://doi.org/10.3389/fpsyg.2022.1006580

Cherchia, G., & Singer, T. (2017). The Neuroscience of compassion and empathy and their link to prosocial motivation and behavior. In J. Dreher & L. Tremblay (Eds.), *Decision neuroscience: An integrative perspective* (pp. 247–257). Elsevier Academic Press. https://doi.org/10.1016/B978-0-12-805308-9.00020-8247-257

Choong, Y. O., Tunku, U., & Rahman, A. (2014). The relationships of intrinsic motivation and job autonomy with organizational commitment: An empirical study. *Australian Journal of Basic and Applied Sciences*, *8*, 343–351.

Cohen-Charash, Y., & Spector, P. E. (2001). The role of justice in organizations: A meta-analysis. *Organizational Behavior and Human Decision Processes*, *86*(2), 278–321. https://doi.org/10.1006/obhd.2001.2958

Colquitt, J. A., Conlon, D. E., Wesson, M. J., Porter, C. O. L. H., & Ng, K. Y. (2001). Justice at the millennium: A meta-analytic review of 25 years of organizational justice research. *Journal of Applied Psychology*, *86*(3), 425–445. https://doi.org/10.1037/0021-9010.86.3.425

Daumiller, M., Stupinsky, R., & Janke, S. (2020). Motivation on higher education faculty: Theoretical approaches, empirical evidence, and future directions. *International Journal of Educational Research*, *99*, 101502. https://doi.org/10.1016/j.ijer.2019.101502

Deci, E. L., & Ryan, R. M. (1985). *Intrinsic motivation and self-determination in human behavior*. Plenum. https://link.springer.com/book/10.1007/978-1-4899-2271-7

Deci, E. L., & Ryan, R. M. (2009). The "what" and "why" of goal pursuits: Human needs and the self-determination of behavior. *Psychological Inquiry*, *11*(4), 227–268. https://doi.org/10.1207/S15327965PLI1104_01

Deng, C., Liao, S., & Liu, Z. (2019). When does status turn into proactive helping behavior? The moderating role of cooperative/competitive behavior intention. *Frontiers in Psychology*, *10*, 2702. https://doi.org/10.3389/fpsyg.2019.0270248

Derler, A. (2019). *Building brain-friendly leadership models*. NeuroLeadership Institute.

Diabat, O. A., Alhumaid, K., Alawadhi, M., Mouzaek, T., Matri, K. A., Salloum, S. A., & Aburayya, A. (2022). The effect of implementing the scarf model on the perception of patients' aggression among emergency nurses in Dubai Hospitals. *Academy of Strategic Management Journal*, *21*(6), 1–14.

Donde, R., & Williams, C. R. (2012). Mapping leadership behaviors to NeuroLeadership models: A NASA case study. *NeuroLeadership Journal*, *4*, 1–21.

Edmondson, A. C., & Lei, Z. (2014). Psychological safety: The history, renaissance, and future of an interpersonal construct. *Annual Review of Organizational Psychology & Organizational Behavior*, *1*(1), 23–43. http://dx.doi.org/10.1146/annurev-orgpsych-031413-091305

Eka, F., & Anik, H. (2020). The effect of organizational communication and job satisfaction on employee engagement and employee performance at PT. Abyor International. *Dinasti International Journal of Education Management and Social Science*, *1*(4), 479–489. http://dx.doi.org/10.31933/dijemss.v1i4.216

Festinger, L. (1954). A theory of social comparison processes. *Human Relations*, *7*(2), 117–140. https://doi.org/10.1177/001872675400700202

Festinger, L. (1957). *A theory of cognitive dissonance*. Stanford University Press.

Gagné, M., & Bhave, D. P. (2011). Autonomy in the workplace: An essential ingredient to employee engagement and well-being in every culture. In V. I. Chirkov, R. M. Ryan, & K. M. Sheldon (Eds.), *Human autonomy in cross-cultural context: Perspectives on the psychology of agency, freedom, and well-being* (pp. 163–187). Springer Science + Business Media. https://doi.org/10.1007/978-90-481-9667-8_8

Gagné, M., & Deci, E. L. (2005). Self-determination theory and work motivation. *Journal of Organizational Behavior*, *26*(4), 331–362. https://doi.org/10.1002/job.322

Gkintoni, E., Dimakos, I., Halkiopoulos, C., & Antonopoulou, H. (2023). Contributions of neuroscience to educational praxis: A systematic review. *Emerging Science Journal, Special Issue: Current Issues, Trends, and New Ideas in Education*, *7*, 146–158. http://dx.doi.org/10.28991/ESJ-2023-SIED2-012

Herzberg, F. (1959). *The motivation to work*. John Wiley & Sons.

Hirsh, J. B., Mar, R. A., & Peterson, J. B. (2012). Psychological entropy: A framework for understanding uncertainty-related anxiety. *Psychological Review*, *119*(2), 304–320. https://doi.org/10.1037/a0026767

Hughes, S., & Lewis, H. (2020). Tensions in current curriculum reform and the development of teachers' professional autonomy. *The Curriculum Journal*, *31*, 290–302. https://doi.org/10.1002/curj.25

Hwang, Y. K., & Lee, C. S. (2015). Structural relationship between authentic leadership, organizational communication, organizational effectiveness, and psychological capital of office workers. *Indian Journal of Science and Technology*, *8*(57), 292–298. http://dx.doi.org/10.17485/ijst/2015/v8iS7/69993

Itzchakov, G., Weinstein, N., Vinokur, E., & Yomtovian, A. (2022). Communicating for workplace connection: A longitudinal study of the outcomes of listening training on teachers' autonomy, psychological safety, and relational climate. *Psychology in the Schools*, *60*(4), 1279–1298. https://doi.org/10.1002/pits.22835

Javadizadeh, B., Aplin-Houtz, M., & Casile, M. (2022). Using SCARF as a motivational tool to enhance students' class performance. *International Journal of Management Education*, *20*(1), 100594. https://doi.org/10.1016/j.ijme.2021.100594

Jordan, S. J., Sivanathan, N., & Galinsky, A. D. (2011). Something to lose and nothing to gain: The role of stress in the interactive effect of power and stability on risk taking. *Administrative Science Quarterly*, *56*(4), 530–558. https://doi.org/10.1177/0001839212441928

Kahn, W. A. (1990). Psychological conditions of personal engagement and disengagement at work. *Academy of Management Journal*, *33*(4), 692–724. https://psycnet.apa.org/doi/10.2307/256287

Kringelbach, M. L., & Berridge, K. C. (2009). Towards a functional neuroanatomy of pleasure and happiness. *Trends in Cognitive Sciences*, *13*(11), 479–487. https://doi.org/10.1016/j.tics.2009.08.006

Lartey, F. M. (2021). Impact of career planning, employee autonomy, and manager recognition on employee engagement. *Journal of Human Resource and Sustainability Studies*, *9*, 135–158. https://doi.org/10.4236/jhrss.2021.92010

Lee, N., Senior, C., & Butler, M. J. R. (2012). The domain of organizational cognitive neuroscience: Theoretical and empirical challenges. *Journal of Management*, *38*(4), 921–934. https://doi.org/10.1177/0149206312439471

Li, H., Li, F., & Chen, T. (2018). A motivational-cognitive model of creativity and the role of autonomy. *Journal of Business Research*, *9*, 177–198. https://doi.org/10.1016/j.jbusres.2018.07.025

Li, T., & Foung, S. (2019). SCARF education model and happiness index modelling, the 3rd Sriwijaya University learning and education international conference. *IOP Conference Series: Journal of Physics*, *1166*, 012038. https://doi.org/10.1088/1742-6596/1166/1/012038

Lieberman, M. D., & Eisenberger, N. I. (2009). Pains and pleasures of social life. *Science*, *323*(5916), 890–891. https://doi.org/10.1126/nauka.1170008

Liu, Y., Yin, X., Li, S., Zhou, X., Zhu, R., & Zhang, F. (2021). The relationship between employee's status perception and organizational citizenship behaviors: A psychological path of work vitality. *Psychology Research and Behavior Management*, *14*, 743–757. http://dx.doi.org/10.2147/PRBM.S307664

Magee, J. C., & Galinsky, A. D. (2008). Social hierarchy: The self-reinforcing nature of power and status. *Academy of Management Annals*, *2*, 351–398. https://doi.org/10.1080/19416520802211628

Maslow, A. H. (1943). A theory of human motivation. *Psychological Review*, *50*(4), 370–396. https://psycnet.apa.org/doi/10.1037/h0054346

Masten, C., Eisenberger, N., Pfeifer, J., & Dapretto, M. (2010). Witnessing peer rejection during early adolescence: Neural correlates of empathy for experiences of social exclusion. *Social Neuroscience*, *5*(5–6), 496–507. http://dx.doi.org/10.1080/17470919.2010.490673

McGrath, E., Cooper-Thomas, H. D., Garrosa, E., Sanz-Vergel, A. I., & Cheung, G. W. (2017). Rested, friendly, and engaged: The role of daily positive collegial interactions at work. *Journal of Organizational Behavior*, *38*(2), 1213–1226. http://dx.doi.org/10.1002/job.2197

Newman, J., & Purnell, K. (2023). Reshaping leadership in schools: A social neuroscience lens. *Archives in Neurology & Neuroscience*, *14*(1), 1–5. https://doi.org/10.33552/ANN.2023.13.000829

Orazbayeva, B., Van der Sijde, P., & Baaken, T. (2021). Autonomy, competence and relatedness – The facilitators of academic engagement in education-driven university-business cooperation. *Studies in Higher Education*, *46*(7), 1406–1420. https://doi.org/10.1080/03075079.2019.1679764

Owens, B. P., Baker, W. E., Sumpter, D. M., & Cameron, K. S. (2016). Relational energy at work: Implications for job engagement and job performance. *Journal of Applied Psychology*, *101*(1), 35–49. https://doi.org/10.1037/apl0000032

Owens, D., & Sutton, R. (2001). Status contests in meetings: Negotiating the informal order. In M. E. Turner (Ed.), *Groups at work: Advances in theory and research* (pp. 299–316). Lawrence Erlbaum Associates Publishers.

Pink, D. H. (2009). *Drive: The surprising truth about what motivates us*. Riverhead Books.

Pollak, A., Chrupała-Pniak, M., Rudnicka, P., & Paliga, M. (2017). Work engagement – A systematic review of polish research. *Polish Psychological Bulletin*, *48*(2), 175–187. https://doi.org/10.1515/ppb-2017-0021

Rajhans, K. (2012). Effective organizational communication: A key to employee motivation and performance. *Interscience Management Review*, *2*(2), 81–85. http://dx.doi.org/10.47893/IMR.2009.1040

Rock, D. (2008). SCARF: A brain-based model for collaborating with and influencing others. *NeuroLeadership Journal*, *1*, 78–87.

Rock, D. (2011). Leadership excellence essentials. *NeuroLeadership Journal*, *28*(8), 11–12.

Rock, D., & Cox, C. (2012). SCARF in 2012: Updating the social neuroscience of collaborating with others. *NeuroLeadership Journal*, *4*, 1–14.

Ryan, R. M., & Deci, E. L. (2000). Self-determination theory and the facilitation of intrinsic motivation, social development, and well-being. *American Psychologist*, *55*(1), 68–78. https://doi.org/10.1037/0003-066X.55.1.68

Ryan, R. M., & Deci, E. L. (2020). Intrinsic and extrinsic motivation from a self-determination theory perspective: Definitions, theory, practices, and future directions. *Contemporary Educational Psychology*, *61*, 101860. https://doi.org/10.1016/j.cedpsych.2020.101860

Schaufeli, W. B., Bakker, A. B., & Salanova, M. (2006). The measurement of work engagement with a short questionnaire. *Educational and Psychological Measurement*, *66*(4), 701–716. http://dx.doi.org/10.1177/0013164405282471

Schaufeli, W. B., Salanova, M., González-Romá, V., & Bakker, A. B. (2002). The measurement of engagement and burnout: A two sample confirmatory factor analytic approach. *Journal of Happiness Studies*, *3*, 71–92. http://dx.doi.org/10.1023/A:1015630930326

Sekiguchi, T., Li, J., & Hosomi, M. (2017). Predicting job crafting from the socially embedded perspective: The interactive effect of job autonomy, social skill, and employee status. *The Journal of Applied Behavioral Science*, *53*(4), 470–497. https://doi.org/10.1177/0021886317727459

Sia, S. K., & Appu, A. (2015). Work autonomy and workplace creativity: Moderating role of task complexity. *Global Business Review*, *16*, 772–784. https://doi.org/10.1177/0972150915591435

Tang, M., Wang, D., & Guerrien, A. (2020). A systematic review and meta-analysis on basic psychological need satisfaction, motivation, and well-being in later life: Contributions of self-determination theory. *PsyCh Journal*, *9*(1), 5–33. https://doi.org/10.1002/pchj.293

Tortoriello, M., Perrone, V., & McEvily, B. (2011). Cooperation among competitors as status-seeking behavior: Network ties and status differentiation. *European Management Journal*, *29*, 335–346. https://doi.org/10.1016/j.emj.2011.02.001

Van den Bos, K., & Lind, E. A. (2002). Uncertainty management by means of fairness judgments. In M. P. Zanna (Ed.), *Advances in experimental social psychology* (Vol. 34, pp. 1–60). Academic Press. http://dx.doi.org/10.1016/S0065-2601(02)80003-X

Van den Broeck, A., Vansteenkiste, M., De Witte, H., & Lens, W. (2008). Explaining the relationships between job characteristics, burnout and engagement: The role of basic psychological need satisfaction. *Work and Stress*, *22*, 277–294. http://dx.doi.org/10.1080/02678370802393672

Van den Broeck, M., Vansteenkiste, M., De Witte, H., Soenens, B., & Lens, W. (2010). Capturing autonomy, competence, and relatedness at work: Construction and initial validation of the work-related basic need satisfaction scale. *Journal of Occupational and Organizational Psychology*, *83*, 981–1002. http://dx.doi.org/10.1348/096317909X481382

Vansteenkiste, M., & Ryan, R. M. (2013). On psychological growth and vulnerability: Basic psychological need satisfaction and need frustration as a unifying principle. *Journal of Psychotherapy Integration*, *23*(3), 263. https://doi.org/10.1037/a0032359

Vroom, V. H. (1964). *Work and motivation*. John Wiley & Sons.

Waldman, D. A., Wang, D., & Fenters, V. (2019). The added value of neuroscience methods in organizational research. *Organizational Research Methods*, *22*(1), 223–249. https://doi.org/10.1177/1094428116642013

Worth, J., & Van den Brande, J. (2020). *Teacher autonomy: How does it relate to job satisfaction and retention*? National Foundation for Educational Research.

Zak, P. (2018). The neuroscience of high-trust organizations. *Consulting Psychology Journal: Practice and Research*, *70*(1), 45–58. https://doi.org/10.1037/cpb0000076

Zeijen, M. E., Petrou, P., Bakker, A. B., & van Gelderen, B. R. (2020). Dyadic support exchange and work engagement: An episodic test and expansion of self-determination theory. *Journal of Occupational and Organizational Psychology*, *93*, 687–711. https://doi.org/10.1111/joop.12311

# 5 Harmony at Work

## Work–Life Balance as a Component of Psychosocial Support in Organizations

*Justyna Pawlak*

### Introduction

One of the significant challenges of human resource management in modern organizations is to foster employees' quality of life and well-being. Numerous studies have shown the importance of these factors for the level of engagement in fulfilling a professional role. The search for the determinants of such well-being has shown that employees' ability to maintain a work–life balance (WLB) is the crucial one among them. It is important to emphasize that WLB is much more than maintaining a balance between the hours spent in the workplace and leisure time. It is a comprehensive concept that includes psychological, social, and individual aspects that determine the harmonious functioning of an individual in both professional and personal areas. In light of the research by Greenhaus and Beutell (1985) and Kossek et al. (2006), WLB is becoming an important area of focus not only for employees themselves but also for those organizations that are aware of the impact of work–life balance on employee engagement and performance.

This problem has currently gained another dimension due to the advances in communication and remote working technology, which has changed the way we perceive the boundary between work and personal life. Studies have shown (e.g., Derks et al., 2016; Allen et al., 2015) that the development of mobile technology and remote work tools can be both a blessing and a curse for achieving WLB. On the one hand, it allows for flexibility and autonomy in the performance of professional duties, and this can help improve WLB. On the other hand, constant access to work via mobile devices can lead to technology overload, making it difficult for an individual to draw clear boundaries between work and personal life. This was particularly evident during the pandemic, when both employees and their families stayed at home working and studying remotely (Pawlak, 2021). Working from home has eliminated the traditional division between work and non-work. In addition, as information and communication technologies have enabled employees to work anywhere, there has also emerged an expectation that they will work at any time, meaning that the boundary between work

DOI: 10.4324/9781032715407-6

time and personal time has all but disappeared (e.g., de Wet & Koekemoer, 2016; Carlson et al., 2018). Studies indicate that being constantly connected has led to an actual increase in working hours (e.g., Senarathne Tennakoon et al., 2013; Thomas, 2014).

According to Mesmer-Magnus and Viswesvaran (2005), the blurring of the boundaries between work and personal life can aggravate work–family conflict (WFC), and work intruding into personal life is often the cause of tensions with partners, family members, and significant others (Kossek & Lautsch, 2008; Leonardi et al., 2010), which in turn negatively affects employee engagement and mental well-being. This phenomenon poses a challenge for both individuals and organizations, which must strike a balance between the use of modern technology and the protection of employees' privacy and WLB.

This chapter focuses on the factors shaping WLB in terms of their impact on work engagement while taking into consideration the growing challenges of technological change. Based on a critical analysis of the literature, it not only presents the essence and determinants of WLB but also provides practical guidelines for organizations on what measures are worth taking in an era when the boundaries between work and personal life are becoming increasingly blurred. The chapter will present WLB and its determinants. Subsequently, the benefits of employees maintaining WLB and the consequences of a failure to do so will be discussed. The final section will offer solutions to support employees and their overall well-being in a way that will ensure their ability to maintain WLB while increasing their engagement.

## Work–Life Balance

### *The Essence of Work–Life Balance*

Work–life balance is a comprehensive process that aims to achieve harmony between professional demands and aspects of an individual's private life. When describing WLB, it is important to consider the dynamic nature of the phenomenon, as it evolves with career development, life changes, and individual preferences. This concept is not limited to the division of time between work and personal life, for it also entails mental, emotional, and social aspects. A person achieving WLB recognizes that work and private life can function in symbiosis, mutually supporting and enriching each other.

In the literature, WLB is defined from various angles. Noon and Blyton (2007, p. 356) define work–life balance as "the ability to successfully sustain one's work and non-work life." Some describe it as a kind of a friendly coexistence of the two main areas of human existence: work and non-work life (Smoder, 2012). Attention is also paid to the capability to achieve goals in various spheres of life (Chirkowska-Smolak, 2008) and the ability to meet the demands of work and personal life and gain satisfaction in all areas of life (Bulger & Fisher, 2012).

WLB can be achieved through attentive involvement in multiple roles (Marks & MacDermid, 1996) in which time allocation and engagement are roughly equal (Kirchmeyer, 2000). According to Wilson, an analysis of the various areas of human activity leads to the conclusion that to achieve balance in life, one should strive for a harmonious coexistence of personal needs and ambitions, family responsibilities and duties, professional tasks and duties, social obligations, moral and spiritual obligations, and imaginary duties and responsibilities (Wilson, 2012, p. 31).

However, it should be emphasized that WLB is a subjective concept that can mean something slightly different for each person. For some, harmony may be a flexibility in working hours, while for others, it may mean being able to spend more time with family or pursuing their passions. The essence of WLB is to achieve a state in which the individual feels satisfied with both their professional achievements and the quality of their personal life. The sense of this state of balance is determined largely by a person's awareness of their individual desires and values. In practice, achieving WLB requires not only effective time management but also a mindful approach to one's own priorities, as well as the ability to cope with stress and build healthy relationships both at work and in private life. It is also particularly important to feel that one has enough control over their life to make decisions independently and on their own and act accordingly (Clutterbuck, 2005, p. 76).

Some researchers, however, in the very definition of WLB, emphasize not so much the balance as the tension that often accompanies the attempts to maintain it. Clark (2000) defines it as functioning well at work and home, accompanied by minimal role conflict. While discussing the problem of maintaining WLB, Clutterbuck too defines it as "a state where an individual manages real or potential conflict between different demands on his or her time and energy in a way that satisfies his or her needs for well-being and self-fulfilment" (Clutterbuck, 2005, p. 26). Therefore, this means not only that the conflict is non-existent but also that the individual copes with its effects or maintains the tension at a level that does not interfere with their need for psychological well-being.

There are many different approaches to achieving WLB, which is due to the individual traits, preferences, and life context of each person. These differences range from subjective feelings and understanding of work–life harmony to strategic approaches to time management. The variety of subjective feelings of harmony is due to the unique priorities, values, and goals of each individual. For one person, harmony may mean active participation in social life, while for another, it may mean quiet time spent at home. Those pursuing WLB may engage in non-work activities, such as sports, art, or volunteering, which are important parts of their personal lives. Others focus on creating strong family bonds and spending time with loved ones. In addition, as Borkowska (2010) notes, the point of work–life balance is not uniform but depends on many factors, such as the characteristics of a given person (age, gender, education, or family situation), the organizational and economic situation of the country, and especially the situation in the labor market.

The diversity of strategic approaches to WLB includes preferences related to the way professional responsibilities are carried out so that they can be fulfilled efficiently while preserving time and energy resources for non-work life. The variety of these approaches and solutions chosen indicates that WLB is not a homogeneous model, but a dynamic process in which individuals create their own unique balances, taking into account the diversity of areas of life that are important to them. This approach allows WLB strategies to be adapted to changing needs and priorities at different phases of professional and personal life.

### *Determinants of WLB*

The key WLB determinants are organizational culture and the integration of life variables. In organizations where practices and values support work–life balance, employees are more likely to experience harmony. However, in workplaces where a culture of overload and expectation of constant availability prevails, WLB becomes harder to achieve. Research proves that employees are increasingly responding or being encouraged to respond to emails, text messages, or professional phone calls in their free time. This leads to work overload, role ambiguity, and work–life conflict, resulting in technostress and burnout (e.g., Kossek & Lautsch, 2008; Leonardi et al., 2010; Thomas, 2014).

Questions about boundaries and work–life balance have led to discussions about the "right to disconnect" during leisure time (Vayre & Vonthron, 2019). Fenner and Renn (2010) proved that the organization's expectations and the social norms it communicates are interpreted by employees as pressure to use technology to continue working from home after hours, and a study by Allen et al. (2015) showed that the provision of technological devices by the employer increases the pressure for accessibility, regardless of whether this is explicitly expected. Although employees are aware of the negative consequences of prolonging work via information and communications technology, they often succumb to pressure to stay connected to work (Waller & Ragsdell, 2012).

A second key determinant of the ability to achieve WLB is the effective integration of life variables, such as child care, education, and elderly care. Individuals with multiple life roles must skillfully manage these variables to achieve harmony. It is worth noting that despite many measures taken related to distributing responsibilities more equally, studies still show that the burden of work related to family care rests disproportionately on women (Witkowska et al., 2019).

Organizations that offer support for integrating various aspects of life can contribute to employee performance and overall satisfaction. It should be noted that the integration of life variables is closely related to the ability to use the resources available to the individual, both inside and outside of work. The appropriate selection and effective use of non-work resources can increase an individual's work efficiency and, in the case of heavy non-work loads, offset their adverse effects on work engagement. As shown by Sanhokwe (2022), non-work resources were positively related to work engagement, while external support moderated the negative relationship between non-work demands and work engagement.

This mutual influence and tension between the area of life and the area of work have influenced the emergence of a number of WLB-related terms to indicate various aspects of this mutual relationship. Despite its popularity and certainly its greatest recognition also in everyday language, the work–life balance term has been criticized as misleading because it suggests that harmony can be achieved between the conflicting spheres of work and life (Crompton, 2006). This criticism can be supported by empirical research on WLB, which has shown that the balance achieved is very often precarious and requires great effort. Many alternative discourses have emerged, such as work–life articulation (Crompton, 2006), work–life integration (e.g., Kossek & Lambert, 2006), or work–family enrichment (Greenhaus & Powell, 2006), allowing a shift away from the metaphor suggesting that restoring "balance" for individual employees will solve more complex problems. The WLB concept alone does not exhaust the entire spectrum of understanding of work–life relationship issues, so the related concepts that have emerged enable us to look at other aspects of this tension accompanying many employees or to highlight the possibility of mutual enrichment of the two areas.

## Benefits of Achieving Work–Life Balance

Many studies indicate that achieving WLB has a significant impact on employee productivity, motivation, and satisfaction (Quoc Viet Nguyen et al., 2023; Yadav et al., 2022; Kossek & Lambert, 2006). Work–life balance also has a significant moderating effect on the relationship between work engagement, perceived organizational support, and intent to stay with a company (Weng et al., 2023).

One of the theoretical approaches that demonstrates the mechanisms that enable the aforementioned benefits is the conservation of resources (COR) theory (Hobfoll, 1989, 1998), which assumes that existing resources can, by their very presence, enable additional resources to emerge. This means that those with more resources are more ready to be proactive and solve problems. Maintaining WLB increases the sense of self-efficacy, energy, and positive attitude that can intrinsically motivate and stimulate employees to engage in their work (Niessen et al., 2018).

This dependence also occurs in the opposite direction and leads to an enrichment of work–family relations (Chen & Powell, 2012) and mutual reinforcement (Wood et al., 2020). Non-work resources, which, however, can support an employee in the professional area, are treated in this approach as valuable, psychosocial, symbolic, or economic assets (Chen & Fellenz, 2020; Hobfoll, 1989). Such resources may include the emotional support of a spouse or other loved one, information support, or the availability of information and communication technologies (Sanhokwe, 2022).

In turn, according to the job demands-resources (JD-R) model, substantial workplace resources can increase work engagement. These resources include a culture conducive to WLB and family-supportive supervisor behaviors (FSSB), which play an important role in enhancing work engagement (Peeters et al., 2009; Qing & Zhou, 2017), while a lack of resources and a work culture that supports role conflict (WFC, FWC) can reduce work engagement and well-being (Opie & Henn, 2013; Wood et al., 2020).

Among the most important benefits of achieving WLB is its impact on employee productivity and well-being. Employees who manage to maintain WLB are more likely to work focused, make creative decisions, and solve problems effectively. Minimizing feelings of overload and stress related to work–life imbalance promotes a more productive work environment. Innovative and friendly WLB policies help employees to be more productive, dedicated, and committed, resulting in stronger engagement. In the long term, this benefits the company in terms of efficiency (Yadav et al., 2022). In addition, work–life balance promotes the development of diverse skills and interests, which translates into a creative approach to professional challenges. Furthermore, employees who feel that the organization respects their personal lives and puts their work and personal responsibilities on an equal footing are often more motivated and committed to performing their tasks and achieving company goals. A study by Liu et al. (2021) found that work–life balance had a significant impact on organizational commitment. In the long term, this can translate into a willingness to stay longer in the organization (Santhanam et al., 2020), which affects organizational stability and minimizes costs related to staff turnover.

Achieving WLB also turns out to be an important factor influencing employee satisfaction and is sometimes a moderating and mediating variable (Ford et al., 2007; Rashmi & Kataria, 2021). According to research by Crompton and Brockmann (2006), flexibility in working conditions, a key element of WLB, affects subjective assessment of job satisfaction. Employees who are allowed to customize their schedules show higher levels of job satisfaction.

Employee autonomy is also an important factor influencing job satisfaction. Deci and Ryan's research (1985) indicates that individuals who have more control over their work responsibilities and combine them with their private lives experience higher levels of job satisfaction. In turn, studies by Greenhaus and Beutell (1985) focus on the aspect of counteracting work–family conflict as a key factor affecting job satisfaction.

It should be remembered that a proper work–life balance also translates into improved mental and physical health of employees. Eliminating the excessive stress of work overload and being able to focus on aspects of personal life contribute to an individual's overall well-being. Employees who experience WLB are less likely to suffer from burnout syndrome, stress-related health problems, and other negative consequences of an overly intense work life (Hämmig et al., 2012). Research findings indicate that, especially for young employees, supervisors play a key role in enhancing their ability to balance work and personal responsibilities, which improves their well-being and, in turn, affects how they perceive the organization (Nabawanuka & Ekmekcioglu, 2021).

## Consequences of Lack of Work–Life Balance and Effects of Work–Family Conflict

Work–life imbalance and the occurrence of work–family conflict (WFC) have significant consequences for both the individual and the organization (e.g., Vayre & Vonthron, 2019; Anderson et al., 2002; Demerouti et al., 2004). Analysis of these effects is an important area of research related to human resource management. WFC harms work efficiency and employee engagement, as it contributes to lower job and personal satisfaction. Consequently, this may lead to a decrease in the quality of work and a decline in self-esteem. Additionally, physical and emotional exhaustion can occur due to the overload of responsibilities. As a result, it is difficult to rest and regenerate, which leads to a build-up of stress and burnout (Piecuch & Szczygieł, 2019). The following are the main aspects of the effects of imbalance and the presence of work–family conflict.

### *Consequences for the Individual*

Research by Frone et al. (1997) indicates that a lack of work–life balance can lead to deterioration in an individual's mental health. Over-commitment to work at the expense of one's private life can generate stress, frustration, and feeling of being overloaded. Employees experiencing a lack of WLB and increasing work–life conflict are at greater risk of health problems, both mental and physical. The stress of the constant pressure of responsibilities and the difficulty of balancing different roles can lead to burnout syndrome, insomnia, and serious health problems (Hämmig et al., 2012; Hughes & Bozionelos, 2007). Hämmig and Bauer (2009) found that WLB instability is a risk factor affecting employees' mental health, job performance, and families. Imbalance can also negatively affect interpersonal relationships, both professionally and privately, which further negatively affects mental well-being.

The presence of work–family conflict often correlates with reduced satisfaction with an individual's life. Research by Greenhaus and Beutell (1985) emphasizes that individuals experiencing difficulty balancing work and family responsibilities may feel a general dissatisfaction with life. Additionally, the work–life imbalance often translates into problems in family relationships. Work–family conflict can lead to limited time availability for the family, which in turn affects the quality of relationships. As a result, a person may not only experience frustration and lack of satisfaction in their personal life but also feel deprived of an important part of non-work resources that can positively affect their commitment and performance at work (Greenhaus & Powell, 2006).

### *Consequences for the Organization*

One of the direct effects of the lack of WLB is reduced employee productivity. The constant overload of responsibilities and no recovery time lead to a decrease in efficiency in the performance of professional tasks. Employees may be less focused, more error-prone, and less motivated to achieve goals and innovate (Wang et al., 2021; Yadav et al., 2022). Reduced productivity affects not only the individual but also the entire organization, generating potential financial losses and hurting competitiveness. In turn, research by Wang et al. (2021) proved that family–work conflict has a significant negative impact on both work engagement and innovative behavior. The consequences of a work–life imbalance can also manifest themselves through increased absenteeism and staff turnover. Employees experiencing difficulties balancing work and family responsibilities may be more prone to illness and may be inclined to seek more flexible and friendly workplaces. This in turn affects the stability of the team and the costs related to employee turnover.

Organizations that fail to promote work–life balance may also experience image damage among employees and the business community. Companies considered unfriendly to employees' private lives risk losing talent and hiring difficulties. The effects of the lack of work–life balance and the occurrence of work–family conflict are multidimensional and harm individuals and organizations. Companies that focus on supporting WLB can minimize these negative effects while contributing to employee well-being and engagement.

## Factors Supporting Work–Life Balance

In the search for solutions to effectively build strategies to support employee WLB, it is important for HR specialists and managers to first and foremost understand the relationship between WLB and work engagement and look at it from a holistic perspective, rather than treat them as two separate entities, as only such a perspective allows adequate practices to be implemented (Wood et al., 2020). As Rothwell et al. (2010) note, it is important to be aware of the need to change and evolve one's culture, systems, and policies to effectively facilitate higher levels of work engagement and WLB, as they are intertwined. By strategically and proactively applying policies and systems that support WLB, employees can feel valued and engaged at work, which in turn helps achieve more desirable individual and organizational outcomes (Wood et al., 2020). To that effect, HR professionals and organizations can effectively address retention and engagement issues through the lens of WLB.

Research and practice indicate several factors supporting the achievement of WLB, which contributes to improving employee well-being, and increasing engagement and organizational efficiency. Kelly and Moen (2007) showed that companies offering specific solutions supporting WLB gain employee trust and build a positive image. Efforts to develop appropriate strategies should be made with a long-term perspective in mind, and consideration should be given to linking actions to strengthen organizational culture (e.g., supporting a work–family culture) with the organization's development prospects (Wood et al., 2020). The solutions undertaken may concern various levels of the organization's functioning and involve both immediate support and long-term building of organizational culture.

### *Flexible Working Conditions*

One of the most frequently cited ways to support WLB is to create flexible working conditions. Flexibility in terms of working hours, job location, or form of employment is an important factor supporting WLB. Research by Kelly and Moen (2007) indicates that allowing employees to customize their work schedules contributes to increased work–life satisfaction.

A study by Hill et al. (2010) on more than 24,000 employees suggests that one of the key elements of flexibility in the context of WLB are adjustable working hours. Employees who have the option to customize their work time experience higher levels of WLB. Flexible working hours allow for a better fit between professional duties and private life, which translates into a positive employee experience. This solution makes it possible to respond to the needs of employees, as well as to react agilely to change. It is not uncommon for such forms of work to become a key factor in the decision to take up employment. Research conducted as part of the social diagnosis showed that flexible working hours are an important factor in the decision to become active in the labor market for 41.7% of non-working men and as many as 58.3% of women (Czapiński & Panek, 2009). A group for whom flexible working hours proved particularly important were parents of young children. They pointed to this way of organizing work as one of the key tools that allows them to combine work with having a family. Meanwhile, a study by Kelly and Moen (2007) showed the importance of being able to adjust work schedules to individual employee preferences.

However, it is also necessary to take into account the specific duties/position of a particular employee in order to implement optimal solutions for them. A study by Kossek and Lautsch (2018) shows that giving employees control over schedule variability (flextime) can benefit lower-level employees the most. Part-time work, on the other hand, which allows control over the workload, is potentially the most damaging for this group of workers due to the involuntary loss of income and benefits. However, the same practices that allow for part-time work increase recruitment and retain employees in higher positions.

Another aspect of flexibility in achieving WLB is the introduction of the possibility of at least partial remote work. Research by Gajendran and Harrison (2007) indicates that remote work can be an effective tool to support work–life balance. Individuals who work remotely often experience greater autonomy in managing their time and space, which contributes to improved WLB. A particular form of managing one's working time is *time banking*. It is a system in which employees accumulate time worked beyond the norm and can later use it as additional days off, at a time that optimally allows them to combine their professional and personal responsibilities.

However, when implementing time and workplace flexibility solutions, one should be aware of the risks involved. The research by Greenhaus et al. (2003) points out the problematic consequences of flexibility for WLB. Employees who can flexibly set their work time and/or workplace often experience difficulties in establishing work–life boundaries, which can lead to overload. While the new work arrangements provide employees with more freedom to organize their day, many complain about the difficulty of breaking away from work and report that they work longer hours, in the evenings or on weekends at home (Fenner & Renn, 2010).

### *Supportive Organizational Culture*

Improperly implemented solutions that were intended to support employees' WLB can, as indicated above, sometimes have the opposite effect, accelerating employee exhaustion and burnout. That is why it is so important to take action on a broader level and create a work culture that promotes respect for work–life balance. Key aspects related to organizational culture that support WLB include the following:

- *Acceptance of diversity of work styles*: Organizations promoting WLB should emphasize acceptance of diverse work styles. Enabling employees to choose the work methods that are most effective for them allows for customization according to individual preferences and needs.
- *Value-oriented leadership* plays a key role in shaping organizational culture. Value-oriented leaders support values related to work–life balance. By setting an example and promoting the importance of WLB, they shape an atmosphere conducive to the harmonious coexistence of the two areas of life.
- *Clearly communicated expectations* regarding work and achieving WLB are crucial to implementing optimal solutions. Research by Kossek and Lambert (2006) emphasizes that organizations should provide clear information on expected efficiency and flexibility in work organization. This communication allows employees to better plan and adjust their work time as needed.
- *Monitoring stress levels and workload*: The research underscores that organizations should take care of employees' mental health by responding to signals of stress and overload. Mechanisms for employees to express their needs

and concerns are an integral part of a culture that supports WLB. In addition, analyzing employee workloads to remove unnecessary meetings and minimize administrative processes may be beneficial in achieving a more conducive WLB culture and work engagement (Wood et al., 2020).

- *Personal development programs*: A supportive work culture views employees not only in terms of their usefulness for achieving organizational goals but also as individuals developing and seeking balance in their lives. Personal development programs, such as stress management or time management skill training, help employees achieve WLB more effectively.

#### ***Employee Autonomy and Support Programs***

Giving employees more autonomy in their work decisions contributes to WLB. Deci and Ryan's research (1985) indicates that individuals with greater control over their work and private responsibilities experience higher levels of job and life satisfaction. In addition, increasing employees' sense of influence over their organizational environment further enhances their engagement (Pawlak & Adamska-Chudzińska, 2023). Granting the employee adequate autonomy for their position may also mean including them in the process of developing the most appropriate strategies so that, depending on current life variables, which may change during their employment, "tailor-made" solutions can be selected that meet their needs and those of the employer.

Organizations that introduce programs to support employees in achieving WLB, such as childcare programs, psychological support, or mentoring, are effective in building positive employee experiences. Research by Kossek and Lambert (2006) indicates that organizations offering this type of support record higher levels of work engagement. Some researchers and practitioners also point to the importance of increasing the resources and competencies that employees need in their private lives by providing family counseling services, on such issues as marriage, children, and other relevant family matters (e.g., Peeters et al., 2009). Companies can offer online courses as well as offline seminars or workshops that help develop and maintain self-esteem, provide prevention and coping mechanisms for WFC, and provide the skills required to communicate effectively with a spouse and children (Chan et al., 2017; Wood et al., 2020).

Introducing educational and awareness programs on WLB can also be helpful. Organizations should consider providing appropriate information and training to help employees understand the importance of work–life balance and provide practical tools to achieve it. Also, the importance of implementing wellness and healthcare programs to support WLB should not be overlooked. The proposed range of options for supporting employee WLB is presented in Table 5.1.

Thus, depending on the industry, the specifics of the position, the size of the organization, and the individual situation of the employee, a solution can be chosen to benefit both parties.

*Table 5.1* Solutions supporting WLB

| *Solutions supporting WLB* | *Examples* |
|---|---|
| Flexible working conditions | Flexible working hours |
| | Remote work |
| | Reduced working hours |
| | Part-time work |
| | Time banking |
| Supportive organizational culture | Promoting work–life balance |
| | Acceptance of diversity of work styles |
| | Value-oriented leadership |
| | Clearly communicating expectations regarding work and achieving WLB |
| | Monitoring stress levels and workload |
| | Personal development programs |
| Employee autonomy | Independence in organizing working time |
| | Right to make decisions in undertaking tasks and projects |
| | Right to make decisions in the selection of solutions to support WLB |
| Employee support programs | Family and employee support programs |
| | Initiatives promoting a healthy lifestyle |
| | Social and welfare benefits |
| | Access to psychological and counseling assistance |

*Source:* Own compilation

## Conclusions

In conclusion, it should be stated that at a time when more and more employees experience the phenomenon of work spilling over into personal life, concern for work–life balance requires that organizations take a conscious approach to creating conditions conducive to the harmonious coexistence of employees' professional and personal lives and improving their well-being. This chapter identified a number of possible organizational interventions designed to support WLB, the achievement of which stimulates work engagement. These include flexible working hours, the option of remote work, stress and workload monitoring, and personal development programs. It is also important to build an organizational culture that supports autonomy and respect toward employees' private lives.

On the one hand, the implementation of such solutions may seem like a costly undertaking, but on the other hand, studies show that work–life balance is not just a matter of the individual employee and their subjective feelings. The benefits of maintaining WLB are multifaceted, successively affecting the functioning of the entire organization. Organizations that undertake such initiatives gain employee loyalty, improving job satisfaction and reducing the risk of burnout. Employees who are in control of their time and the boundaries between work and non-work and effectively manage their professional and personal responsibilities demonstrate a better mental and emotional state, which significantly affects their ability to engage in work. Maintaining a work–life balance promotes their willingness to stay with the organization and their productivity, which in turn lowers labor costs and increases the efficiency of economic processes, ultimately contributing to higher profit (Clutterbuck, 2005). By implementing the right strategies and programs, organizations can not only increase the engagement and well-being of their employees but also reap the benefits of improving business performance, increasing employee retention, and enhancing the organization's image as an employer. Investing in improving work–life balance is therefore mutually beneficial.

Thus, the harmony at work from the title does not only mean skillfully combining the work and personal lives of employees allowing them to promote their well-being but also mean harmonizing individual and organizational benefits.

## References

Allen, T. D., Golden, T. D., & Shockley, K. M. (2015). How effective is telecommuting? Assessing the status of our scientific findings. *Psychological Science in the Public Interest*, *16*(2), 40–68. https://doi.org/10.1177/1529100615593273

Anderson, S. E., Coffey, B. S., & Byerly, R. T. (2002). Formal organizational initiatives and informal workplace practices: Links to work-family conflict and job-related outcomes. *Journal of Management*, *28*(6), 787–810. https://doi.org/10.1177/014920630202800605

Borkowska, S. (2010). Równowaga między pracą a życiem pozazawodowym. *Acta Universitatis Lodziensis Folia Oeconomica*, *240*.

Bulger, C. A., & Fisher, G. G. (2012). Ethical imperatives of work/life balance. In N. P. Reilly, M. J. Sirgy, & C. A. Gorman (Eds.), *Work and quality of life*. Springer.

Carlson, D. S., Thompson, M. J., Crawford, W. S., Boswell, W. R., & Whitten, D. (2018). Your job is messing with mine! The impact of mobile device use for work during family time on the spouse's work life. *The Journal of Occupational Health Psychology*, *23*, 471–482.

Chan, X. W., Kalliath, T., Brough, P., O'Driscoll, M., Siu, O.-L., & Timms, C. (2017). Self-efficacy and work engagement: Test of a chain model. *International Journal of Manpower*, *38*(6), 819–834.

Chen, I. S., & Fellenz, M. R. (2020). Personal resources and personal demands for work engagement: Evidence from employees in the service industry. *International Journal of Hospitality Management*, *90*, 102600.

Chen, Z., & Powell, G. (2012). No pain, no gain? A resource-based model of work-to-family enrichment and conflict. *Journal of Vocational Behaviour*, *81*(1), 89–98.

Chirkowska-Smolak, T. (2008). Równowaga między pracą a życiem osobistym. *Ruch prawniczy, ekonomiczny i socjologiczny*, *70*(1), 235–249.

Clark, S. C. (2000). Work/family border theory: A new theory of work/family balance. *Human Relations*, *53*(6), 747–770.

Clutterbuck, D. (2005). *Równowaga między życiem zawodowym a osobistym*. Oficyna Ekonomiczna.

Crompton, R. (2006). *Employment and the family: The reconfiguration of work and family life in contemporary societies*. Cambridge University Press.
Crompton, R., & Brockmann, M. (2006). Class, gender, and work-life balance. In D. Perrons, C. Fagan, L. McDowell, K. Ray, & K. Ward (Eds.), *Gender divisions and working time in the new economy: Changing patterns of work, care and public policy in Europe and North America* (pp. 103–122). Edward Elgar Publishing Ltd.
Czapiński, J., & Panek, T. (2009). *Diagnoza społeczna 2009. Warunki i jakość życia Polaków. Raport.* Rada Monitoringu Społecznego.
de Wet, W., & Koekemoer, E. (2016). The increased use of information and communication technology (ICT) among employees: Implications for work–life interaction. *The South African Journal of Economic and Management Sciences*, *19*(2), 264–281.
Deci, E. L., & Ryan, R. M. (1985). *Intrinsic motivation and self-determination in human behavior*. Springer Science & Business Media.
Demerouti, E., Geurts, S. A. E., Bakker, A. B., & Euwema, M. (2004). The impact of shiftwork on work–home interference, job attitudes and health. *Ergonomics*, *47*, 987–1002.
Derks, D., Bakker, A. B., Peters, P., & van Wingerden, P. (2016). Work-related smartphone use, work–family conflict and family role performance: The role of segmentation preference. *Human Relations*, *69*, 1045–1068.
Fenner, G. H., & Renn, R. W. (2010). Technology-assisted supplemental work and work-to-family conflict: The role of instrumentality beliefs, organizational expectations and time management. *Human Relations*, *63*(1), 63–82.
Ford, M. T., Heinen, B. A., & Langkamer, K. L. (2007). Work and family satisfaction and conflict: A meta-analysis of cross-domain relations. *Journal of Applied Psychology*, *92*(1), 57–78.
Frone, M. R., Yardley, J. K., & Markel, K. S. (1997). Developing and testing an integrative model of the work–family interface. *Journal of Vocational Behavior*, *50*(2), 145–167.
Gajendran, R. S., & Harrison, D. A. (2007). The good, the bad, and the unknown about telecommuting: Meta-analysis of psychological mediators and individual consequences. *Journal of Applied Psychology*, *92*(6), 1524–1541. https://doi.org/10.1037/0021-9010.92.6.1524
Greenhaus, J. H., & Beutell, N. J. (1985). Sources of conflict between work and family roles. *Academy of Management Review*, *10*(1), 76–88.
Greenhaus, J. H., Collins, K. M., & Shaw, J. D. (2003). The relation between work–family balance and quality of life. *Journal of Vocational Behavior*, *63*(3), 510–531.
Greenhaus, J. H., & Powell, G. N. (2006). When work and family are allies: A theory of work-family enrichment. *The Academy of Management Review*, *31*(1), 72–92.
Hämmig, O., & Bauer, G. (2009). Work-life imbalance and mental health among male and female employees in Switzerland. *International Journal of Public Health*, *54*(2), 88–95. https://doi.org/10.1007/s00038-009-8031-7
Hämmig, O., Brauchli, R., & Bauer, G. F. (2012). Effort-reward and work-life imbalance, general stress and burnout among employees of a large public hospital in Switzerland. *Swiss Medical Weekly*, *142*, 13577. https://doi.org/10.4414/smw.2012.13577
Hill, E. J., Erickson, J. J., Holmes, E. K., & Ferris, M. (2010). Workplace flexibility, work hours, and work-life conflict: Finding an extra day or two. *Journal of Family Psychology*, *24*(3), 349–358. https://doi.org/10.1037/a0019282
Hobfoll, S. E. (1989). Conservation of resources: A new attempt at conceptualizing stress. *American Psychologist*, *44*, 513–524.
Hobfoll, S. E. (1998). *Stress, culture, and community*. Plenum Press.
Hughes, J., & Bozionelos, N. (2007). Work-life balance as source of job dissatisfaction and withdrawal attitudes: An exploratory study on the views of male workers. *Personnel Review*, *36*(1), 145–154. https://doi.org/10.1108/00483480710716768

Kelly, E. L., & Moen, P. (2007). Rethinking the clockwork of work: Why schedule control may pay off at work and at home. *Advances in Developing Human Resources*, *9*(4), 487–506. https://doi.org/10.1177/1523422307305489

Kirchmeyer, C. (2000). Work-life initiatives: Greed or benevolence regarding workers time? *Trends in Organizational Behavior*, *7*, 79–94.

Kossek, E., & Lambert, S. (2006). *Work and life integration: Organizational, cultural and individual perspectives*. Lawrence Erlbaum Associates.

Kossek, E. E., & Lautsch, B. A. (2008). *CEO of me: Creating a life that works in the flexible job age*. Pearson.

Kossek, E. E., & Lautsch, B. A. (2018). Work–life flexibility for whom? Occupational status and work–life inequality in upper, middle, and lower level jobs. *Academy of Management Annals*, *12*, 5–36. https://doi.org/10.5465/annals.2016.0059

Kossek, E. E., Lautsch, B. A., & Eaton, S. C. (2006). Telecommuting, control, and boundary management: Correlates of policy use and practice, job control, and work–family effectiveness. *Journal of Vocational Behavior*, *68*(2), 347–367.

Leonardi, P. M., Treem, J. W., & Jackson, M. H. (2010). The connectivity paradox: Using technology to both decrease and increase perceptions of distance in distributed work arrangements. *Journal of Applied Communication Research*, *38*(1), 85–105. https://doi.org/10.1080/00909880903483599

Liu, T., Gao, J., Zhu, M., & Jin, S. (2021). Women's work-life balance in hospitality: Examining its impact on organizational commitment. *Frontiers in Psychology*, *12*, Article 625550. https://doi.org/10.3389/fpsyg.2021.625550

Marks, S. R., & MacDermid, S. M. (1996). Multiple roles and the self: A theory of role balance. *Journal of Marriage and the Family*, *58*(2), 417–432. https://doi.org/10.2307/353506

Mesmer-Magnus, J., & Viswesvaran, C. (2005). Convergence between measures of work-to-family and family-to-work conflict: A meta-analytic examination. *Journal of Vocational Behavior*, *67*(2).

Nabawanuka, H., & Ekmekcioglu, E. B. (2021). Millennials in the workplace: Perceived supervisor support, work-life balance and employee well-being. *Industrial and Commercial Training*, *54*(1), 123–144.

Nguyen, Q. V., Nguyen, H. N., & Phan, T. U. (2023). Unveiling the dynamics of motivation, work-life balance, and work engagement among Vietnamese employees in multinational corporations. *Problems and Perspectives in Management*, *21*(3), 629–641.

Niessen, C., Müller, T., Hommelhoff, S., & Westman, M. (2018). The impact of preventive coping on business travellers' work and private life. *Journal of Organizational Behavior*, *39*(1), 113–127.

Noon, M., & Blyton, P. (2007). *The realities of work*. Macmillan.

Opie, T., & Henn, C. M. (2013). Work-family conflict and work engagement among mothers: Conscientiousness and neuroticism as moderators. *Journal of Industrial Psychology*, *39*(1), 1–12.

Pawlak, J. (2021). Work, life czy balans? Łączenie życia zawodowego i prywatnego przed oraz w czasie pandemii. In P. Walentynowicz & W. Machel (Eds.), *Narzędzia i rozwiązania wykorzystywane w kreowaniu sukcesu organizacji w warunkach gospodarki cyfrowej* (pp. 143–160). Uniwersytet Gdański.

Pawlak, J., & Adamska-Chudzińska, M. (2023). Supporting employee autonomous motivation: Does the sense of influence increase organisational commitment? *International Journal of Work Organisation and Emotion*, *14*(3), 241–257.

Peeters, M. C. W., Wattez, C. J. P., Demerouti, E., & de Regt, W. (2009). Work-family culture, work-family interference and well-being at work: Is it possible to distinguish between a positive and a negative process? *Career Development International*, *14*(7), 700–713.

Piecuch, T., & Szczygieł, E. (2019). *Work-life balance w teorii i praktyce funkcjonowania współczesnych organizacji*. Oficyna Wydawnicza Politechniki Rzeszowskiej.

Qing, G., & Zhou, E. (2017). Bidirectional work-family enrichment mediates the relationship between family-supportive supervisor behaviors and work engagement. *Social Behaviour and Personality*, *45*(2), 299–308.

Rashmi, K., & Kataria, A. (2021). The mediating role of work-life balance on the relationship between job resources and job satisfaction: Perspectives from Indian nursing professionals. *International Journal of Organizational Analysis*. Advance online publication. https://doi.org/10.1108/IJOA-04-2021-2722

Rothwell, W. J., Stavros, J. M., & Sullivan, R. L. (2010). Organization development and change. In W. J. Rothwell, J. M. Stavros, R. L. Sullivan, & A. Sullivan (Eds.), *Practicing organization development: A guide for leading change* (3rd ed., pp. 11–42). Pfeiffer.

Sanhokwe, H. (2022). The influence of nonwork resources, nonwork demands and external support on work engagement and productivity: A moderated mediation model. *Journal of Industrial Psychology*, *48*, a1957. https://doi.org/10.4102/sajip.v48i0.195

Santhanam, N., Kumar, J. R., Kumar, V., & Saha, R. (2020). Employee turnover intention in the milieu of human resource management practices: Moderating role of work-life balance. *International Journal of Business Innovation and Research*, *24*(1), 57–75.

Senarathne Tennakoon, K. L. U., da Silveira, G. J. C., & Taras, D. G. (2013). Drivers of context-specific ICT use across work and nonwork domains: A boundary theory perspective. *Information and Organisation*, *23*, 107–128.

Smoder, A. (2012). Elastyczne formy pracy jako instrument work-life balance. *Polityka społeczna*, *1*.

Thomas, K. J. (2014). Workplace technology and the creation of boundaries: The role of VHRD in a 24/7 work environment. *Advances in Developing Human Resources*, *16*(3), 281–295. https://doi.org/10.1177/1523422314532092

Vayre, E., & Vonthron, A.-M. (2019). Identifying work-related internet's uses – At work and outside usual workplaces and hours – And their relationships with work–home interface, work engagement, and problematic internet behavior. *Frontiers in Psychology*, *10*, Article 2118. https://doi.org/10.3389/fpsyg.2019.02118

Waller, A. D., & Ragsdell, G. (2012). The impact of e-mail on work–life balance. *Aslib Proceedings*, *64*, 154–177. https://doi.org/10.1108/00012531211215178

Wang, X., Zhang, Z., & Chun, D. (2021). How does mobile workplace stress affect employee innovative behavior? The role of work-family conflict and employee engagement. *Behavioral Sciences (Basel)*, *12*(1), 2.

Weng, T.-C., Shen, Y.-H., & Kan, T.-T. (2023). Talent sustainability and development: How talent management affects employees' intention to stay through work engagement and perceived organizational support with the moderating role of work–life balance. *Sustainability*, *15*, 13508. https://doi.org/10.3390/su151813508

Wilson, P. (2012). *Idealna równowaga. Jak znaleźć czas i sposób na pełnię życia*. MT Biznes.

Witkowska, D., Kompa, K., & Matuszewska-Janica, A. (2019). *Sytuacja kobiet na rynku pracy: Wybrane aspekty*. Wydawnictwo Uniwersytetu Łódzkiego.

Wood, J., Oh, J., Park, J., & Kim, W. (2020). The relationship between work engagement and work–life balance in organizations: A review of the empirical research. *Human Resource Development Review*, *19*(3), 240–262. https://doi.org/10.1177/1534484320917560

Yadav, A., Pandita, D., & Singh, S. (2022). Work-life integration, job contentment, employee engagement and its impact on organizational effectiveness: A systematic literature review. *Industrial and Commercial Training*, *54*(3), 509–527. https://doi-1org-10000084n012b.hanbg.uek.krakow.pl/10.1108/ICT-12-2021-0083

# 6 The Influence of Development Opportunities on Work Engagement

## The Example of Young Employees

*Alicja Szczygieł*

### Introduction

Dynamic technological advancements and the evolution of the job market result in organizations facing grave challenges related to meeting the needs of a multi-generational workforce. Among them, special attention is due to Generation Z, who are estimated to constitute a fifth of the total workforce employed by 2025 (Deloitte, 2018; Czyczerska et al., 2020). Young persons who enter the job market formulate new demands regarding the work environment and employment conditions, with a particular emphasis on professional development opportunities (Ławińska & Korombel, 2023; Parmelee, 2022). Because of their expectations, development and creation of learning opportunities becomes one of the more important factors influencing work engagement, which is essential for both individual effectiveness and organizational success. Failure to meet the demands of young employees leads to a decline in their loyalty and increases their willingness to change jobs (Ragin-Skorecka et al., 2023). Enterprises that are successful in implementing development strategies are better equipped to deal with the challenges of modern job market and are able to sustainably expand their operation and, above all, build their work engagement. One of the ways to enhance the competencies of employees is to have them participate in a training process that should be carefully planned and tailored to the individual needs of employees and the strategic goals of the organization. Even though organizations are aware of the major significance of recognizing the needs of employees, for various reason, they happen to limit the active role of employees, reducing it to merely participating in trainings selected by the organization (Przewoźnik & Górczyńska, 2021).

The aim of the chapter is to study whether or not and in what way opportunities for professional development influence Gen Z employees' work engagement, analyzed through the lens of three components: vigor, dedication, and absorption. The Utrecht Work Engagement Scale (UWES) was used in the study, as well as an original survey questionnaire, which was composed of questions about participation in the training process, including ways to identify the developmental needs and expectations of the respondents. The study is divided into six sections. The first of these discusses the training process, treating it as a

DOI: 10.4324/9781032715407-7

major part of employee development within the organization. In the second section of the chapter, the focus shifts to the characteristics of Gen Z in the workplace and their expectations regarding professional development. The third part presents the issues related to the level of work engagement among young workers. Part four outlines the methodology of the investigation conducted, while part five reports the results of an original research carried out among Gen Z employees. The chapter closes with a discussion and conclusions. The results of this study may enable organizations to gain a more in-depth understanding of the importance of the training process factors that successfully enhance the level of engagement of this demographic group, which in turn may contribute to improving the loyalty and lowering the turnover, currently observed among Gen Z as the youngest cohort in the workplace (Ragin-Skorecka et al., 2023).

## Training Process as a Development Path for Organizational Employees

Employee development is considered to be one of the foundations of human resources management today and plays a key role in organizations achieving long-term success. Rapid changes in the global economy accelerate the process of skill obsolescence among employees which results in the need for constant development.

According to Reg Revens, "the learning in the organization must be equal to or greater than the rate of environmental change. If the learning rate inside is *less* than the rate of external change, then the organization is declining or dying" (Pedler & Aspinwall, 1998, p. 12). Literature on the topic highlights that flexibility and willingness to learn are crucial in the face of rapid market changes (Pocztowski, 2007; Król & Ludwiczyński, 2007; Pasieczny & Rosiek, 2021; Alerasoul et al., 2022; Dziura, 2022).

Human resource development is defined as "a deliberate arrangement of undertakings for enriching knowledge, developing capabilities, shaping values, attitudes, motivations, and skills, as well as fostering a good mental and physical condition of workers, which lead to improved work efficiency and increased value of human resources" (Pocztowski, 2007, p. 274). It involves "introducing, eliminating, modifying, directing and guiding processes in such a way that all individuals and teams are equipped with the skills, knowledge and competences they require to undertake current and future tasks required by the organization" (Amstrong, 2001, p. 425). It is an integral part of human resource management, which consists in organizations attracting and maintaining highly capable workforce, best equipped to achieve their goals (Pocztowski, 2007).

Training practices are among the basic tools to develop employees and are defined as "the entirety of deliberate and systematic activities in an organization aimed at advancing and broadening certain aspects of human resources as well as furnishing employees with new skills, indispensable in view of the current and future needs of the organization" (Pocztowski, 2007, p. 277). Training programs are an investment that contributes to the growth of employee productivity and is intended to bring about a lasting change in their skills, knowledge, and attitudes (Rodriguez & Walters, 2019; Kuruppu et al., 2021). They should be seen as a process, not a one-off learning event – meeting, and held according to predetermined plans, because the incessant changes in the company environment require ongoing adjustment (Kroenke, 2015).

The following are identified as components of the training process:

- Training needs assessment
- Training plan preparation
- Execution of the planned training sessions
- Evaluation of training practices and results

A training needs' analysis helps identify competence gaps, that is, the instances of divergence between the current and the desired state of skills of employees. These are determined on two primary levels. One of these involves the analysis of an employee's position, which is to ascertain the knowledge, skill, capabilities, and behavior requirements, crucial for the successful performance of a given job, in view of the goals and the mission of the organization. The other focuses on identifying the individual training needs of employees. At this stage, information is obtained with the active participation of the employee by such methods as surveys and interviews (Pocztowski, 2007; Amstrong, 2001; Neczaj, 2005). The identification is meant to indicate the direction for competency development of the participants in the training process. A failure to adjust the types of training activities to the actual needs of the organization and expectations on the part of the employee is likely to lead, in the case of the company, to no return on investment, and in the case of the employee, the discouragement from participating in another learning process (Serafin, 2011; McGuinness & Luis, 2015).

The phase of training plan preparation involves setting training goals, choosing the method and medium, arranging the schedule, and selecting trainers. It is also important to specify a budget and secure the assets required to conduct the training.

The execution of planned training activities consists in the implementation of a training plan, with employees participating in training designed to develop their skills and knowledge in line with the predetermined objectives. Training implies using various teaching methods to enhance employee qualifications for specific tasks (Nechirwan et al., 2021).

Evaluation of training and training results involves measuring the extent to which learning objectives have been achieved. This assessment can be conducted with regard to several aspects, including participant reaction, change in employee knowledge and qualifications, practical application of new skills, and the ultimate influence on organizational performance. The training process ends with monitoring and maintaining results (Phillips et al., 2009; Gajewska & Piskrzyńska, 2016; Lewicka et al., 2019).

All stages of a successful training process are crucial and should be taken into considerations in planning. From the point of view of employees, the most important stages are the initial two, that is, the training needs identification and the participation in a relevant learning process that is tailored to competency gaps.

## Developmental Expectations of Gen Z in the Workplace

In the analysis of job market dynamics, special attention is given to generational differences, which have been the subject of numerous studies and publications. The literature identifies four main generations active in the workplace today: Baby Boomers, Generation X, Generation Y, and Generation Z. The birth years of these demographic cohorts vary depending on the country, social experiences, and authors (Gruszczyńska-Malec & Waligóra, 2019; Ragin-Skorecka et al., 2023). Baby Boomers, that is, people born in the years 1946–1969, display a strong attachment to traditional work values. The next group, Generation X (born between 1970 and 1979), is considered to act as a bridge between the older and the younger generations. It is believed that people from this demographic group are able to adapt to both traditional and modern work culture. Generation Y, also known as the Millennials, consists of individuals born in the years 1980–1994, who stand out because of their high level of digital literacy and pursuit of work–life balance. The final group are the members of Generation Z, born after 1995, also referred to as the "Children of the Internet," Native Users, iGeneration, Gen Tech, and Generation C (Gajda, 2017; Otieno & Nyambegera, 2019; Czyczerska et al., 2020; Wasiluk & Bańkowska, 2021; Skowronek, 2022; Ławińska & Korombel, 2023). The youngest generation is the first to have been born in a technology-dominated world (Czyczerska et al., 2020).

The current data suggests that Generation Z already accounts for the third of the global population, and their number is estimated to soon surpass that of members of the millennial generation. In the United States, Generation Z makes up a quarter of the population, being the most varied generation in the history of the country, while by 2030, almost all level jobs will be filled by the members of Generation Z (Ławińska & Korombel, 2023; Buchko & Gabrielova, 2021). In Great Britain, meanwhile, the population of Generation Z reaches approximately 10 million people, which accounts for 15% of the total population (Ławińska & Korombel, 2023). The demographic transformation discussed signals major shifts in the job market, with an emphasis on the need to adjust the management strategies to the dynamically evolving expectations of the younger generations of the workforce.

Market analysts predict that Generation Z may enter the job market directly, bypassing the conventional path of higher education (Otieno & Nyambegera,

2019). Employees from this cohort are interested in building a professional career and pursuing rapid success, which marks a fundamental difference between them and their predecessors, who were often prepared to adopt a long-term approach to shaping their career paths. Gen Zers are not focused on stability in their professional life (Wasiluk et al., 2021). They value autonomy and openness to change and exhibit lower levels of loyalty toward their employers compared with the earlier generations (Czyczerska et al., 2020; Ragin-Skorecka et al., 2023). Based on their findings, scholars highlight the role of creating conditions that foster development as one of the essential aspects that do matter for Generation Z (Gajda, 2017; Lutyńska & Wasiluk, 2023; Ławińska & Korombel, 2023; Czyczerska et al., 2020).

According to the young generation, the employer "should not only provide handsome remuneration and powerful non-financial incentives, but also respect them, maintain a good atmosphere in the workplace, create opportunities for personal development, and be adept at harnessing their potential" (Ławińska & Korombel, 2023, p. 13). Lutyńska and Wasiluk claimed that freedom and autonomy are of great importance for young workers, while "their personal development is absolutely crucial" (Lutyńska & Wasiluk, 2023, p. 65). An analysis of the report from "Global 2022 Gen Z and Millennial Survey" conducted by Deloitte (2022) on a sample of 14,808 Gen Z respondents hailing from various geographical locations revealed this generation's inclination to change jobs in order to seek better learning and development opportunities (Deloitte, 2022), which constitutes a major challenge for employers in preventing a young talent drain from their organizations. Gen Zers are characterized by their pursuit of instant professional success without long-term effort, value self-development, and stress the importance of easy access to knowledge and information, preferring the principle of "just-in-time learning" (Kukla & Nowacka, 2019). Furthermore, they expect managers to not only be the sole source of their knowledge but also complement their learning – by providing guidance and asking questions (Otieno & Nyambegera, 2019).

## Generation Z and Work Engagement

Work engagement plays an important role in any organization as it influences its operation and performance. The model developed by Meyer and Allen posits that "organizational commitment is the level of identification with and commitment to a specific organization and the willingness to remain in it" (Chrupała-Pniak & Grabowski, 2014, p. 85). Thus understood, organizational commitment comprises three components, namely, the affective, normative, and emotional attachment (Meyer et al., 1993).

Schaufeli and Bakker (2004) define work engagement as "a positive, fulfilling, work-related state of mind that is characterized by vigor, dedication, and absorption" (Rakowska & Mącik, 2016). According to them, engaged employees work hard not because of a powerful compulsion but because they find their work pleasing (Schaufeli & Bakker, 2004). Vigor in the workplace is characterized by a substantial level of energy and resilience while performing work tasks, unwavering persistence, and the readiness to exert work effort despite the difficulties encountered. Professional dedication is related to a strong involvement that is manifested through a sense of enthusiasm, inspiration, pride, and the ability to approach work as a challenge. Absorption is defined as a state of complete focus and involvement in one's job, which makes the passage of time imperceptible and detaching oneself from work tasks especially difficult (Schaufeli & Bakker, 2004).

According to Gallup's "State of the Global Workplace: 2023 Report," the younger group of Millennials and Gen Zers (born in 1989 or later) recorded a five-point decrease in engagement, from 40% to 35%. For comparison, the representatives of the demographic boom generation (born in the years 1946–1964) recorded a two-point increase in engagement, from 34% to 36%, whereas Generation X also saw a decline, from 35% to 31% (Harter, 2024).

Work engagement depends on a number of conditions. Based on the conducted literature review, Juchnowicz (2012) distinguished ten most important factors that influence engagement. Among them, she mentions the relationship with the direct superior and an interesting and challenging job that offers opportunities for development (Juchnowicz, 2012). The results of a study conducted on young employees (Szymankowska & Bartczak, 2020) are a testament to the belief that an organization's failure to offer opportunities for employee development ranks among factors that discourage them from working and engagement (Szymankowska & Bartczak, 2020). The research by Domagalska-Grędys (2017) determined that the core values for Generation Z are self-actualization and personal development. Gruszczyńska-Malec and Waligóra (2019) emphasize that steps taken by employers who wish to enhance work engagement among the members of Generation Z should include opportunities, professional growth, project autonomy, and control over their career path (Gruszczyńska-Malec & Waligóra, 2019).

A literature review of academic sources substantiates the claim that for Gen Z employees the ability to develop their competencies is among the most important factors that influence work engagement. Therefore, an attempt was made to explore the gap by studying selected aspects of the training process and its impact on work engagement among the young workforce, whoever, without limiting the perspective on development to the category of employee development. During the research, special attention was paid to the significance of the active participation of young workers in the training process and the impact it may have on their work engagement.

## Methodology

A survey was conducted to find the answer to the following research question: Does the implementation of opportunities for professional development by an organization influence the level of work engagement among the members of Generation Z?

With this question, two research hypotheses have been formulated:

- H1 – There is a positive correlation between young employees' participation in the training process and their work engagement.
- H2 – There is a positive correlation between the alignment with the development expectations of Gen Z employees and their work engagement.

The exploration was conducted using two research instruments. One of these was the Utrecht Work Engagement Scale (UWES), developed by Schaufeli et al. (2006). The shorter version of the questionnaire was adopted for the study, UWES-9, which comprises nine questions that measure the three items of work engagement, that is, vigor, dedication, and absorption. The respondents rated their answers on a scale from one to seven, with one meaning "never," and seven – "always, everyday" (Schaufeli et al., 2006; Rakowska & Mącik, 2016). A reliability analysis of the work engagement scale was performed using Cronbach's alpha coefficient, which allowed for the assessment of both the entire scale and its three distinct components. The result for all nine questions (0.8945) indicates the high reliability of the scale and internal consistency of the test (Table 6.1). For the purpose of interpreting the study results regarding work engagement, a scale was used in the questionnaire, on which the average level of engagement was set at 3.5 points. Consequently, values above that line were interpreted as higher than the average level of engagement, whereas values below it indicate levels of engagement that are lower than the average.

*Table 6.1* Assessment of the reliability of the Work Involvement Scale

| *Dimensions* | *Statement* | *Cronbach's α* | *Cronbach's α entire scale* |
|---|---|---|---|
| Vigor | At my work, I feel bursting with energy. | 0.7811 | 0.8945 |
| | At my job, I feel strong and vigorous. | | |
| | When I get up in the morning, I feel like going to work. | | |
| Dedication | I am enthusiastic about my job. | 0.7990 | |
| | My job inspires me. | | |
| | I am proud of the work that I do. | | |
| Absorption | I am immersed in my work. | 0.7301 | |
| | When I am working, I forget everything else around me. | | |
| | I feel happy when I am working intensely. | | |

*Source:* Own work based on Schaufeli et al. (2006)

The other research instrument was a survey questionnaire in which questions were separated into three thematic groups:

- The respondents' participation in the development processes in their organization
- The respondents' expectations and suggestions regarding the organizational support for their development
- Demographic information section

As a research instrument, the questionnaire comprised 12 substantive questions and 4 additional questions about demographic data. In seven questions, a Likert scale was used as the measurement method, and these were analyzed for reliability using Cronbach's alpha coefficient, which was 0.8025. The remaining four were multiple-choice questions.

In the analysis of statistical data, a number of research instruments was used to assess the reliability, independence, and the strength of associations between the research variables. The first instrument used was the Cronbach's alpha method for assessing the internal consistency of a set of items (questions) in a measurement scale. It is a standard procedure for scale reliability assessment, where a higher value of Cronbach's alpha (approaching 1) indicates a better consistency and credibility of the measurement instrument. Subsequently, a chi-square test for independence was performed, as it enables researchers to establish whether or not there is a significant association between two categorical variables. This test is used for comparing the distribution of the observed and expected values, assuming the variables are independent. The rejection of this hypothesis suggests that there is a statistically significant dependence between the variables. An assessment of the strength of association was performed using Cramer's V coefficient. It is a measure of the strength of association between categorical variables, which assumes the values between 0 and 1, where 0 indicates no association, whereas 1 indicates a perfect association. Importantly, Cramer's V coefficient determines not only the existence (or lack thereof) but also the strength of association.

Over the course of the research, 199 members of Generation Z, defined as people born after 1995, were studied. The sample had the following demographic structure: women accounted for 62.81%, while men for 37.19%. The majority of the respondents (79.90% of the sample) have had partial tertiary education, while 20.10% have completed secondary education. The employment pattern among the respondents comprised short employment periods. Similar sized groups of respondents were employed for a period of between six months and two years (48.24% of the sample), and less than six months (45.73%). A small fraction worked for a period of between three and five years. All the persons whose data was subject to analysis participated in professional training programs offered by their employers.

## Professional Development Opportunities and Work Engagement of Gen Z: Research Results

An analysis of the data shows that 72.36% of the respondents displayed an above average level of work engagement, with 27.64% reporting lower results. A detailed analysis of the three dimensions of work engagement (vigor, dedication, absorption) had the following form:

- Vigor: 67.84% of respondents had an above average score, while the score of 32.16% of respondents was below the average.
- Dedication: 76.38% of respondents had an above average score, while the score of only 23.62% was below the average.
- Absorption: 69.35% of respondents had an above average score, with 30.65% falling below this threshold.

No statistically relevant dependence between the level of work engagement and demographic data – such as gender, work experience, and education level – was found.

### *Participation in Training Process and Work Engagement Among Young Employees: Research Results*

Before participating in training activities, 38% of respondents received relevant information with an outline of the training from their superiors. A smaller fraction of respondents (15%) was informed by their direct superiors about the reasons behind their participation in the learning process. Some employees (11%) were interviewed by the higher-ups about their training/development needs, while only 4% of respondents had a chance to design their own development paths. The remaining persons (6% of respondents) were assigned to training programs without any additional information. The statistical analysis conducted enabled the identification of a (low level) correlation between being provided with information about the training program and the level of work engagement. A reflection on the connection between receiving information and the respective dimensions of engagement, that is, vigor, dedication, and absorption, revealed that the access to information is only to a minor extent correlated with the levels of vigor and dedication, while for absorption, this correlation turned out to be a little more pronounced than for the remaining pair (Table 6.2).

Respondents expressed varied preferences in relation to the types of training activities offered by their companies. The highest number of indications (76% of respondents) pointed to participation in on-the-job and on-line learning (75%), as well as in conferences (70%). Additionally, coaching as a learning method was opted for by 67% of respondents. A similar fraction (65%) recognized job rotation as a desired form of development offered by their companies, whereas webinars and mentoring were indicated by 65% and 64% of respondents, respectively.

*Table 6.2* Influence of studied factors on work engagement

| | Engagement | Vigor | Dedication | Absorption |
|---|---|---|---|---|
| Before I am assigned to a training session, I am provided with the outline of it. | | | | |
| | Engagement | Vigor | Dedication | Absorption |
| $chi^2$ | 6.6223 | 3.0244 | 3.9273 | 9.4252 |
| *p* value | 0.01 | 0.082 | 0.046 | 0.002 |
| Cramer's V | 0.1824 | 0.1233 | 0.1414 | 0.2177 |
| I am satisfied with the types of training provided by my company. | | | | |
| | Engagement | Vigor | Dedication | Absorption |
| $chi^2$ | 18.5534 | None | 21.6352 | 25.0773 |
| *p* value | <0.001 | None | <0.001 | <0.001 |
| Cramer's V | 0.3053 | None | 0.3297 | 0.3550 |
| I can influence the choice of training programs to participate in. | | | | |
| | Engagement | Vigor | Dedication | Absorption |
| $chi^2$ | 11.1172 | 13.1340 | 8.5922 | 12.7366 |
| *p* value | 0.004 | 0.001 | 0.014 | 0.002 |
| Cramer's V | 0.2364 | 0.001 | 0.2078 | 0.2530 |
| Training sessions in which I participated have influenced my professional development. | | | | |
| | Engagement | Vigor | Dedication | Absorption |
| $chi^2$ | 15.9266 | 1.7467 | 22.9686 | 22.9686 |
| *p* value | <0.001/0 | 0.418 | 0.028 | <0.001/0 |
| Cramer's V | 0.2829 | 0.0937 | 0.1898 | 0.3397 |
| I am satisfied with the number of training events that I am offered by my company. | | | | |
| | Engagement | Vigor | Dedication | Absorption |
| $chi^2$ | 21.4587 | 7.5139 | 23.6332 | 23.4967 |
| *p* value | <0.001 | 0.023 | <0.001 | <0.001 |
| Cramer's V | 0.3285 | 0.1943 | 0.3446 | 0.3436 |
| Participation in the training sessions offered by my company has a positive influence on the level of my engagement at work. | | | | |
| | Engagement | Vigor | Dedication | Absorption |
| $chi^2$ | 14.1968 | 8.7943 | 18.1723 | 19.6604 |
| *p* value | 0.001 | 0.012 | 0.0001 | 0.00005 |
| Cramer's V | 0.2671 | 0.2102 | 0.2671 | 0.3143 |

*Source:* Own work based on the research

A fraction of study participants (38%) expressed satisfaction with the methods of professional development they were afforded. A similar group of respondents (33%) offered no opinion on the training opportunities at their disposal. A lesser proportion of participants (29%) was not satisfied with the training forms provided. A moderate correlation was established between the level of satisfaction with the offered training opportunities and general work employment, as well as two dimensions thereof, namely, devotion and absorption. No statistically significant connection between the level of satisfaction with training methods and vigor was detected during the analysis.

The level of decision-making in the context of employees' choice of training activities to participate in was distributed evenly among the respondents. Precisely 41% of respondents stated that they have influence on the selection of training practices, while an equal fraction of respondents (41%) admitted to not having had the ability to impact the process of training selection. The remaining proportion of respondents (18%) was unable to determine their position on the issue. A weak correlation was observed between the autonomy in selecting training methods and the general level of work engagement, and its three components: vigor, dedication, and absorption, with a slightly stronger association detected for absorption.

A little more than half of the sample (51%) considered it beneficial for their professional development to participate in the training activities provided by their organizations. A dissatisfaction with the results of participating in these development programs was expressed by 21% of respondents. A similar number of subjects under study (26%) did not decide to give an unequivocal evaluation of the influence of training on their career development. A statistically significant dependence between the sense of personal development stemming from participating in a training process and work engagement was found, with the most accurate correlation observed for absorption.

Young employees expressed diverse views about their satisfaction with the number of training events contracted by their companies. On the one hand, a part of the sample (37%) is content with the number of training sessions offered; on the other hand, however, a similar fraction of respondents does not share that opinion. The remainder of respondents (27%) expressed no clear opinion on the issue, which may imply the ambiguity of their training experience or a lack of sufficient awareness of the benefits of participating in training activities. There is a connection between employee satisfaction with the number of training events offered and their work engagement. Furthermore, a moderate correlation between this aspect of satisfaction and the three dimensions of engagement, namely, vigor, absorption, and dedication, was observed. In 2023, the majority of respondents (75.37%) did participate in training opportunities offered by their companies. The largest proportion participated in two to four training events (42.71%), and a little less in a single one (32.66%). Those participating in five to seven training sessions comprised 11.06% of study subjects, and the range of eight to ten such events was attended by 4.52%, while above ten of these saw the participation of 6.53%. According to the results gathered, the number of training sessions attended by the study participants in 2023 did not influence their work engagement.

More than half of study participants (52.26%) voiced the belief that participation in training activities contributed to improving work engagement among them. Meanwhile, the other group of respondents (21.11%) saw no significant impact of participation in development programs on their level of work engagement or did not share their opinion on the topic (26.63%). The study detected a correlation between the subjective opinions of employees about the impact of training participation on their actual work engagement and its three dimensions:

vigor, dedication, absorption, with the association being the strongest for absorption. Table 6.2 presents the statistics of the variables analyzed.

### *Association Between Alignment with Development Expectations of Gen Z Employees and Their Work Engagement: Research Results*

A larger proportion of respondents (57.78%) sided with the claim that broadening of the variety of the training programs on offer would contribute to improved work engagement. A relatively smaller percentage of respondents (18.60%) took the opposite stance or reported difficulties in assessing the influence of the training offer on their level of work engagement (23.62%). The majority of study participants (57.29%) further believed that the identification of their learning and development needs and the opportunity to have their development expectations heard would also cause an improvement in work engagement. A smaller part of the sample (30.65%) found it difficult to respond, whereas 12.06% believed that such activities had no influence on their work engagement.

Research respondents were most likely to voice willingness to take part in specialist training courses, focused on specific industry or technical knowledge, as declared by 43.22% of participants. Foreign language courses were seen as attractive by 30.65% of the study subjects. Training courses on using modern information tools and development of soft skills were less popular, accounting for respectively 10.55% and 10.05% respondents' choices. A small group showed interest in personal development programs (3.02%) and courses on how to comply with legal regulations and industry standards (2.51%).

The young employees under study were willing to implement changes and improvements to the training processes conducted by the organizations that employ them. A third of respondents (33.01%) advocated an increase in the number of practical courses and on-the-job workshops. Some (16.99%) stressed the need to identify individual training expectations of employees before they are assigned to participate in specific training projects. The expansion of e-learning and digital learning platforms was indicated as a desired change by a fraction of respondents (10.68%), while better mentoring support and coaching was considered to be essential by 9.22% of study participants. It seems noteworthy that during the study no one mentioned the need to introduce changes regarding personalized development paths. Other individual changes proposed by another group of respondents (28.64%) include holding integration meetings–training events not directly related to the industry, psychological support for employees, and the general enhancement of the quality of training practices offered.

## Inferences and Discussion

The study results obtained are likely to have been prone to the influence of subjective factors in the answers given by respondents. Therefore, the data was subject to careful interpretation to avoid drawing erroneous conclusions, on the basis of potentially distorted information.

An analysis of the research question indicates that Gen Z employees subject to study are committed at work. The majority of employees recorded above average scores for overall engagement, as well as in the three components studies: vigor, dedication, and absorption. Such a state implies work engagement and interest in job tasks and readiness to undertake activities that require great efforts and sacrifices. It should be underscored, however, that all study participants were characterized by short period of employment due to their age, which calls for great caution when formulating such conclusions.

As for the verification of the H1 hypothesis regarding the existence of a positive correlation between young employees' participation in the training process and their work engagement, it has been demonstrated that the identification of development needs that should involve inquiring about development needs, providing information motivating the training participation of employees, and setting individual development paths had no significant effect on work engagement among them. Being provided with information about the outline of the learning process marked a departure from the above situation, as it did cause an increase in work engagement. In a reflection on the significance of the opportunity to get acquainted with the outline of a learning event, the strongest (albeit still moderate) correlation among the three components was detected for absorption. This result may imply that employees who are aware of the training activities on offer are slightly more likely to exhibit work engagement, which may be the result of them perceiving training activities as an occasion to develop their competencies. Respondents from Generation Z, however, independent, as they are, seem to value the ability to express their development expectations at the stage of identifying training needs, which they find essential. More than half of the study subjects declared that it was their subjective belief that having such an option would influence their levels of work engagement. Such findings may also point to the organizational implementation of training processes conducted without due diligence, focused mainly on informing employees about the training events they are assigned to, or to the low awareness among young employees of the measures they superiors should undertake to effectively foster learning and development among their subordinates.

Participation in the training process influences the intensity of work engagement among Gen Z respondents. A correlation was discovered between work engagement among young workers and the studied aspects related to participation in training processes, that is, the types of learning methods proposed by the company, the level of decision-making regarding employees' choice of training activities, and their satisfaction with the number of training events offered. Employee participation in the said aspects is also connected to the three essential components of engagement: vigor, absorption, and dedication. The sole exception is the satisfaction with the forms of learning and development provided, as it is related only to a single item of work engagement – vigor, which may indicate that young employees adapt to various training methods and do not feel strongly influenced of these methods on their everyday levels of energy and enthusiasm or that other factors, such as support from colleagues and/or superiors, are more important for maintaining their readiness to perform job tasks. The data suggests that employees who have influence on the choice of training programs to participate in exhibit statistically significantly higher levels of work engagement with its crucial components, vigor, dedication, and absorption. The values recorded point to a moderate strength of this dependence, which suggests that it may be worthwhile to grant employees autonomy in educational decisions as an element of a human resource management strategy aimed at raising the level of work engagement. Gruszczyńska-Malec and Waligóra (2019) corroborated the claim that Generation Z expects to be allowed to carry out projects independently and that it improves their level of engagement. Generation Z is made up of people who want to feel they influence what is happening in the company (Benítez-Márquez et al., 2021).

A statistically significant dependence in the employees studied was found between the sense of professional development and work engagement, which indicates that the ability to perceive the developmental benefits of training participation may have a major impact on work engagement. The strongest correlation here was observed for absorption, which implies that employees who are most positive in their assessment of the influence of training programs on their development at the same time exhibit the highest engagement scores due to being deeply immersed in their tasks.

The persons studied declared that the participation in training activities arranged by their companies has a positive impact on their sense of engagement. The responses elicited were validated by statistical analysis. The strongest connection was observed for absorption, which may suggest that training activities are effective in increasing the level of engagement which in turn implies that investment in the professional development of employees may be a useful tool to increase their engagement and focus on work. Employee satisfaction with the number of training events offered by their companies is reflected in their work engagement in general, including the specific aspects thereof, namely, vigor, dedication, and absorption. It is particularly dedication and absorption, regarded as the components of engagement, that were found to have a greater connection with the satisfaction derived from having access to training programs, which highlights the importance of investment in the professional development of employees for their loyalty and job absorption. It is also a testament to the claim that the perception of an adequate number of training events on offer is a major factor bearing on employees' positive attitude toward their job and organization. It should be underscored that what mattered in relation to work engagement among the group studied was not the specific number of such events but the subjective employee perception of how these may benefits them.

Members of the young workforce regard the active participation in the training process as important, which was corroborated by the statistical analysis. Only approximately a third of respondents were satisfied with the types and number of the training activities proposed and had opportunity to decide whether or not to take part therein. These results may point to the failure to tailor learning and development programs to the individual needs and preferences of staff members, which may have a negative impact on their future work engagement. The Gallup report indicates that in order to trigger engagement among young workers, their interest in development should be considered (Harter, 2024).

The verification of the H2 hypothesis, on the association between alignment with development expectations of Gen Z employees and their work engagement, identified the need to focus more on the hands-on components of training and on-the-job workshops, the identification of training needs, integration of digital technology in the learning process, and soft skills development. The research showed that young people also value mentoring support, as elaborated on in a paper by Mărginean (2021). The willingness of this age group to take part in various training programs was confirmed by the results of a study by Wasiluk and Bańkowska (2021). There may be various circumstances behind the fact that the need for personalized career paths has not been voiced. One of them is the insufficient awareness of the benefits of such an undertaking. Another is the consequence of the characteristics of Generation Z, as its members do not concentrate on long-term career building and instead prefer to acquire knowledge and skills quickly in order to pursue instant success (Czyczerska et al., 2020; Wasiluk & Bańkowska, 2021).

A correlation was found between the alignment of development expectations of the Gen Z employees studied and work engagement among them. Young workers believe that both the participation in diversified training programs and the identification of their training needs would improve their work engagement. Both these matters suggest that young employees expect their employers to not only provide training offers but also embrace an individual approach. They consider such endeavors to have direct influence of their level of work engagement. This interpretation suggests that it is of vital importance, when planning a professional development strategy for employees, to integrate educational solutions with an in-depth understanding of and reacting to individual training needs, which may lay the foundation for building long-term work engagement.

Based on the data obtained, it can be concluded that the participation of Gen Z employees in the training process does influence the level of their work engagement. These results pave the way for further comparative research, some focused on various generational groups and others on the exploration of the ways to identify the development needs of young employees that would meet their expectations. That could, on the one hand, influence their work engagement and, on the other, increase their loyalty toward their organizations.

## Conclusion

The results of the research confirm that organizational implementation of opportunities for professional development may influence the level of work engagement among Gen Zers. The importance of investing in the professional development of employees, particularly from the Gen Z cohort, is invaluable. Not only do successful development programs enhance employee competencies and skills, but they also positively affect work engagement. Young employees should co-participate in the training process, as it has a favorable influence on their level of work engagement. Members of the young workforce want to talk about their needs and identify them in order to participate in a training process tailored to them. Such undertakings of the company will contribute to the sense of fulfillment among young workers, which stems from being recognized in the workplace and having support for ongoing development (Huțanu et al., 2020). Generation Z workers are willing to change jobs (Benítez-Márquez et al., 2021); therefore, treating each of them personally may help increase their loyalty and secure a return on the investment made by employers supporting their development. Employee training and development play a major role in the organization, fostering the opportunity to achieve individual professional goals, and thus improve the level of engagement (Rodriguez & Walters, 2019). The analysis of the data demonstrated that Gen Z employees value access to varied forms of training and potential for growth, which have a direct impact on their improved engagement in professional duties. Furthermore, the study highlights the importance of tailoring development programs to the individual needs and expectations of young workers, which not only increases their job satisfaction but also contributes to their long-term loyalty toward the company.

## References

Alerasoul, S. A., Afeltra, G., Hakala, H., Eliana, M. E., & Strozzi, F. (2022). Organisational learning, learning organisation, and learning orientation: An integrative review and framework. *Human Resource Management Review*, *32*(3), 100854.

Amstrong, M. (2001). *Zarządzanie zasobami ludzkimi*. Dom Wydawniczy ABC.

Benítez-Márquez, M. D., Sánchez-Teba, E. M., Bermúdez-González, G., & Núñez-Rydman, E. S. (2021). Generation Z within the workforce and in the workplace: A bibliometric analysis. *Frontiers in Psychology*, *12*, 736820.

Buchko, A. A., & Gabrielova, K. (2021). Here comes Generation Z: Millennials as managers. *Business Horizons*, *64*(2), 489–499.

Chrupała-Pniak, M., & Grabowski, D. (2014). Motywacyjne i organizacyjne predyktory zaangażowania pracowników. *Prace Naukowe UE we Wrocławiu*, *350*. https://www.dbc.wroc.pl/dlibra/docmetadata?id=27715&from=publication

Czyczerska, K. M., Ławnik, A. J., & Szlenk-Czyczerska, E. (2020). Współczesny rynek pracy w Polsce a generacja. Różnice między pokoleniami X, Y oraz Z. *Rozprawy Społeczne*, *14*(3), 102–125.

*The Deloitte global 2022 Gen Z and Millennial survey*. https://www.deloitte.com/global/en/issues/work/genzmillennialsurvey-2022.html

The Deloitte Millennial Survey. (2018). *Millennials disappointed in business unprepared for Industry 4.0.* https://odpowiedzialnybiznes.pl/wp-content/uploads/2018/06/gx-2018-millennial-survey-report.pdf

Domagalska-Grędys, M. (2017). Wartości pracy młodych pokoleń Y i Z. *Roczniki Naukowe Stowarzyszenia Ekonomistów Rolnictwa i Agrobiznesu, XIX*(2), 40–45.

Dziura, B. (2022). Wykorzystanie kapitału ludzkiego do tworzenia przewagi konkurencyjnej w przedsiębiorstwa województwa podkarpackiego w II dekadzie XXI wieku. In A. Chodyński, F. Dariusz, & M. Leśniewski (Eds.), *Innowacyjność konkurencyjność, jakość, wiedza i uczenie się komponentami rozwoju organizacji w zmiennym otoczeniu* (pp. 99–119). Krakowska Akademia im. Andrzeja Frycza Modrzewskiego.

Gajda, J. (2017). Oczekiwania przedstawicieli pokolenia z wobec pracy zawodowej i pracodawcy. *Prace Naukowe UE we Wrocławiu, 491.*

Gajewska, P., & Piskrzyńska, K. (2016). Efektywność szkoleń pracowniczych na przykładzie przedsiębiorstwa branży motoryzacyjnej. *Zarządzanie. Teoria i Praktyka, 4*(18), 9–16.

Gruszczyńska-Malec, G., & Waligóra, Ł. (2019). Zarządzanie multigeneracyjne – budowanie zaangażowania w zespole zróżnicowanym ze względu na wiek. *Education of Economists and Managers Problems Innovations Projects, 53*(3), 11–24.

Harter, J. (2024). *The new challenge of engaging younger workers.* https://www.gallup.com/workplace/610856/new-challenge-engaging-younger-workers.aspx?utm_source=gallup_brand&utm_medium=email&utm_campaign=gallup_at_work_send_1_february_02272024&utm_term=information&utm_content=heres_how_to_address_it_textlink_1

Huţanu, A., Bertea, P. E., & Iftode, D. (2020). Generation Z is going to work. What are its expectations? The future of education, International conference, Alexandru Ioan Cuza University of Iaşi, Romania. *Journal of Organizational Psychology, 17*(5), 118–128.

Juchnowicz, M. (2012). *Zaangażowanie pracowników.* PWE.

Kroenke, A. (2015). Pokolenie x, y, z w organizacji. *Zeszyty Naukowe Politechniki Łódzkiej, Organizacja i Zarządzanie, 1202*(61).

Król, H., & Ludwiczyński, A. (Eds.). (2007). *Zarządzanie zasobami ludzkimi.* PWN.

Kukla, D., & Nowacka, M. (2019). Charakterystyka podejścia do pracy przedstawicieli pokolenia Z –praca w systemie wartości młodych. Cz.1. *Polish Journal of Continuing Education, 3*, 120–130.

Kuruppu, C. L., Kavirathne, C. S., & Karunarathna, N. (2021). The impact of training on employee performance in a selected apparel sector organization in Sri Lanka. *Global Journal of Management and Business Research: Administration and Management, 21*(2).

Ławińska, O., & Korombel, A. (2023). *Pokolenie Z jako wyzwanie współczesnego zarządzania przedsiębiorstwem.* Politechnika Częstochowskiej.

Lewicka, D., Pec, M., & Wilk, A. (2019). Proces szkoleniowy i jego rezultaty. Studium przypadku przedsiębiorstwa handlowego. *Przedsiębiorczość i Zarządzanie, 20*(6), 105–119.

Lutyńska, K., & Wasiluk, A. (2023). Co motywuje do pracy pracowników różnych pokoleń? *Akademia Zarządzania, 7*(3).

Mărginean, A. E. (2021). Gen z perceptions and expectations upon Entering the workforce. *Sciendo, 14*(22).

McGuinness, S., & Luis, O. (2015). Skill gaps in the workplace: Measurement, determinants and impacts. *IZA Discussion Papers*, 9278. Institute for the Study of Labor.

Meyer, J. P., Allen, N. J., & Smith, C. A. (1993). Commitment to organizations and occupations: Extension and test of a three-component conceptualization. *Journal of Applied Psychology, 78*, 538–551. https://doi.org/10.1037/0021-9010.78.4.538

Nechirwan, B. I., Baban, J. O., Bayar, G., Pshdar, A. H., Sarhang, S., Hassan, M. A., Shahla, A. A., Bawan, Y. S., Bayad, J. A., & Govand, A. (2021). The role of training and development on organizational effectiveness. *International Journal of Engineering, Business and Management*, *5*(3).

Neczaj, R. (2005). Rozpoznanie i analiza potrzeb szkoleniowych organizacji. *E-mentor*, *1*(8). SGH.

Otieno, J. O., & Nyambegera, S. M. (2019). Millennials and generation Z employees are here: Is your organization ready? *Journal of Language, Technology & Entrepreneurship in Africa*, *10*(2).

Parmelee, M. (2022). https://www2.deloitte.com/us/en/insights/topics/talent/deloitte-millennial-survey.html

Pasieczny, J., & Rosiek, T. (2021). *W kierunku organizacji uczącej się. Transformacja organizacyjna na przykładzie jednostki administracji publicznej*. Dom Wydawniczy ELIPSA.

Pedler, M., & Aspinwall, K. (1998). *A concise guide to the learning organization*. Lemos & Crane.

Phillips, P., Phillips, J. J., Stone Ron, D., & Burkett, H. (2009). *Zwrot z inwestycji w szkolenia i rozwój pracowników*. Wolters Kluwer.

Pocztowski, A. (2007). *Zarządzanie zasobami ludzkimi*. Polskie Wydawnictwo Ekonomiczne.

Przewoźnik, J., & Górczyńska, J. (2021). *Raport z wyników badań: Potrzeby szkoleniowe i edukacyjne w opinii pracodawców i pracowników branży handlowej i możliwość ich realizacji*. Projekt „Problemy społeczne pod lupą" Federacji Związków Zawodowych Pracowników Spółdzielczości, Produkcji, Handlu i Usług w Polsce.

Ragin-Skorecka, K., Motała, D., & Boguszewska, K. (2023). Pokolenie z nie jest gotowe na pracę w turkusie. *Zeszyty Naukowe Politechniki Poznańskiej. Organizacja i Zarządzanie*, *87*.

Rakowska, A., & Mącik, R. (2016). Zaangażowanie pracownika a satysfakcja t pracy – modelowanie zależności z wykorzystaniem PLS-SEM. *Przegląd Organizacji*, *5*(916).

Rodriguez, J., & Walters, K. (2019). The importance of training and development in employee performance and evaluation. *World Wide Journal of Multidisciplinary Research and Development*, *3*, 206–212.

Schaufeli, W., & Bakker, A. (2004). *Work engagement scale*. Occupational Health Psychology Unit, Utrecht University.

Schaufeli, W., Bakker, A., & Salanova, M. (2006). The measurement of work engagement with a short questionnaire: A cross-national study. *Educational and Psychological Measurement*, *66*(4), 701–716.

Serafin, K. (2011). Identyfikacja potrzeb szkoleniowych jako istotny obszar działań w zarządzaniu personelem. *Problemy Zarządzania*, *4*(34), 191–203.

Skowronek, A. (2022). Oczekiwania pracowników wielopokoleniowego zespołu wobec kompetencji menedżerów w dobie cyfryzacji. *Zarządzanie Zasobami Ludzkimi*, *146–147*(3–4), 95–111.

Szymankowska, A., & Bartczak, M. (2020). Zapobieganie odejściom młodych pracowników z organizacji – wyniki badań. *Journal of Modern Science*, *1*(44), 107–124.

Wasiluk, A., & Bańkowska, M. (2021). Przesłanki dotyczące wyboru miejsca pracy przez pracowników pokolenia X, Y i Z. *Zeszyty Naukowe PTE*, *14*.

# 7 The Impact of Leadership on Employee Engagement

*Robert Szydło, Małgorzata Tyrańska, Sylwia Wiśniewska, Ireneusz Rynduch and Magdalena Adamczyk-Kowalczuk*

## Introduction

Leadership within organizations has long been the subject of intense study, with scholars drawing upon various psychological and managerial theories and paradigms to understand its complexities. A comprehensive examination of leadership delves into its psychological context, exploring the interplay between individual traits, behaviors, situational factors, and social dynamics. Building upon earlier theories, the concept of transactional and transformational leadership emerged along with the idea of there being a tension between exchanging relationships and inspiring followers, motivating them through higher ideals and values. In today's organizations, fostering employee engagement has become a priority for leaders, given its impact on productivity, morale, and organizational success; it has thus been the job of the leader to employ various tools and techniques in order to build such engagement in the employees' mind. Transformational leadership, in particular, emphasizes individualized consideration, intellectual stimulation, inspirational motivation, and idealized influence as key components for achieving that goal. Combined with the concept of sustainable leadership, this approach might just be the key to developing employee management in a responsible way.

This study is intended as an explorative effort to identify the critical leadership practices that enhance employee engagement. The main objective is to identify and describe the actions that may have a positive impact on employee engagement. The main research question was formulated thus: in the perception of employees, does sustainable leadership have an impact on employee engagement?

There were also two supplementary questions:

- What is the perceived impact of each level of sustainable leadership practices on employee engagement?
- Which elements may affect the perception of the impact of sustainable leadership on employee engagement?

DOI: 10.4324/9781032715407-8

The CSAQ method was used to answer these questions, followed by both descriptive and mathematical statistics. The publication presents the result of the Project no. 068/ZZS/2024/POT financed from the subsidy granted to the Krakow University of Economics.

## Psychological and Managerial Contexts of Leadership

The psychological context of leadership encompasses various theories, models, and perspectives that seek to understand the behaviors, traits, and processes involved in effective leadership. The classic approach to the psychology of leadership focuses on, for example, personal traits, behavioral leadership style, and contingency. A trait-based approach to leadership states that specific innate characteristics or traits predispose individuals to become influential leaders. The traits identified in the Big Five personality dimensions (Costa & McCrae, 1992), that is, agreeableness, extraversion, conscientiousness, emotional stability, and openness to experience, are often associated with leadership effectiveness (Judge et al., 2002). However, contemporary research suggests that while traits may contribute to leadership emergence, they are not the sole determinants of leadership effectiveness. An approach based on behavioral theories focuses on the actions and behaviors of leaders rather than their innate traits. Behavioral theories suggest that influential leaders demonstrate various leadership styles, entailing both initiation of structure (task-oriented behavior) and consideration (relationship-oriented behavior) (Fleishman, 1973; Stogdill, 1974). At the same time, it is essential to mention that influential leaders can exhibit various behavioral styles depending on the situation. According to contingency theories, leadership should be seen as a perfect match between personality and context (Fiedler, 1964). Contingency theories posit that leadership effectiveness depends on the interaction between certain leader traits or behaviors and situational factors.

The above-mentioned aspects are important factors behind the figure of the leader indeed. As has been claimed – leaders are born, not made (Galton, 1892). This approach, however, often leads to stereotypical notions of leaders as having innate charisma, exhibiting certain behaviors, and being surrounded by "followers" whom they inspired. Drawing on earlier theories, Bass (1985) introduced the concepts of transactional and transformational leadership. Transactional leaders focus on relationships of exchange with their followers, providing rewards for performance and correcting deviations. Transformational leaders, on the other hand, inspire and motivate followers by appealing to higher ideals and values, fostering a sense of collective identity and purpose. Bass (1997) and Bass and Riggio (2010) likewise claim that transformational leadership comprises four fundamental components:

- Individualized consideration, which involves attentiveness to the needs, capabilities, and ambitions of followers to facilitate the enhancement of aspirations, skills, and fulfillment of needs

- Intellectual stimulation, wherein followers' fundamental beliefs, assumptions, and approaches are challenged to foster the cultivation of novel and superior perspectives and methods
- Inspirational motivation, that is, charismatic and inspiring leadership, which offers the vigor, rationale, and impetus necessary to inspire transformation among followers
- Idealized influence – admired, respected, and trusted, leaders serve as role models to their followers

In that context, emotional intelligence is an enormously important factor that relates to the ability to recognize, understand, and manage one's own emotions, as well as the emotions of others. Leaders with high emotional intelligence are better equipped to handle interpersonal relationships, inspire trust and confidence, and navigate challenging situations effectively (McClellan et al., 2017). At the same time, the need for authenticity emphasizes the importance of genuineness, self-awareness, transparency, and moral integrity in leadership. Authentic leaders are guided by their core values and beliefs; they lead with honesty, empathy, and purpose (Caza & Jackson, 2011).

Be that as it may, one may find numerous definitions of leadership, including such as: "an individual, or clique, which influences the behavior of another individual or group of individuals" (Hogg, 2007). However, according to the new psychology of leadership, social identity approach is crucial, making organizational life possible in the first place (Haslam et al., 2003). Moreover, leadership, seen as social identity management, focuses on a leader's ability to create, represent, advance, and embed a shared, unique sense of "we" (Haslam et al., 2020). Haslam et al. (2020) pointed out four key aspects of leadership based on social identity that encourage leaders' advocacy: being one of us, doing it for us, crafting a sense of us, and making us matter. The main principle of social identity management asserts that as individuals develop a more robust identification with a group, they become increasingly attentive to the group's prototype and to those who embody it most closely. This is because the prototype represents the essential attributes of the group's membership. In such prominent group settings, being perceived as highly prototypical enhances one's influence (Hogg, 2007).

Understanding the psychological context of leadership involves considering not only individual differences, cognitive processes, and emotional intelligence but also social dynamics and the interplay between leaders and their environments. Effective leadership is often a complex and dynamic process influenced by many factors.

The issue of leadership, widely analyzed in numerous management publications, continues to be an essential and topical one. The importance of leadership is related to its impact on employee engagement, interpersonal relations, work motivation, openness, anticipation of change, and the achievements of teams and organizations. In general, leadership is understood as the ability to influence the behavior of employees to achieve specific goals (Onyekwere et al., 2023). In management science, leadership means the ability to influence, motivate, and enable other members of an organization to act toward its success (Bass & Bass, 2008). It is worth noting that the literature on the subject emphasizes a process-based view of leadership. Leadership is the process by which a person influences others to achieve goals and directs the organization to make it more consistent. Leaders engage in this process using their knowledge and leadership skills (Sharma & Jain, 2013). Moreover, leadership, as a part of management, is defined by the ability to persuade others to engage in a specific form of participation. It is regarded as the process of directing people through communication and beliefs, using an amalgam of influences related to the trust in people heading in the same direction, the mission of the analyzed system, collective decision-making, and motivation of human resources (Răducan & Răducan, 2014).

The evolution of leadership theory is reflected in the periodization offered in the source literature (Van Seters & Field, 1990):

- *The personality era*, with the sub-periods of *the excellent man period* (mainly analyzing the life paths of prominent historical figures) and *the trait period* (pursuing the discovery of the correlation between the leader's various character traits of a leader and leadership effectiveness)
- *The influence era*, which dealt with the sources and use of authority
- *The behavior era*, focusing on typical leadership behavior and identifying the differences between the behaviors of effective and ineffective leaders
- *The situation era*, centered on the context of leadership application
- *The contingency era*, related to leadership's dependence on one or more factors from the set including personality, influence, behavior, and situation
- *The transactional era*, supplementing the previous theories with the aspects of role differentiation and social interaction
- *The anti-leadership era*, promoting views that undermine the meaning of leadership research and seeking potential leadership substitutes
- *The culture era*, looking at how to build a solid organizational culture and stimulate employees to lead themselves
- *The transformational era*, concentrating on leadership behavior in organizational change and processes related to developing a vision for the future to encourage employee commitment to the changes introduced

In light of the multifaceted and holistic character of leadership-related issues, the literature organizes existing leadership concepts according to four paradigms: the classical, the transactional, the visionary, and the organic. These four represent ideas widely accepted at various times (Avery, 2011). The first three paradigms refer to the above periodization, while the fourth can be described as another period in the development of the leadership concept.

The classical paradigm reigned from antiquity until the 1970s. It saw leadership as based on respect and authority. These two elements were essential for giving orders and controlling subordinates (Kark et al., 2018). The transactional paradigm, prevalent from the 1970s to the mid-1980s, assumed that a leader influences subordinates through personal contacts and relationships. Leaders and their employees negotiate, transacting with regard to their expectations, rewards, and goals (Kuhnert, 1994). According to the visionary paradigm, characteristic of the time between the mid-1980s and the turn of the century, leaders use emotions to inspire their subordinates. This type of leadership is characterized by an individualized approach to subordinates, based on the charisma of the leader, who is responsible for the vision of development and motivation of subordinates, as well as meeting their needs (Bass & Avolio, 1990; Stone et al., 2004). The organic paradigm, which has been in effect since the beginning of the 21st century, assumes that the leader acts as a coordinator, creating conditions for cooperation and operating in bilateral interaction with subordinates. Leadership is distributed and formed within the framework of relationships in changing teams (Dang & Basur, 2017).

The paradigms listed are not mutually exclusive; they illustrate the shifting ideas and values underlying the perception of leadership and the expectations voiced for the leader's role and modus operandi. Historically analyzing the ideas embodied in each paradigm, one can see the growing role and significance of subordinates. In the classical perspective, leadership is indivisible; the leader is the key figure, while employees carry out his commands with no right to dissent. Over the subsequent approaches, leadership becomes an increasingly inclusive process in which the contribution and importance of employees and their knowledge become more and more important, and their position vis-à-vis the leader strengthens (Avery, 2011).

The issues related to leadership can also be presented through mutually complementary groups of theories (Biesok & Wyród-Wróbel, 2018), namely: *leadership theories* – based on the personality traits, abilities, and character of leaders – which seek a universal set of leaders' characteristics and their genetic attributes; *behavioral theories*, based on the models of practical leadership actions and behaviors, the so-called leadership styles; *situational leadership theories*, guided by the idea of a leader's decisions and actions being influenced by multiple factors, including situations and circumstances.

Significantly, leaders can intentionally and continuously influence other members of the organization and even impose their will (Avery, 2011). A leader is a person who not only gives orders and coordinates the performance of duties but also sets goals, creates a vision, as well as long-range and long-term assumptions, and then convinces those under her or his authority to implement them. By no means is the work of a leader limited to giving direct orders, ensuring day-to-day coordination, and supervising the bulk of tasks carried out. Instead, it involves building a sense of belonging to the organization and setting its goals (Scott, 2003).

Among the key factors that influence the effectiveness of leaders in organizations are integrity, usefulness, benevolence, reciprocity, and the ability to sustain relationships. Integrity means the alignment of the leader's thoughts, words, and deeds, whose honesty and sincerity in relations with employees are required. Utility is one of the critical factors in exerting influence. Employees should recognize and acknowledge the usefulness of their relationships with the organization and the leader. Interactions must match employees' expectations and be directed toward achieving common goals. Benevolence means the relationship between the leader and employees that should result in the satisfaction and contentment of both parties. Reciprocity means finding a common ground for action, taking action using employees' ideas, and pursuing goals based on transparent relationships. The ability to sustain relationships means maintaining ties that enable efficient communication and interaction between the leader and employees. Employees should see that the leader recognizes their commitment to their work, appreciates their achievements, and knows they are an asset to the organization (Zakrzewski et al., 2014).

## Leadership Tools to Improve Engagement

Contemporary organizations and leaders operating within them face the challenge of shaping lasting bonds with their personnel (Stefańska & Grabowski, 2023; Southgate et al., 2023). The rapidly changing market conditions, including the development of modern technologies and the emergence of alternatives to traditional work methods, such as hybrid and remote work, give employees more significant opportunities to explore offers tailored to their individual preferences (Dabić et al., 2023; Hamouche, 2023; Li et al., 2023). Consequently, uncertainty grows among organizational leaders, who must flexibly adapt to the current demands of the workforce (Waydowicz, 2018; Rahmadani et al., 2020; Al Marshoudi et al., 2023). A practical solution to this situation may be the leaders' adept support for employee engagement (Batista-Taran et al., 2013; Mughal et al., 2020; Southgate et al., 2023).

There is not a single unequivocal definition of employee engagement in either business practice or economic sciences. The Gallup Institute created one of the earliest concepts of employee engagement in 1985 (Mrówka, 2010). They developed a set of 12 questions, called Q12, referring to factors that increase work efficiency and the resulting engagement (Harter et al., 2009). Meanwhile, the Institute for Employment Studies (IES) defines engagement as "the employee's positive attitude towards the organization and its values; an engaged employee is aware of business needs and collaborates with others to increase organizational efficiency; developing and deepening engagement requires a two-way relationship between the employee and the employer" (Skowron-Mielnik, 2016, p. 154). Nowadays, commitment is associated with employees' attitude, a crucial factor here being the strength of psychological identification with or attachment to the organization (Gojny, 2013; Szczepanska-Woszczyna & Bogaczyk, 2023; Šakytė-Statnickė et al., 2023).

Numerous tools and factors influence the level of employee engagement. Borkowska (2014) distinguishes three groups thereof. They may be related to individual personality trait, such as age, gender, health, competencies, and perspectives on professional development. Equally significant is the nature of the job and the working conditions, such as remote work, mental or physical workload, the level of risk associated with responsibilities, quality of team communication, transparent personnel policy, and motivational and reward systems. The third group consists of organizational-situational factors, including interpersonal relationships, alignment with the organizational culture, and self-realization through work. The literature points to solutions leaders representing organizations should implement to build employee engagement. These include the following (Borkowska, 2014):

- Considering organizational culture during employee recruitment
- Specifying employee duties
- Providing conditions and resources suitable for the tasks assigned
- Making efforts to build a friendly organizational culture focused on trust, cooperation, and understanding
- Ensuring the quality of the communication process
- Implementing clear employee assessment and reward systems
- Actively supporting employee development and motivation
- Balancing work and private life for both themselves and their subordinates

Similar conclusions were reached by Wilczyński (2023), who identified an array of vital leader behaviors that build employee engagement. Among them, he highlighted the awareness of organizational values, the ability to explain goals and tasks to subordinates, and effective communication from superiors to subordinates, also emphasizing the role of ethical conduct that strengthens the mutual respect within the organization. International literature also addresses the topic of building employee engagement. Rao (2017) identified 20 tools and techniques for this purpose. He listed building trust in the workplace as the foremost issue, followed by ensuring that employees feel comfortable in the organization and perceive the impact of their work. He then pointed to openness to subordinates' ideas, understanding their aspirations and expectations, assigning tasks based on employees' strengths and fostering their development, encouraging job rotations, actively improving attitudes toward work, creating a healthy organizational culture, expressing recognition for employees' achievements, sharing power, facilitating interaction among employees, promoting creativity, granting significant decision-making freedom, visualizing approaches, being inspirational, ensuring well-being and safety, as well as supporting activities beyond work for the benefit of the environment and providing a job assessment.

Ultimately, it was emphasized that employees should be treated as individuals who voluntarily act for the organization's good, and not merely people who work for an organization. In research on employee engagement and commitment, sustainable leadership has been confirmed as a facilitator (Piwowar-Sulej et al., 2022; Galpin & Whittington, 2012; Sunthonpagasit & Hanson, 2019). Sustainable leadership is a management approach that focuses on balancing organizational goals with the needs of stakeholders and environmental protection (McCann & Holt, 2010). The leader operates so as to achieve the organization's goals while ensuring the well-being of employees, customers, suppliers, society, and the natural environment (Gerard et al., 2017). Sustainable leadership aims to increase organizational profits while minimizing the negative impact on the environment and all within it (Šimanskienė & Župerkienė, 2014). An interesting construct of sustainable leadership pyramid was introduced by Avery and Bergsteiner (2011). It comprises 14 foundation practices, 6 higher-level practices, and 3 key performance drivers. The theory is presented in Figure 7.1.

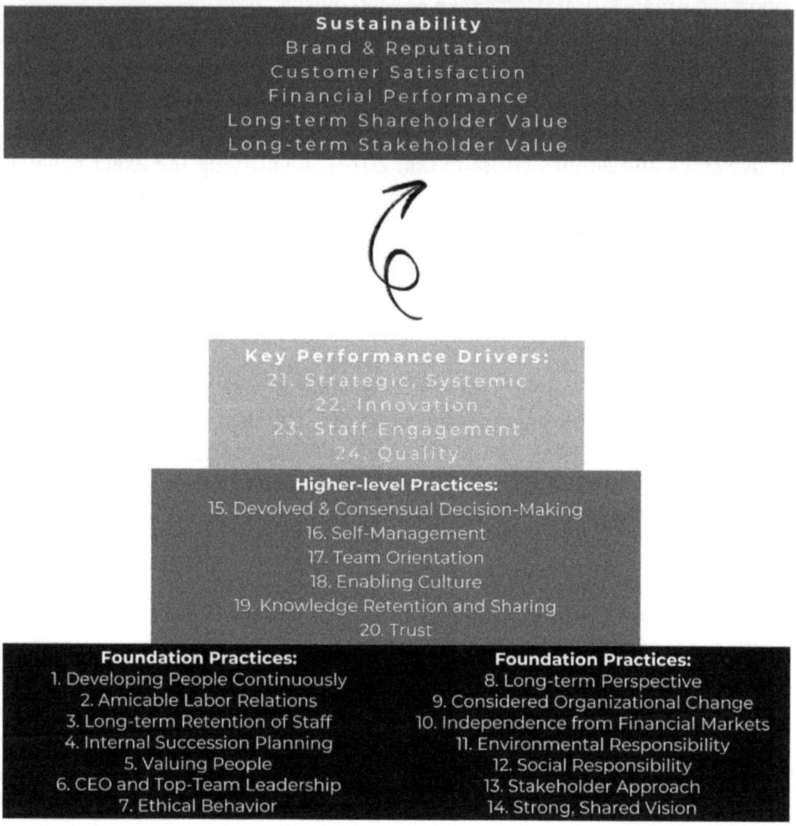


*Figure 7.1* Sustainable leadership practices

*Source:* Own work based on Avery and Bergsteiner (2011).

Organizations also seek to employ creative, productive employees who initiate changes and work with pleasure and enthusiasm (Lewicka & Rakowska, 2016). Research results highlight the relationship between employee engagement and the organization's satisfaction with their effectiveness (Wołpiuk-Ochocińska, 2015). Therefore, a positive correlation is observed between high employee engagement and company's income, business success, and achieved market position (Borkowska, 2014). The absence or low level of employee engagement can lower the efficiency and effectiveness of management and decision-making – employees do not identify with the organization's mission, common goals, and tasks (Juchnowicz, 2010). Consequently, their psychological resilience at work, endurance, and resistance to random events plummets. Work ceases to bring satisfaction or joy, making individuals more inclined to seek new employment opportunities (Juliantara et al., 2020). The lack of efforts invested in building employee engagement can also result in a decline in the emotional aspect associated with the job, such as pride level or willingness to support the organization (Bednarska & Małkowska, 2014).

In short, the degree of employee engagement is considered a key indicator of the effectiveness of management in an organization. Engagement is a significant determinant of the growth of human resource management efficiency. Thus, the type and intensity of employee engagement significantly influence managers' decisions and actions (Borkowska, 2014). Identifying the exact behaviors of leaders that may affect employee engagement seems, therefore, crucial. The arguments above present engagement in organizational management processes as a highly relevant issue in today's job market (Moczydłowska, 2013).

## Materials and Methods

In order to answer research questions, 108 students and employees were asked about various sustainable management practices. The data was collected between February and March 2024 using a dedicated questionnaire created by the authors. The questionnaire consisted of three questions about different levels of leadership activities by Avery and Bergsteiner (2011) and independent variables such as the following:

- Age – coded by research participants according to their age
- Work experience – total length of service in months for every position held until the research
- Gender – participants had the choice between man, female, and others
- Occupation – labor market status identified as: student, working student, employee
- Company size – according to the general scale: micro (1–9 employees), small (10–49 employees), medium (50–249 employees), and large (more than 250 employees)
- Organization type operationalized as: public sector, NGO, private sector – local company, private sector – regional company, private sector – global company

The statistical methods introduced in the research procedure are as follows:

- Shapiro–Wilk test – distribution normality
- Kruskal–Wallis *H* test – for comparing more than two independent samples
- Mann–Whitney *U* test – for comparing two independent samples
- Spearman's Rho – for a correlation check
- Friedman's ANOVA
- Exploratory factor analysis
- General descriptive statistics

All the research and calculations were prepared using the SPSS 27 software.

The researched sample comprised 26 men (23.9%) and 83 women (76.1%). The majority, 46 (42.2%), were working students, there were also 43 (39.4%) students only, and 20 (18.3%) were employees. A total of 51 study participants (46.7%) worked in small and medium enterprises, with 32 (29.4%) in big companies and 26 (23.9%) in micro organizations. Employment in the private sector represented the great majority of 87 respondents (79.4%), the public sector accounted for 17 posts (15.6%), while 5 people (4.6%) worked in NGOs. The average age was $M = 23.51$ years, $SD = 6.521$, and the average work experience was $M = 32.98$ months with $SD = 56.274$.

Within the conducted research, none of the variables describing the practices of sustainable leadership had a normal distribution, $p < 0.05$, for each case in the Shapiro–Wilk test. Non-parametric test results will be presented in the Results section.

## Results

In order to enhance the clarity of the results of statistical analysis, the section will be divided based on the research questions. First research question pertains to the perceived impact of the respective practices of sustainable management on the employee engagement.

**Research question 1.** What is the perceived impact of every level of sustainable leadership practices on employee engagement?

In order to answer this question, a set of tests and analysis were performed. A complete rundown of descriptive statistics will now be presented to introduce the general assessment. These will be followed by the exploratory factor analysis that allows for distinguishing the factors based not on the theoretical framework but on the empirical study. The final element of the research presentation are the results of the Friedman's ANOVA test. These will enable the authors to check the statistically significant differences between the various factors. The results of a descriptive statistics analysis are presented in Table 7.1.

*Table 7.1* Descriptive statistics for the sustainable management practices

| | *Level* | *Mean* | *Mode* | *Std. Dev.* | *Variance* | *Min* | *Max* | *Percentiles* | | |
|---|---|---|---|---|---|---|---|---|---|---|
| | | | | | | | | *25* | *50* | *75* |
| Valuing people | Foundation | 4.77 | 5 | .587 | .345 | 1 | 5 | 5.00 | 5.00 | 5.00 |
| Amicable labor relations | Foundation | 4.66 | 5 | .670 | 449 | 1 | 5 | 4.00 | 5.00 | 5.00 |
| Trust | High | 4.62 | 5 | .704 | 496 | 1 | 5 | 4.00 | 5.00 | 5.00 |
| Developing people | Foundation | 4.41 | 5 | .735 | .541 | 1 | 5 | 4.00 | 5.00 | 5.00 |
| Staff engagement | Key | 4.41 | 5 | .819 | .671 | 1 | 5 | 4.00 | 5.00 | 5.00 |
| Ethical behavior | Foundation | 4.36 | 5 | .811 | .658 | 1 | 5 | 4.00 | 5.00 | 5.00 |
| Knowledge retention and sharing | High | 4.34 | 5 | .830 | .689 | 1 | 5 | 4.00 | 4.00 | 5.00 |
| Quality | Key | 4.17 | 4 | .826 | .682 | 1 | 5 | 4.00 | 4.00 | 5.00 |
| International succession planning | Foundation | 4.15 | 5 | .961 | .923 | 1 | 5 | 4.00 | 4.00 | 5.00 |
| Long-term staff retention | Foundation | 4.11 | 4 | .875 | .766 | 1 | 5 | 4.00 | 4.00 | 5.00 |
| Strong, shared vision | Foundation | 4.04 | 4 | .892 | .795 | 1 | 5 | 4.00 | 4.00 | 5.00 |
| Enabling culture | High | 4.00 | 4 | .991 | .981 | 1 | 5 | 4.00 | 4.00 | 5.00 |
| Team orientation | High | 3.93 | 4 | .879 | .772 | 1 | 5 | 3.00 | 4.00 | 5.00 |
| Long-term perspective | Foundation | 3.90 | 4 | .942 | .888 | 1 | 5 | 3.00 | 4.00 | 5.00 |
| Strategic, systemic innovation | Key | 3.85 | 4 | .859 | .738 | 1 | 5 | 3.50 | 4.00 | 4.00 |
| Devolved & consensual decision-making | High | 3.78 | 4 | .916 | .840 | 1 | 5 | 3.00 | 4.00 | 4.00 |
| CEO and top-team leadership | Foundation | 3.63 | 4 | .988 | .975 | 1 | 5 | 3.00 | 4.00 | 4.00 |
| Considered organizational change | Foundation | 3.63 | 4 | .959 | .920 | 1 | 5 | 3.00 | 4.00 | 4.00 |
| Social responsibility | Foundation | 3.49 | 4 | 1.068 | 1.141 | 1 | 5 | 3.00 | 4.00 | 4.00 |
| Self-management | High | 3.46 | 4 | 1.041 | 1.084 | 1 | 5 | 3.00 | 4.00 | 4.00 |
| Stakeholder approach | Foundation | 3.43 | 3 | 1.066 | 1.136 | 1 | 5 | 3.00 | 3.00 | 4.00 |
| Environmental responsibility | Foundation | 3.15 | 4 | 1.161 | 1.349 | 1 | 5 | 2.00 | 3.00 | 4.00 |
| Dependence from financial markets | Foundation | 3.12 | 3 | 1.069 | 1.143 | 1 | 5 | 2.50 | 3.00 | 4.00 |

*Source:* Own study

Twenty-three different practices were investigated. The perceived impact on employee engagement for all of them was recorded on a level above 3.0, meaning all have positive impact. The minimum value of the assessment of each practice was equal to 1, whereas the maximum was 5. It is important to observe that the impact of three practices was assessed above the 4.5 mark. These practices are as follows:

- Valuing people – $M = 4.77$, SD = 0.587, Mdn = 5
- Amicable labor relations – $M = 4.66$, SD = 0.670, Mdn = 5
- Trust – $M = 4.62$, SD = 0.704, Mdn = 5

The top two are included among the foundation practices, whereas trust is a higher-level one. Meanwhile, the impact of six kinds of practices was assessed below the level of 3.5:

- Social responsibility – $M = 3.49$, SD = 1.068, Mdn = 4
- Self-management – $M = 3.46$, SD = 1.041, Mdn = 4
- Stakeholder approach – $M = 3.43$, SD = 1.066, Mdn = 3
- Environmental responsibility – $M = 3.15$, SD = 1.161, Mdn = 3
- Independence form financial markets – $M = 3.12$, SD = 1.069, Mdn = 3

Out of the five lowest ranked practices, four are foundational, and one is higher-level practice.

The second element of the data analysis was the exploratory factor analysis (principal component analysis, varimax rotation with Kaiser normalization). The results are as follows:

- Factor 1 – comprises seven foundation practices and one key practice, all reported on a five-point Likert scale that explained 30.64% of the variance with factor loadings ranging from 0.460 to 0.757. The said practices are environmental responsibility, stakeholder approach, social responsibility, independence from financial markets, strong, shared vision, considered organizational change, long-term retention of staff, and strategic systemic innovation. The Cronbach's alpha is 0.842, which can be considered a very good reliability for an organizational factor that is characterized by $M = 3.56$, SD = 0.7094, and Mdn = 3.55.
- Factor 2 – comprises seven foundation practices and two key practices, all reported on a five-point Likert scale that explained 10.01% of the variance with factor loadings ranging from 0.365 to 0.822. The practices included valuing people, international succession planning, ethical behavior, staff engagement, developing people, quality, long-term perspective, CEO and top-team leadership, and amicable labor relations. The Cronbach's alpha is 0.793; it can be considered a good reliability of an employee factor characterized by $M = 4.32$, SD = 0.5076, and Mdn = 4.37.

- Factor 3 – comprises six higher-level practices, all reported on a five-point Likert scale that explained 7.35% of the variance with factor loadings ranging from 0.532 to 0.678. It includes devolved and consensual decision-making, team orientation, enabling culture, knowledge retention and sharing, trust, and self-management. The Cronbach's alpha is 0.756, it can be considered an acceptable level of reliability for a factor of higher-level practices characterized by $M = 3.56$, SD = 0.7094, and Mdn = 3.55.

The final step of the analysis involved testing the differences between the factors. Friedman's ANOVA revealed differences between the perceived impact of the respective organizational practices on employee engagement with $\chi^2(2) = 199.501$ and $p < 0.001$. The Wilcoxon test revealed differences between the following factors:

- Organizational (Mdn = 3.55) and higher-level factors (Mdn = 4.06), T = −0.711, z = −5.249, $p < 0.001$
- Organizational (Mdn = 3.55) and employee factors (Mdn = 4.37), T = −1.339, z = −9.888, $p < 0.001$
- Employee (Mdn = 4.37) and higher-level factors (Mdn = 4.06), T = 0.628, z = 4.639, $p < 0.001$

The results of the above tests are presented in Figure 7.2.

The second research question refers to the variables that may affect the perceived impact of sustainable management factors on employee engagement.

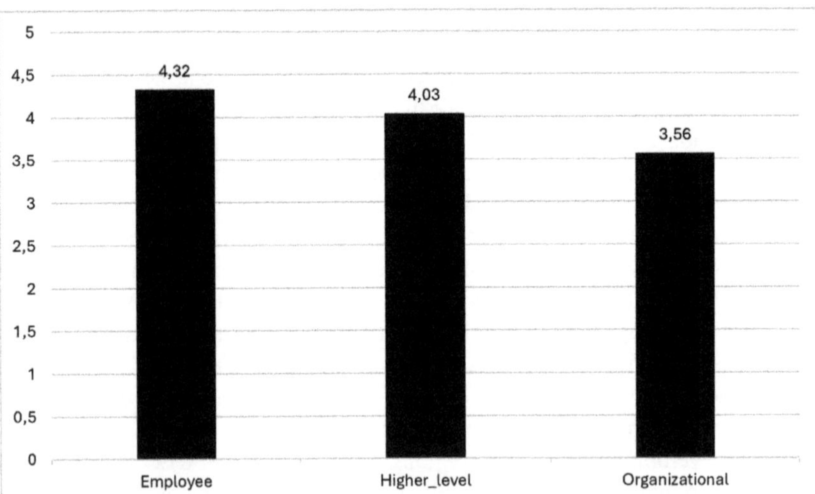


*Figure 7.2* The differences between mean values of sustainable managements practices

*Source:* Own work

*Table 7.2* Results of the statistical tests performed

| *Variable* | *Employee* | *Higher level* | *Organizational* |
|---|---|---|---|
| Spearman's rho – non-parametric correlation | | | |
| Age | $\rho = -0.047, p = 0.625$ | $\rho = 0.169, p = 0.078$ | $\rho = -0.076, p = 0.431$ |
| Work experience | $\rho = -0.063, p = 0.517$ | $\rho = 0.274, p = 0.004$ | $\rho = -0.018, p = 0.852$ |
| Mann–Whitney *U* test | | | |
| Gender | U = 811.5, z = −1.902, $p = 0.057$ | U = 1108.0, z = 0.206, $p = 0.837$ | U = 842.5, z = −1.682, $p = 0.093$ |
| | Independent-Samples Kruskal–Wallis *H* test | | |
| Occupation | $H_{(2,n = 109)} = 1.397$, $p = 0.497$ | $H_{(2,n = 109)} = 1.405$, $p = 0.495$ | $H_{(2,n = 109)} = 2.026$, $p = 0.363$ |
| Company size | $H_{(3,n = 109)} = 0.502$, $p = 0.918$ | $H_{(3,n = 109)} = 6.441$, $p = 0.092$ | $H_{(3,n = 109)} = 1.483$, $p = 0.686$ |
| Type of the organization | $H_{(5,n = 109)} = 16.772$, $p = 0.005$ | $H_{(5,n = 109)} = 12.533, p =$ 0.028 | $H_{(5,n = 109)} = 3.710$, $p = 0.592$ |

*Source:* Own study

**Research question 2.** Which elements may affect the perception of the impact of sustainable leadership on employee engagement?

There are six variables: age, work experience, gender, occupation, company size, and the type of organization. The results of the tests conducted are presented in Table 7.2. Red values mean that there is no statistically significant difference, and green values indicate such differences.

Most of these variables do not have a statistically significant influence on the perceived impact of factors of sustainable management practices on employee engagement. There are, however, three exceptions:

- Work experience has a moderate positive correlation with the assessment of the impact of higher-level practices factors.
- The type of the organization has influence in terms of the employee factor. There is a statistically significant difference between the government sector and global organizations $U_{(\text{Ngovernment} = 17, \text{ Nglobal} = 26)} = 33.298$, z = 3.377, $p =$ 0.011.
- People from global companies assess the impact of employee factor higher (4.43) than those from the governmental sector (3.95). Similar situation is connected with the higher-level factor, although the Mann–Whitney *U* test with the Bonferroni correction results do not allow for a deeper analysis.

## Discussion and Conclusions

The research presented above allowed for an answer to the research questions posed. These questions are going to serve as the basis for the discussion. The procedure is prone to certain limitations, the most important of which is the size of the research sample. As it is rather small, the research results can only be treated as a pilot study witnessing only general implications for practical use.

Now, to answer the first supplementary research question: "What is the perceived impact of each level of sustainable leadership practices on employee engagement?" The highest assessed practice is that of valuing people. Its importance corresponds with the results obtained by Catteeuw et al. (2007) who pinpoint valuing people as one of the key pillars of their employee engagement model, much like Marcos and Sridevi (2010). At the same time, Davis and Van der Heijden (2023) suggest that an internal context should be created for employees to show their engagement in the organization. Amicable labor relations are also important for Suriyankietkaew and Avery (2014), as well as Amoako (2015). Additionally, trust is widely described as an important instrument for enhancing engagement (Wilkins, 2018; Payne et al., 2022). The research revealed that the most important factors are the ones connected with employees, not with the organization. Hence, it is vital that leaders get to know their employees (Kisi, 2023). Jose et al. (2024), meanwhile, suggest that ensuring workers' personal safety is the most important of employee-related activities. A similar observation is offered by Andrlić et al. (2023), with the difference being that the latter points specifically to mental care.

Let us now turn to the second supplementary research question: "Which elements may affect the perception of the impact of sustainable leadership on employee engagement?" It seems to be rather uniform with regard to the various criteria that may affect the perception of the impact of different sustainable leadership practices on employee engagement. Firstly, gender, age (Abidin, 2017), occupation, and company size do not have any impact at all; work experience is merely correlated, whereas the type of organization is limited to the employee factor only.

Nevertheless, the research results obtained allow for a positive answer to the main research question, as they lead to the conclusion that sustainable leadership does have an impact on employee engagement, as perceived by employees themselves, especially when leaders' actions are related to the employee factor.

The presented research, as well as other studies analyzed in the literature review, presents a picture of business implications to be suggested, which boils down to the following:

- Prioritize valuing people – the implementation of recognition or appreciation programs will boost positive motivation and enhance engagement
- Promote amicable relations – together with organizational climate and empowering culture, these elements will build a management system in which people are at the center of importance

- Place emphasis on ethical behaviors – importantly, these cannot be limited to declarations and theories only, but they must involve live actions
- Demonstrate leadership engagement – lead by example and let employees feel that engagement is not required from them only but is a part of the entire organizational ecosystem

The above recommendations may be implemented at a fast pace. It has to be emphasized that these do not involve profound changes, procedures, or internal systems. They are all related to the mutual respect and open communication within the company. Enhancing employee engagement is, therefore, only a tip of the iceberg for each and every organization.

## References

Abidin, S. (2017). The effect of perceived authentic leadership on employee engagement. *Journal of Tourism, Hospitality and Environment Management*, *2*(4), 29–47.

Al Marshoudi, F. B., Jamaluddin, Z., Aween, A. M. B., Al Balushi, F. I., & Mohammad, B. A. (2023). The mediating role of employee engagement in the relationship between leadership styles and organizational performance. *International Journal of Management Thinking*, *1*(2), 34–55.

Amoako, G. (2015). Striking where it hurts: The political economy of graduate teachers strikes and labour relations in Ghana's public education sector. *African Review of Economics and Finance*, *7*(2).

Andrlić, B., Priyashantha, K. G., & De Alwis, A. C. (2023). Employee engagement management in the COVID-19 pandemic: A systematic literature review. *Sustainability*, *15*(2), 987. https://doi.org/10.3390/su1502098

Avery, G. C. (2011). *Understanding leadership: Paradigms and cases*. SAGE Publications Ltd. https://doi.org/10.4135/9781446215487

Avery, G. C., & Bergsteiner, H. (2011). Sustainable leadership practices for enhancing business resilience and performance. *Strategy & Leadership*, *39*, 5–15. https://doi.org/10.1108/10878571111128766

Bass, B. M. (1985). Leadership: Good, better, best. *Organizational Dynamics*, *13*(3), 26–40.

Bass, B. M. (1997). Does the transactional–transformational leadership paradigm transcend organizational and national boundaries? *American Psychologist*, *52*(2), 130–139. https://doi.org/10.1037/0003-066X.52.2.130

Bass, B. M., & Avolio, B. J. (1990). Developing transformational leadership: 1992 and beyond, *Journal of European Industrial Training*, *14*(5), 21–27. https://doi.org/10.1108/03090599010135122

Bass, B. M., & Bass, R. (2008). *The Bass handbook of leadership: Theory, research, and managerial applications* (4th ed.). Free Press.

Bass, B. M., & Riggio, R. E. (2010). The transformational model of leadership. *Leading Organizations: Perspectives for a New Era*, *2*(1), 76–86.

Batista-Taran, L. C., Shuck, M. B., Gutierrez, C. C., & Baralt, S. (2013). The role of leadership style in employee engagement. In M. S. Plakhotnik, S. M. Nielsen, & D. M. Pane (Eds.), *Proceedings of the eighth annual college of education & GSN research conference*. Florida International University.

Bednarska, M., & Małkowska, K. (2014). Zaangażowanie pracowników w procesie kształtowania satysfakcji i lojalności klientów biur podróży. *Folia Turistica*, *32*, 145–157.

Biesok, G., & Wyród-Wróbel, J. (Eds.). (2018). *Człowiek w organizacji. Zaufanie, przywództwo, zaangażowanie, satysfakcja*. Wydawnictwo CeDeWu.

Borkowska, S. (2014). Rola zaangażowania pracowników. *Zarządzanie Zasobami Ludzkimi*, *2*, 9–26.

Catteeuw, F., Flyn, E., & Vonderhorst, J. (2007). Employee engagement: Boosting productivity in turbulent times. *Organization Development Journal*, *25*(2), 151–158.

Caza, A., & Jackson, B. (2011). Authentic leadership. In A. Bryman, D. Collinson, K. Grint, B. Jackson, & M. Uhl-Bien (Eds.), *Sage handbook of leadership* (pp. 350–362). Sage.

Costa, P. T., & McCrae, R. R. (1992). Normal personality assessment in clinical practice: The NEO personality inventory. *Psychological Assessment*, *4*(1), 5.

Dabić, M., Maley, J. F., Švarc, J., & Poček, J. (2023). Future of digital work: Challenges for sustainable human resources management. *Journal of Innovation & Knowledge*, *8*(2), 100353.

Dang, G. P., & Basur, P. (2017). Organic leadership style and employee engagement: The mediating effect of the social relevance of work in the context of faculty members in higher education. *Purushartha: A Journal of Management, Ethics and Spirituality*, *10*(1), 107–116.

Davis, A., & Van der Heijden, B. (2023). Launching the dynamic employee engagement framework: Towards a better understanding of the phenomenon. *Employee Relations: The International Journal*, *45*(2), 421–436.

Fiedler, F. E. (1964). A contingency model of leadership effectiveness. *Advances in Experimental Social Psychology*, *1*, 149–190.

Fleishman, E. A. (1973). Twenty years of consideration and structure. In E. A. Fleishman & J. F. Hunt (Eds.), *Current developments in the study of leadership*. South Illinois University Press.

Galpin, T., & Whittington, J. L. (2012). Sustainability leadership: From strategy to results. *Journal of Business Strategy*, *33*(4), 40–48.

Galton, F. (1892). *Hereditary genius: An inquiry into its laws and consequences*. Macmillan.

Gerard, L., McMillan, J., & D'Annunzio-Green, N. (2017). Conceptualizing sustainable leadership. *Industrial and Commercial Training*, *49*(3), 116–126.

Gojny, M. (2013). Znaczenie zaangażowania i intencji odejścia dla retencji pracowników w kontekście postrzeganego wsparcia organizacji (POS). Zeszyty Naukowe. *Organizacja i Zarządzanie*, *51*, 1146.

Hamouche, S. (2023). Human resource management and the COVID-19 crisis: Implications, challenges, opportunities, and future organizational directions. *Journal of Management & Organization*, *29*(5), 799–814.

Harter, J. K., Schmidt, F. L., Killham, E. A., & Agrawal, S. (2009). *Q12 meta-analysis: The relationship between engagement at work and organizational outcomes*. Gallup.

Haslam, S. A., Postmes, T., & Ellemers, N. (2003). More than a metaphor: Organizational identity makes organizational life possible. *British Journal of Management*, *14*(4), 357–369.

Haslam, S. A., Reicher, S. D., & Platow, M. J. (2020). *The new psychology of leadership: Identity, influence and power*. Routledge.

Hogg, M. A. (2007). Social psychology of leadership. In A. W. Kruglanski & E. T. Higgins (Eds.), *Social psychology: Handbook of basic principles* (pp. 716–733). The Guilford Press.

Jose, G., Nimmi, P. M., & Kuriakose, V. (2024). HRM practices and employee engagement: Role of personal resources: A study among nurses. *The International Journal of Productivity and Performance Management*, *73*(1), 1–17.

Juchnowicz, M. (2010). Zarządzanie kapitałem ludzkim a poziom zaangażowania pracowników. *Zarządzanie Zasobami Ludzkimi, 3–4*, 57–66.

Judge, T. A., Bono, J. E., Ilies, R., & Gerhardt, M. W. (2002). Personality and leadership: A qualitative and quantitative review. *Journal of Applied Psychology*, *87*(4), 765.

Juliantara, I. K., Sihombing, I. H. H., & Sulistyawati, N. L. K. S. (2020). *The effect of employee engagement on turnover intention* [Conference session]. The International Conference on Business and Management Research (ICBMR 2020), pp. 300–305. Atlantis Press.

Kark, R., Van Dijk, D., & Vashdi, D. R. (2018). Motivated or demotivated to be creative: The role of self-regulatory focus in transformational and transactional leadership processes. *Applied Psychology: An International Review*, *67*(1), 186–224. https://doi.org/10.1111/apps.12122

Kisi, N. (2023). Analysis and visualization of global, research on employee engagement. *Sustainability*, *15*, 10196.

Kuhnert, K. W. (1994). Transforming leadership: Developing people through delegation. In B. M. Bass & B. J. Avolio (Eds.), *Improving organizational effectiveness through transformational leadership* (pp. 10–25). Sage Publications, Inc.

Lewicka, D., & Rakowska, A. (2016). Wpływ praktyk ZZL na zaangażowanie pracowników w innowacyjnych przedsiębiorstwach. *Nauki o zarządzaniu*, *2*, 102–115.

Li, M., Fu, N., Chadwick, C., & Harney, B. (2023). Untangling human resource management and employee well-being relationships: Differentiating job resource H.R. practices from challenge demand H.R. practices. *Human Resource Management Journal*, *34*(1), 214–235.

Marcos, S., & Sridevi, M. S. (2010). Employee engagement: The hay to improving performance. *International Journal of Business and Management*, *5*(12), 89–96.

McCann, J. T., & Holt, R. A. (2010). Defining sustainable leadership. *International Journal of Sustainable Strategic Management*, *2*(2), 204–210.

McClellan, J., Levitt, K., & DiClementi, G. (2017). Emotional intelligence and positive organizational leadership: A conceptual model for positive emotional influence. *Journal of Behavioral and Applied Management*, *17*(3), 2626.

Moczydłowska, J. M. (2013). Zaangażowanie pracowników–aspekty psychologiczne i organizacyjne. *Myśl ekonomiczna i polityczna*, *4*(42), 162–171.

Mrówka, R. (2010). Pojęcie zaangażowania pracowników we współczesnych naukach ekonomicznych i praktyce gospodarczej. *Nauki ekonomiczne w świetle nowych wyzwań gospodarczych*, *1*, 405–416.

Mughal, M. U., & Iraqi, K. M. (2020). The impact of leadership, teamwork, and employee engagement on employee performances. *Saudi Journal of Business and Management Studies*, *5*(3), 233–244.

Onyekwere, L. A., Ogona, I. K., & Ololube, N. P. (2023). Leadership and management of change in organizations. *South Asian Research Journal of Humanities and Social Sciences*, *5*(3), 96–106. https://doi.org/10.36346/sarjhss.2023.v05i03.012

Payne, A. L., Stone, C., & Bennett, R. (2022). Conceptualising and building trust to enhance the engagement and achievement of under-served students. *The Journal of Continuing Higher Education*, *71*(2), 134–151. https://doi.org/10.1080/07377363.2021.2005759

Piwowar-Sulej, K., Bąk-Grabowska, D., Grzesik, K., & Zając, C. (2022). *Zrównoważone Zarządzanie Zasobami Ludzkimi–wybrane zagadnienia*. Wydawnictwo Uniwersytetu Ekonomicznego we Wrocławiu.

Răducan, R., & Răducan, R. (2014). Leadership and management. *Procedia – Social and Behavioral Sciences*, *149*, 808–812. https://doi.org/10.1016/j.sbspro.2014.08.322

Rahmadani, V. G., Schaufeli, W. B., & Stouten, J. (2020). How engaging leaders foster employees' work engagement. *Leadership & Organization Development Journal, 41*(8), 1155–1169.

Rao, M. S. (2017). Innovative tools and techniques to ensure effective employee engagement. *Industrial and Commercial Training, 49*(3), 127–131.

Šakytė-Statnickė, G., Bilan, S., & Savanevičienė, A. (2023). The impact of work engagement of different generations on organizational engagement. *Journal of International Studies, 16*(4), 136–152.

Scott, W. R. (2003). *Organizations: Rational, natural, and open systems* (5th ed.). Prentice Hall.

Sharma, M. K., & Jain, S. (2013). Leadership management: Principles, models, and theories. *Global Journal of Management and Business Studies, 3*(3), 309–318.

Šimanskienė, L., & Župerkienė, E. (2014). Sustainable leadership: The new challenge for organizations. *Forum Scientiae Oeconomia, 2*(1), 81–93.

Skowron-Mielnik, B. (2016). Paradoks efektywności pracy–między budowaniem zaangażowania a wypaleniem zawodowym. *Nauki o Zarzadzaniu, 27*, 151–163.

Southgate, G., Aderibigbe, J. K., Balogun, T. V., & Mahembe, B. (2023). Leadership styles as predictors of employee engagement at a selected tertiary institution. *SA Journal of Human Resource Management, 1*, 21.

Stefańska, M., & Grabowski, G. (2023). Zaangażowanie pracowników a satysfakcja z pracy w warunkach pracy zdalnej. *e-mentor, 98*(1), 13–21.

Stogdill, R. (1974). *Handbook of leadership*. Free Press.

Stone, G. A., Russell, R. F., & Patterson, K. (2004). Transformational versus servant leadership: A difference in leader focus. *Leadership & Organization Development Journal, 25*(4), 349–361. https://doi.org/10.1108/01437730410538671

Sunthonpagasit, J., & Hanson, B. (2019). Developing sustainable leadership practices to improve employee engagement through ODI: A case study of Thai family-owned business. *ABAC ODI Journal Vision Action Outcome, 6*(1), 40.

Suriyankietkaew, S., & Avery, G. C. (2014). *Do certain leadership practices raise stakeholder satisfaction? An investigation of managers in Thai SMEs*. 9th International Symposium on Sustainable Leadership.

Szczepanska-Woszczyna, K., & Bogaczyk, R. (2023). Organisational climate and employee engagement – A case study of international corporations. *Forum Scientiae Oeconomia, 11*(3), 9–29.

Van Seters, D. A., & Field, R. H. G. (1990). The evolution of leadership theory. *Journal of Organizational Change Management, 3*(3), 29–45. https://doi.org/10.1108/09534819010142139

Waydowicz, E. (2018). Przywództwo jako czynnik wzmacniający zaangażowanie pracowników w organizacji uczącej się na przykładzie podmiotu gospodarczego prowadzącego działalność w branży IT. *Przedsiębiorstwo we współczesnej gospodarce– teoria i praktyka, 25*(2), 63–78.

Wilczyński, A. (2023). Umiejętności lidera budujące zaangażowanie pracowników w okresie pandemii. *Nowoczesne Systemy Zarządzania, 18*(2), 47–62.

Wilkins, C. H. (2018). Effective engagement requires trust and being trustworthy. *Medical Care, 56*(10), 6–8. https://doi.org/10.1097/MLR.0000000000000953

Wołpiuk-Ochocińska, A. (2015). *Motywacje do pracy i zaangażowanie w nią młodych pracowników na rynku pracy*. Zeszyty Naukowe WSOP w Katowicach.

Zakrzewski, B., Zakrzewska, D., & Brdulak, J. (2014). Przywództwo i jego rola w funkcjonowaniu przedsiębiorstwa logistycznego – ujęcie teoretyczne. *Logistyka, 6*, 11617–11629.

# 8 Emotional Intelligence in Managers and Work Engagement

## The Crucial Role of Empathy

*Lech Górniak and Marian Bursztyn*

*The world we live in arises from the quality of our relationships.*

Martin Buber

### Introduction

Interpersonal relations, whether private or professional, are shaped by the social context and interpersonal communication. A very important role within interpersonal communication is played by the emotional sphere. It is the consequence of the original function of emotions, which consist in providing direction to our actions toward the other person – whether to approach (positive emotions) or avoid (negative motions) them. The term "emotion" (from Latin *movere*) denotes the state of "being moved" experienced in the mind, which drives all human behavior. One should bear in mind, however, that a precise psychological account of these states entails the distinction between "emotions" and "feelings," based on their contribution to interpersonal interactions. It is believed that emotions regulate the course of an interaction, whereas feelings provide feedback on how the interaction is progressing. Both these components of the emotional state are used in assessing the environment, which enables the individual to undertake the most beneficial course of action in the adaptive sense (Cookson, 2015).

There can be no doubt that many important emotions emerge on the basis of interpersonal relationships, where they serve an evolutionary function, for they enable man to adapt to the environmental – especially social – conditions. Emotions also motivate the individual to take a specific action. At the root of every thought, every decision, and every behavior, there is an emotion that in its own unique way leaves a mark on the experience of the individual, thus determining their future conduct, behavior, and perception of relationships (Lewis & Haviland-Jones, 2004). Deftness in incorporating emotions in contacts with other people lies at the core of emotional intelligence.

It should be emphasized that from the point of view of psychology, when examining the role of emotions in interpersonal relations, it is of no consequence whether we consider private or professional environment. That physically or

DOI: 10.4324/9781032715407-9

"mentally" (remote work) someone finds her- or himself in the place where what they do is referred to as "work" does not alter the fact that their expectations as to how they – as the human persons – are to be treated by others will be the same. What can change are merely the forms and/or the content of communications which pertain to interpersonal behaviors, and the psychological mechanism that provokes emotional responses to these communications remains the same in both cases. Therefore, while seeking ways to build positive work-related emotions, ensure respectful treatment, and foster mental well-being and good mood of workers, it is necessary to generate high levels of work engagement (as understood in this study, following Schaufeli et al., 2002), which is inherent to the role of manager, which should be the same in professional and private contexts.

The aim of this study is to identify the psychosocial conditions of effective use of emotional intelligence (EI) of managers, with a special emphasis on empathy, to enhance work engagement. To accomplish this goal, a literature review was conducted, which focused mainly on the period between 2013 and 2024, using the Web of Science, Scopes, and EBSCO database, as well as additional secondary sources. Earlier academic contributions relevant to the subject of the study were also consulted.

The title of the chapter refers the discussed issues to managerial activities. As it is commonly known, the basic task of a manager is the execution of the management process, namely, planning, organizing, decision-making, monitoring, and leadership, which entails, among other things, engaging employees in their work. In organizational realities, these two roles coexist with one another in such a way as though they were – metaphorically speaking – inexorably intertwined. Depending on the situation – itself composed of time, place, task type, employee maturity, and so on (cf. Blanchard, 2020) – some of their behaviors can be attributed to their managerial while others to their leadership role. It can be assumed that a manager whose employee management practices are guided by emotional intelligence at the same time becomes a leader. In line with this assumption, the two terms – manager and leader – will be used interchangeably.

## Shaping Work Engagement as a Challenge for Modern Managers

The scholar who made an effort to provide a precise definition of engagement as a psychological state of employees was Kahn (who termed it at the time as "personal engagement"). As he himself put it: "I defined personal engagement as the harnessing of organization members' selves to their work roles; in engagement, people employ and express themselves physically, cognitively, and emotionally during role performances" (Kahn, 1990, p. 694).

This contributed volume uses the concept of work engagement developed by Schaufeli et al. (2002). The authors describe it as a positive work-related cognitive state, characterized by vigor, dedication, and absorption. It is not a momentary or idiosyncratic experience; instead, it refers to a lasting and pervasive affective-cognitive state, which does not focus on a single concrete object, event, person, or behavior. Vigor implies high energy and mental resilience levels at work, readiness to invest effort in one's work, and persistence in spite of difficulties. Dedication refers to a sense of meaning, enthusiasm, inspiration, pride, and the propensity to take on challenges, whereas absorption involves being completely focused and deeply immersed in one's job, which makes time feel like it is moving faster and job difficult to put down (Schaufeli et al., 74–75). The common ground between the definition by Schaufeli et al. and that by Kahn is the element of an autonomous decision to engage, that is, from the standpoint of psychology, the crucial factor in this emotional-cognitive-behavioral inner state. It should be emphasized, however, that Schaufeli's account reveals a stronger connection between engagement and psychological presence in the workplace than those by other scholars do.

A study of the signs of engagement can be conducted in two ways. One involves collecting information from employees, either through interviews in which employees describe at length their experiences related to their attitude toward job (cf. Van Roekel et al., 2024) or through questionnaire surveys (cf. Kahn, 1990; Schaufeli et al., 2002). The other consists in observing behaviors conditioned by a mental state that corresponds to what the scholars assumed as defining work engagement. The list of such behaviors can be assumed to include expressed job satisfaction, innovation, willingness to remain in the organization, sense of community, high productivity, participation in extra-contractual tasks, speaking with respect about one's job and employer, and improvement in work–life balance, which is a major contributor to psychological well-being and nurturing a culture of responsibility and care. As much research incontrovertibly shows, all these benefits are evidently connected with empathetic behaviors of managers (Murugesan & Sankaran, 2018).

Organizational leadership seeking ways to incite work engagement has become a crucial challenge for human resource management today. There are two reasons for that. One is that the COVID-19 pandemic resulted in a peaked interest in the issues related to involving employees in activities aimed at maintaining companies' performance at a level that would ensure their continued existence in difficult conditions. The other are the ongoing changes in employee attitudes, predominantly of the younger generation, toward seeking and continuing employment. We have been observing a decline in employee resilience, substantial employment instability, and other post-phenomena phenomena that are unfavorable for organizations, such as "The Great Resignation" (Serenko, 2023; Cohen, 2021), and the subsequent "quiet quitting" Klotz & Bolino, 2022).

Given the psychological underpinnings of human activity outlined above, the basic solution for fostering work engagement to be implemented by organizational leaders turned out to lie in building such manager–employee relationships that would be as close as possible to those encountered in everyday interpersonal contacts in which people feel safe and are willing without external compulsion to engage in various activities aimed at realizing coherent individual and organizational values. This task, however, requires that managers possess the necessary dispositions and competencies allowing them to adroitly develop supportive relationships with employees. Of these, one of the most important appears to be high level of emotional intelligence (EI).

## Emotional Intelligence in the Context of Organizational Management

The term "intelligence," which emerged in the nomenclature of the sciences of man at the outset of the 20th century, is currently used to denote the level of efficiency of the mental sphere in humans. Psychologists adopt a tripartite division of the mind into the cognitive (thinking), the affective (includes emotions), and the motivational components. As the above division suggests, emotions belong to the second, that is, affective, sphere of mental operation. Besides emotions, it comprises moods, evaluations, and emotional states. Thus, the definition of emotional intelligence should combine the notions of emotions and intelligence but without altering the meaning of these terms. Motivation falls within the third sphere of the mind. It is associated with biological needs and learned behavior directed at achieving goals. It should be considered secondary to emotional intelligence. There is more that connects emotions with cognition, however, than emotional intelligence (Salovey & Sluyter, 1997).

Generally speaking, emotional intelligence is the ability to recognize, understand, and manage your emotions and the emotions of others, both individually and in social relationships. Emotional intelligence is also the basis for the ability to monitor thinking and actions both in ourselves and in others (Mayer & Geher, 1996). Thus, this disposition facilitates human use of emotional processes to build sound interpersonal relationships, based on a rational thought process (cf. Salovey & Mayer, 1990; Mayer et al., 2000).

Salovey and Mayer initially described EI as "a type of social intelligence that involves the ability to monitor one's own and others' emotions, to discriminate among them, and to use the information to guide one's thinking and actions" (1990). The original definition was subsequently complemented with the knowledge of emotions and the ability to understand them, factors which are to facilitate emotional regulation and foster "emotional and intellectual development" (Salovey & Sluyter, 1997). Everyone has the capacity to use their emotions in order to improve their thinking, judgment, and behavior (Brackett et al., 2024).

Salovey and Mayer, when providing their detailed account of what emotional intelligence is and what domains of individual's functioning it encompasses, identified the following components:

- The knowledge of one's emotions, also referred to as self-awareness of emotions
- The regulation of emotions, also referred to as emotional management

- The ability to self-motivate, associated with subordinating emotions to chosen goals
- Empathy, enabling one to, that is, recognize emotions in others and utilizing it in practice, for example, in a situation of cooperation
- The ability to establish and maintain contacts with others in order to build good relationships

The ability to establish contacts with others is largely based on appraising and incorporating the emotions of others in building good relationships. Classified as a component of social competence, it is a set of skills critical in performing leadership roles and being efficient in interpersonal relationships (Goleman, 1998).

Goleman (1998) developed the most elaborate, while still synthetic, model of components of emotional intelligence, dominant in the source literature, particularly in relation to leadership competencies. His account is presented in Table 8.1.

The organizational context is a very specific environment as regards the number and intensity of interpersonal contacts. When looking for factors that could improve the efficiency of the organization, one cannot overestimate those related to building good relationships between organizational leaders and their subordinates. One course of action that makes the realization of this task possible involves considering the possibility of the improvement of skills related to emotional intelligence and practical application of this knowledge (Alotaibi et al., 2020). As indicated by numerous research studies and observations made by practitioners, in light of the challenges facing organizations today, one of the essential skills in this field turns out to be empathy, particularly regarding the need to enhance employee engagement (Jin & Ikeda, 2023; Jonsdottir & Kristinsson, 2020; Kock et al., 2019; Rahman & Castelli, 2013; Van Bommel, 2021; Vladić et al., 2021; Zivkovic, 2022).

We should bear in mind, however, that the impact made on employees by the actions of an empathetic leader may be enhanced or reduced depending on her or his general level of EI as such, in line with Goleman's model of EI components presented in Table 8.1. Our study focuses mainly on the importance of empathy, as research results demonstrate that it plays a key role in building work engagement (Murugesan & Sankaran, 2018).

## Empathy as the Core Component of Emotional Intelligence of Managers

Empathy, in the interpretation that was popularized by Goleman (1998), is the awareness of the feelings, needs, and concerns of others, the understanding of others, the ability to sense feelings and points of view (perspectives) of other people, and active interest in their worries, anxieties, and concerns. Davis (1996), who is regarded as the pioneer of the research on empathy, defines it as

*Table 8.1* Model of connections between emotional intelligence components and leadership-management skills

| *Emotional intelligence component* | *Leadership skills* | *Competence description* |
|---|---|---|
| Self-awareness<br>Knowledge of the inner states, preferences, capabilities, and intuitive judgments | Emotional self-awareness | Recognition of one's emotions and their consequences, alignment with one's core values and signals of emotions. |
| | Accurate self-assessment | Awareness of one's strengths and weaknesses, recognition of one's limitations. |
| | Self-confidence | Self-assuredness, sound self-esteem, awareness of one's capabilities and skills, deriving pleasure from confronting difficult challenges, and a sense of satisfaction from overcoming them. |
| Self-management (self-regulation)<br>Ability to control inner states, impulses, and capabilities | Self-control | Finding ways to control emotion and direct them toward positive outcomes. |
| | Transparency | Living true to accepted values in transparency, expressing genuine openness to others in terms of emotions, beliefs, and actions, and admitting to mistakes and failures. |
| | Adaptability | Meeting demands without a loss of focus and energy, flexibility in adjusting to changes and new challenges. |
| | Achievement | Making an ongoing effort to improve one's performance and that of the team, pragmatism, setting ambitious goals, and permanent learning. |
| | Initiative | Ability to seize or create opportunities due to high level of self-efficacy. |
| | Optimism | Adjustment to the changing circumstances of life while noticing more opportunities than threats. Positive outlook on the surrounding reality. |
| Social awareness | Empathy | Awareness of emotions, needs, and anxieties of others, understanding of others, ability to sense emotions and points of view (perspectives) of others, and active interest in their worries, anxieties, and concerns. |
| | Organizational awareness | Ability to understand political forces at work in the organization, as well as the fundamental values and principles held by employees. |
| | Teamwork | Promoting positive emotional climate in the workplace. |
| Relationship management | Inspiration | Crating resonance and mobilizing people toward an attractive vision or a shared mission. |
| | Influence | Influencing others by being convincing and engaging. |
| | Developing others | Showing genuine interest in the team and willingness to support the group. |
| | Change catalyst | Ability to recognize the need for change and to find practical ways to solve/overcome challenges. |
| | Conflict management | Understanding of diverse perspectives and ability to discover common ideals that all parties can share, capacity to get everyone involved in the talks. |
| | Teamwork and collaboration | Persuasiveness, active and enthusiastic involvement in a joint effort. Going beyond professional relationships and simple work tasks. |

*Source:* Own elaboration based on Goleman (1998)

a complex set of mental processes emerging in man's reaction to the experiences of others. These processes have both affective and non-affective consequences. Davis (1996) believes that after the observer encounters the observed person, certain (cognitive, affective, and/or behavioral) reactions are triggered on the part of the observer. He developed the Interpersonal Reactivity Index, which is a multi-dimensional instrument for measuring empathetic skills, based on the assumption that empathy comprises several distinct but interconnected elements that are emotional and cognitive in nature. These are as follows:

- *Perspective taking*: This reflects the ability and propensity to spontaneously assume someone else's point of view in everyday situations. It measures the ability to "go beyond one's self" in communication with other people.
- *Empathetic concern*: This refers to the feelings that are "oriented toward others": tendency for compassion toward and sharing feelings of people suffering misfortunes.
- *Personal distress*: This entails tuning into one's internal states, that is, feelings "oriented toward oneself," for example, a proclivity to experience fear, anxiety, concern, or discomfort in response to powerful negative experiences (suffering) of other people.
- *Fantasy*: This is related to individual ability to be imaginarily transported into fictitious situations, particularly into the sphere of emotions and behaviors of literary and cinematic characters.

Referring these elements to the managerial context, it should be noted that the manager's ability to "go beyond her or his self" and look at a problem from employee's point of view is crucial for building trust and strengthening relationships. Such a manager is better equipped to understand the needs of her or his team which contributes to more efficient decision-making and better communication in the organization.

Meanwhile, managers showing empathetic concern are able to extend compassion and support toward employees who are facing problems. In practice, this results in creating atmosphere where employees feel understood and supported, which has a direct influence on their engagement and loyalty toward the organization.

The third component, "personal distress," involves the ability to feel negative emotions in response to the suffering of others. While excessive feeling of personal discomfort might seem an undesirable trait in a manager, in fact, using it appropriately can help managers build genuine relationships and react to difficult situations in a more balanced and empathetic manner.

The final element of empathy, according to Davis, is "fantasy," which refers to the ability to be imaginarily transported into fictitious situations, particularly the emotional sphere of literary and cinematic characters. This factor might, admittedly, seem less important in the context of managers' work, and it is worth noting, however, that the ability to imagine various scenarios and emotions that can be experienced by members of the team can foster the development of creativity and empathy, particularly in situations that require problem solving.

The fact that leadership yielding the best results for organizations is associated with acknowledging emotions in the relationship between the leader and employees was recognized many years ago, all the way back to the pioneering research at Western Electric's Hawthorne Plant, conducted in the interwar period. It revealed, among other things, that the very fact that management took actions signaling interest in employee needs resulted in their increased productivity, regardless of whether or not the intended changes were implemented. Nevertheless, the authors of these studies made no effort to explore the deeper roots of the researched phenomena.

Along with the development of the scientific trend of research on the influence of leadership behavior on organizational efficiency, new methodological approaches emerged to which we owe our better understanding of the nature of these correlations. Kock et al. (2019), relating the history of the phrase "empathetic leader," pointed out that the recognition of the role of emotions in the relationship between the leader and employees has its origins in studies on emotions in the workplace (Edmondson & Lei, 2014; Goleman, 2007), leadership-embracing emotions (Cornelis et al., 2013; Kellett et al., 2006), and motivational language of leaders (Mayfield & Mayfield, 2017b; Sullivan, 1988). The work on the role of emotional support in management conducted by the Ohio State University and the University of Michigan (Miner, 2002, 2003) was another instance of a large-scale study in the field. Since then, much evidence has been discovered to bolster the claim that emotional support improves workplace performance.

During the 1980s, Kouzes and Posner, together with the team of the Center for Creative Leadership, carried out a large-scale research project (several thousand subjects in a dozen or so countries), aimed at answering the question of how ordinary people performing leadership roles can achieve extraordinary results (Kouzes & Posner, 1987, 1999). They were able to reach managing members of various organizations, both small firms and large enterprises, commercial and non-commercial institutions. The analysis of the results revealed that the most frequently repeated success factor for the leaders studied were their employee relationships, particularly the care they had for the feelings of their employees. This is how the study authors wrote about it:

> What was the factor that distinguished highest-performing managers from lowest-performing? The popular assumption about managers is that they have a high need to express control. So you might think that's the factor that distinguishes highest-performing from lowest-performing managers. . . . But the single factor that differentiated the top from the bottom was higher scores on affection – both expressed and wanted. Contrary to the myth of the cold-hearted boss who cares very little about people's feelings, the

> highest-performing managers show more warmth and fondness toward others. . . , they get closer to people, and they're significantly more open in sharing thoughts and feelings than their lower-performing counterparts.
>
> (Kouzes & Posner, 1999, p. 9)

The results of the research by Kouzes and Posner (1999) clearly indicate that the crucial trait that makes the best managers stand out is their ability to show care about the feelings of their employees. This ability, a major sign of empathy, plays the decisive role in effective team management. Empathy not only facilitates the understanding of employees' point of view but also helps foster a work environment where everyone feels appreciated and understood.

A leader's empathetic approach builds trust and openness in professional relationships, which has a direct influence on employee well-being. When employees feel that their emotions and needs are acknowledged, they experience greater psychosocial support, which organically contributes to their increased engagement and loyalty toward the organization. Thus, empathy becomes the foundation for building enduring and healthy relationships in the workplace.

## Empathy and Relationship Building

There is a psychological correlation between empathy in relationships with other people and the readiness to pursue a common good together, including common organizational goals. Empathy offered is perceived by the other side as evidence that she or he has been recognized as a person, that is, as something more than the "role" they perform in a given situation, for example, a colleague, an employee, a boss.

Empathy, regardless of how it is defined – whether as a factor fostering mutual understanding, a knowledge about what the other person feels, as feeling what the other person feels, as a compassionate reaction to the emotions of the other person, or the ability to assume the other person's point of view (perspective) – always entails the appreciation of the other party. In this sense, it works analogously to the effect of trust (Górniak, 2012).

The act of showing empathy toward someone, much like the acts of respect or trust, is a testament to treating the recipient as a subject, which may signal to them that someone recognizes them in their uniqueness. This impression may result from the perception made at that very moment that the person offering empathy (or trust) makes an effort (in the case of trust – takes a risk), expends some internal resources, and engages in order to reach their uniqueness. This observation encourages reciprocity expressed through, among other things, a kind of engagement that could be referred to as relational engagement – in the relationship being established. Relational engagement entails a decision to form a closer – psychologically speaking – attachment to the other person, which in turn triggers commitment (Górniak, 2012).

Respectful treatment is a sign of honoring the freedom and dignity of other people. The most important difference between the notions of subjecthood and objecthood in relation to people can be identified through the perceived source of man's activity, whether they themselves are the agent or whether they are the object of someone else's action (cf. Maslow, 2011).

The category of subjecthood (respect) is the opposite of instrumental treatment of persons. In order to show the difference more clearly, it is worth looking more closely at this antithesis. Treating someone instrumentally is manifested by reducing them to a specific function, role, or urging them – without allowing room for dialogue – to react in a desired way using all available means of influence (plea, command, threat, blackmail, manipulation, etc.). It also involves disregarding their feelings, needs, value system, and the consequences of forced decisions for their well-being (cf. Mudyń, 2012).

Instrumental treatment means appropriating the right to unilaterally command and take advantage of a person. Thus, it is associated with the use of power, understood as the effort to subjugate and control people, which, though admittedly ordinary and natural in the organizational context, may be abused. The other party is given no margin of freedom, which – according to the "abuser" – is aimed at lowering the uncertainty of the outcomes of the actions undertaken by the "abused" party. With the knowledge that the predictability of the "abused" person increases as a result of these machinations, the need to trust in their decision whether or not to act in line with the expectations dissipates. Thus, the higher the level of control stemming from instrumental behaviors, the lesser the room for trust (cf. Górniak & Motyka, 2012) and the need to be empathetic.

This situation as a matter of course limits the readiness of the "abused" party to spontaneously engage in the activities proposed (or, indeed, imposed) by the "abuser." In order to develop the attitude of objectification (instrumental treatment) of others, the "abuser" does not need any knowledge about the "abused" as a person – their individual needs, the emotions they go through at that moment, their opinions of the goals of the manipulation, their understanding of what is expected of them, and so on. Therefore, to a person who treats people "instrumentally," empathy does not appear to be "compulsory."

Respectful treatment is founded on the assumption that man is a free agent. It precludes any temptations to manipulate and is manifested in respecting and the autonomy of others, allowing them freedom of action and of choice. It is also associated with creating conditions in which the individual has access to personal (informational, intellectual, emotional, motivational) resources. It also implies the respect for feelings, long-term goals, and personal values of other people. To be able to speak of the subjecthood to the person, one has to acknowledge that she or he is someone sufficiently "inner-directed" and autonomous; therefore, as long as we remain in the position of an external observer, we are unable to get inside their inner world or gain a proper insight into their needs, intentions, and feelings. This problem can be solved by empathy, which transforms a passive external observer into an active individual who makes an effort to reach the "interior" of another person. Consequently, empathy is by its very nature a phenomenon of subjecthood.

## Characteristics of Empathetic Leadership

Berendt et al. (2018), organizational coaching professionals, have an interesting way to describe empathy-based leadership. They claim that it can take the form of an attitude displayed by the leader. Such an attitude can be manifested in how one looks at oneself, others, and the reality around, in the awareness of feelings and needs, including empathetic presence with oneself, one's colleagues, and the organization. The cited authors stress that within this account, "empathetic" does not mean "emotional," "sentimental," or "compassionate." On the contrary, empathetic leaders are those who understand themselves, their emotions, and the needs behind them. They are able to constructively express themselves in contact with other people. They are also able to read what goes on in other people and their team's emotions, and they are always ready to verify and test whether their assumptions about others are true. Empathetic leaders do more than just sympathize with team members. They use their knowledge to subtly but significantly build the organization. This does not mean that they want to please or tend to agree with everyone. Instead, in the process of wise decision-making, they thoughtfully consider the facts *and* employee moods (Goleman, 2004).

Empathetic leaders may have a vision they will encourage others to follow, but at the same time, they do not lose sight of the uniqueness of the members of their team, people who support them in realizing it. This attitude is particularly useful when dealing with all kinds of organizational changes, which are virtually everyday affairs in today's organizations. When "new rules of the game" are being established in an ever-changing situation, the sphere of emotions also needs to be managed (Berendt et al., 2018, p. 81). Showing interest, engaging in conversations, dialogue, checking the needs, all of these ensure employee stability in the process of change and give them a sense of being acknowledged and important. Meanwhile, efficient switching between various perspectives of needs gives the leader insights and the opportunity to find a different, perhaps entirely novel, perception of reality. In such an atmosphere of greater trust and exchange, there emerges room for seeking creative solutions, while engagement and motivation increase (Berendt et al., 2018).

During the COVID-19 pandemic, when, due to the unfolding crisis, every uptick in organizational efficiency was closely observed by both practitioners and researchers, the interest in the connection between leaders' showing empathy and their effectiveness clearly surged. It was mainly focused on the influence such behaviors had on work engagement (Blikle, 2014; Jonsdottir & Kristinsson, 2020; Van Bommel, 2021; Kaiser, 2024), including, that is, general performance (Zivkovic, 2022), willingness to innovate (Vladić et al., 2021; Wu & Wu,

2019), job satisfaction (Jin & Ikeda, 2023), and employee retention (Van Bommel, 2021). In that very difficult social and economic situation, leaders' abilities to express empathy proved more useful than ever before. This state of affairs was further corroborated by numerous practitioners, members of the executive staff of well-known companies and organizations (cf.: Berendt et al., 2017; Blikle, 2014; Parish, 2024; Pfejfer-Buczek, 2021). Empathetic leadership has become a sought after and effective crisis response strategy (Van Bommel, 2021). A synthesis of the results of the aforementioned studies is presented in Table 8.2.

The results of the cited studies convincingly demonstrate that empathy can enhance the effectiveness of managerial activity in terms of building and supporting work engagement. Relationships based on empathy not only strengthen team bonds but also constitute a form of psycho-social support, which fosters creating a healthy sustainable work environment. This kind of support is

*Table 8.2* Selected studies on the positive influence of a leader's empathy on various aspects of work engagement

| *Study authors* | *Results* |
|---|---|
| Jin and Ikeda (2023) | Association between empathy leadership and employees' transition from workplace loneliness to job satisfaction ($N = 267$). |
| Jonsdottir and Kristinsson (2020) | Association between supervisor's active-empathetic listening and work engagement ($N = 548$). |
| Kock et al. (2019) | Association between leader's empathetic behaviors and increased employee performance, greater job satisfaction, and enhanced innovation ($N = 257$). |
| Van Bommel (2021) CATALYST organization | Association between empathetic leaders' behavior and increased work engagement, manifested by positive work related emotions, increased productivity and innovation, improvement in work–life balance, greater employee integration, and lowered turnover rate ($N = 889$). |
| Vladić et al. (2021) | Association between empathetic leaders' behavior and enhanced innovation capability. (qualitative research) |
| Zivkovic (2022) | Confirmed by a systematic review of 24 academic papers, association between empathetic leaders' behavior and increased work engagement, manifested in greater well-being, higher retention rates, enhanced innovation, and fostering a culture of responsibility and care. |
| Rahman and Castelli (2013) | Association between empathetic leadership and the increase in productivity, as measured by the increase in task-oriented employee mobilization, that is, an aspect of work engagement ($N = 216$). |

*Source:* Own work

indispensable in today's organizations, striving for lasting success in a rapidly changing business environment.

The research studies presented point to the need to gain an even more in-depth understanding of how the empathy of leaders can be developed and cultivated in organizations. It is particularly worth exploring how the various forms of training and development programs can support managers in building empathetic relationships with employees. Furthermore, future studies can focus on the long-term effects of empathetic leadership, analyzing its influence on innovation, employee retention, and general organizational productivity in the changing market conditions.

Another important direction for further investigation can be the analysis of cultural differences in perceiving and practicing empathy in management. Understanding how various organizational cultures influence the effectiveness of empathetic leadership may help develop more individualized management strategies, which will successfully foster employee development in a variety of contexts.

## Conclusion

This chapter of the contributed volume addressed the issue of the significance of emotional intelligence (EI) for work engagement, with a special focus on the role of empathy as the core component of EI. Empathy, a major element of social skills, plays a central role in building relationships and collaboration in the organization. It has been pointed out that the empathy offered by leaders not only fosters better understanding and communication within the team but also constitutes a form of psycho-social support, which directly influences employee well-being and their level of work engagement. These issues have become especially important in the context of challenges in retaining employees who are highly engaged and genuinely attached to the organization. In a dynamically changing work environment, which more and more often sees the problems with professional burnout, employee turnover, and plummeting work engagement, managers' ability to show empathy has become one of the essential elements supporting employees in their everyday work trials. This chapter is an analysis of the essence and significance of empathy both in the general context of everyday interpersonal relations and, in particular, of team management. Indeed, empathy is more than a tool for building good relationships, as it is also a major factor influencing employee well-being, motivation, and engagement. Empathetic leadership, characterized by the ability to tune into the situation of other people and react to their emotional needs, turns out to be crucial in the process of creating an environment.

The chapter cites the results of empirical research that unequivocally demonstrate a beneficial influence of the empathy offered by managers on increased employees' work engagement. It has been observed that empathetic leadership not only contributes to improved employee well-being but also positively impacts organizational effectiveness, both in terms of productivity and the quality of teamwork. The analysis performed also points to the need of further investigation in this field to verify the long-term effects of the influence of empathetic leadership on various aspect of organizational functioning. Furthermore, we suggest that research on optimization of training programs for managers be carried out, as these could be aimed at developing empathetic leadership skills and their influence on the organizational culture.

In the context of the above considerations, it should be underscored that empathetic leadership constitutes the dominant aspect of emotional intelligence in managers as regards building relationships that foster employees' work engagement and the success of the organization. Not only does implementing and promoting empathy in management improve employees' well-being and work engagement, but it also leads to long-term benefits, such as enhanced innovation capability, productivity, and team stability. Empathy, therefore, should be treated as a strategic element of leadership development in every organization striving to achieve sustainable success.

## References


Alotaibi, S., Amin, M., & Winterton, J. (2020). Does emotional intelligence and empowering leadership affect psychological empowerment and work engagement? *Leadership & Organization Development Journal*, *41*(8), 971–991.

Berendt, J., & Panas, M. (2017). *Budowanie motywacji wewnętrznej poprzez przywództwo oparte na empatii*. Poltext.

Berendt, J., Panas, M., & Lorenc, V. (2018). Przywództwo oparte na empatii w systemowych zmianach w organizacji. [Empathy-based leadership in systemic changes in organizations]. *Coaching Review*, *1*(10), 73–99.

Blanchard, K. (2020). *Leading at a higher level: Blanchard on leadership and creating high performing*. Pearson Education.

Blikle, A. (2014). *Doktryna jakości – rzecz o skutecznym zarządzaniu*. Wydawnictwo Helion.

Brackett, M., Delaney, S., & Salovey, P. (2024). *Inteligencja emocjonalna*. Retrieved June 21, 2024, from https://nobaproject.com/modules/emotional-intelligence

Cohen, A. (2021). How to quit your job in the great post-pandemic resignation boom. *Bloomberg*. https://www.bloomberg.com/news/articles/2021-05-10/quit-your-job-how-to-resign-after-covid-pandemic

Cookson, L. J. (2015). Differences between feelings, emotions and desires in terms of interactive quality. *Advances in Social Sciences Research Journal*, *2*(7) 108–119.

Cornelis, I., Van Hiel, A., De Cremer, D., & Mayer, D. M. (2013). When leaders choose to be fair: Follower belongingness needs and leader empathy influences leaders' adherence to procedural fairness rules. *Journal of Experimental Social Psychology*, *49*, 605–613.

Davis, M. H. (1996). *Empathy: A social psychological approach*. Westview Press.

Edmondson, A. C., & Lei, Z. (2014). Psychological safety: The history, renaissance, and future of an interpersonal construct. *Annual Review of Organizational Psychology and Organizational Behavior*, *1*, 23–43. https://doi.org/10.1146/annurevorgpsych-031413-091305

Goleman, D. (1998). *Working with emotional intelligence*. Bantam Books.

Goleman, D. (2004). *What makes a leader?* https://hbr.org/2004/01/what-makes-a-leader
Goleman, D. (2007). *Social intelligence: The new science of human relationships*. Bantam Dell.
Górniak, L. (2012). Społeczna i ekonomiczna wartość zaufania w organizacji. In M. Motyka & J. Pawlak (Eds.), *Podmiotowość człowieka w organizacji*. Wydawnictwo Uniwersytetu Ekonomicznego w Krakowie.
Górniak, L., & Motyka, M. (2012). Wymiar zaufanie-kontrola, jako dwubiegunowy czynnik efektywności organizacji. *Psychologia Ekonomiczna*, *2*.
Jin, J., & Ikeda, H. (2023). The role of empathic communication in the relationship between servant leadership and workplace loneliness: A serial mediation model. *Behavioral Sciences*, *14*, 4. https://doi.org/10.3390/bs14010004
Jonsdottir, I. J., & Kristinsson, K. (2020). Supervisors' active-empathetic listening as an important antecedent of work engagement. *International Journal of Environmental Research and Public Health (IJERPH)*, *17*(21), 7976. https://doi.org/10.3390/ijerph17217976
Kahn, W. A. (1990). Psychological conditions of personal engagement and disengagement at work. *The Academy of Management Journal*, *33*(4), 692–724.
Kaiser, R. B. (2024). Has empathy really become more important to leadership since the COVID-19 pandemic? *Consulting Psychology Journal*. Advance online publication https://doi.org/10.1037/cpb0000273
Kellett, J. B., Humphrey, R. H., & Sleeth, R. G. (2006). Empathy and the emergence of task and relations leaders. *Leadership Quarterly*, *17*, 146–162.
Klotz, A. C., & Bolino, M. C. (2022). When quiet quitting is worse than the real thing. *Harvard Business Review: Managing Employees*. https://hbr.org/2022/09/when-quiet-quitting-is-worse-than-the-real-thing
Kock, N., Mayfield, M., Mayfield, J., Sexton, S., & De La Garza, L. M. (2019). Empathetic leadership: How leader emotional support and understanding influences follower performance. *Journal of Leadership & Organizational Studies*, *26*(2), 217–236.
Kouzes, J. M., & Posner, B. Z. (1987). *The leadership challenge: How to get extraordinary things done in organizations*. Jossey-Bass.
Kouzes, J. M., & Posner, B. Z. (1999). *Encouraging the heart: A leader's guide to rewarding and recognizing others*. Jossey-Bass Inc Pub.
Lewis, M., & Haviland-Jones, J. M. (2004). *Handbook of emotions* (2nd ed.). The Guilford Press.
Maslow, A. H. (2011). *Toward a psychology of being*. Wilder Publications.
Mayer, J. D., & Geher, G. (1996). Emotional intelligence and the identification of emotion. *Intelligence*, *22*, 89–113.
Mayer, J. D., Salovey, P., & Caruso, D. R. (2000). Emotional intelligence as Zeitgeist, as a personality, and a mental ability. In R. Bar-On & J. D. A. Parker (Eds.), *The handbook of emotional intelligence* (pp. 92–117). Jossey-Bass.
Mayfield, J., & Mayfield, M. (2017b). *Motivating language theory: Effective leader talk in the workplace*. Springer.
Miner, J. B. (2002). *Organizational behavior* (1st ed.). Oxford University Press.
Miner, J. B. (2003). The rated importance, scientific validity, and practical usefulness of organizational behavior theories: A quantitative review. *Academy of Management Learning and Education*, *2*, 250–268.
Mudyń, K. (2012). Podmiotowość. Co to może znaczyć? [Subjectivity. What could this mean?]. *Psychologia społeczna*, *7*(2 (21)), 151–157.
Murugesan, V., & Sankaran, H. (2018). A study on the need and impact of emotional intelligence with special reference to managerial effectiveness in the organization. *International Journal of Engineering & Technology*, *7*(1.7), 223–226.

Parish, K. (2024). *The importance of empathy in leadership*. Retrieved July 1, 2024, from https://6q.io/blog/empathy-in-leadership/

Pfejfer-Buczek, A. (2021). *Empatia w zarządzaniu ludźmi. Czy to sprawa oczywista?* Retrieved July 3, 2024, from https://hrinfluencers.pl/empatia-w-zarzadzaniu-ludzmi-czy-to-sprawa-oczywista/

Rahman, W. A., & Castelli, P. A. (2013). The impact of empathy on leadership effectiveness among business leaders in the United States and Malaysia. *International Journal of Economics Business and Management Studies*, *2*(3), 83–97.

Salovey, P., & Mayer, J. D. (1990). Emotional intelligence. *Imagination, Cognition, and Personality*, *9*(3), 185–211.

Salovey, P., & Sluyter, D. J. (Eds.). (1997). *Emotional development and emotional intelligence: Educational implications*. Basic Books.

Schaufeli, W. B., Salanova, M., Gonzalez-Roma, V., & Bakker, A. B. (2002). The measurement of engagement and burnout: A two sample confirmatory factor analytic approach. *Journal of Happiness Studies*, *3*, 71–92.

Serenko, A. (2023), The great resignation: The great knowledge exodus or theon set of the great knowledge revolution? *Journal of Knowledge Management*, *27*, 1042–1055.

Sullivan, J. (1988). Three roles of language in motivation theory. *Academy of Management Review*, *13*, 104–115.

Van Bommel, T. (2021). The power of empathy in times of crisis and beyond. *Catalyst*. Retrieved July 1, 2024, from https://www.catalyst.org/reports/empathy-work-strategy-crisis

Van Roekel, H., Wigger Enno, F. J., Veldkamp, B. P., & Bakker, A. B. (2024). What is work engagement? A text mining approach using employees' self-narratives. *Applied Psychology*, *73*, 1071–1102. https://doi.org/10.1111/apps.12501

Vladić, N., Maletič, D., & Maletič, M. (2021). Determinants of innovation capability: An exploratory study of inclusive leadership and work engagement. *Quality Innovation Prosperity/Kvalita Inovácia Prosperita*, *25*(2), 130–152. https://doi.org/10.12776/QIP.V25I2.1596

Wu, T.-J., & Wu, Y. J. (2019). Innovative work behaviors, employee engagement, and surface acting A delineation of supervisor-employee emotional contagion effects. *Management Decision*, *57*(11), 3200–3216. https://doi.org/10.1108/MD-02-2018-0196

Zivkovic, S. (2022, April 1–2). *Empathy n leadership: How it enhances effectiveness*. Post-Conference Materials, 80th International Scientific Conference on Economic and Social Development and 10th International OFEL Conference "Diversity, Equity and Inclusion: The Essence of Organisational Well-Being", Dubrovnik, pp. 454–456.

# 9 Neurodiverse Persons in Their Workplace

## Productive Behaviors and Task Engagement

*Maria Foryś*

### Introduction

The issue of neurodiversity in an occupational context is increasingly becoming the subject of scientific research. This is because diagnostics for ADHD, dyslexia, or autism spectrum disorder are increasingly available. Those who were diagnosed in childhood usually received some form of support and adjustment of learning conditions during their education, and then in recent years, they entered the labor market (Kostrzewa et al., 2023). This created challenges for managers. Employers must skillfully cope with these challenges and take advantage of opportunities resulting from them. Neurodiversity means the diversity in the way people function and think due to differences in brain structure and function. It may include differences in learning styles, information processing, approaches to problem-solving, and other aspects related to brain functioning. Individuals are defined as neurodiverse[1] if their neurological systems work differently from those of neurotypical persons. Neurodiverse are the ones with neurodevelopmental disorders such as dyslexia, dysgraphia, dyscalculia, ADHD, autism spectrum disorder, or Tourette's syndrome.

Neurodiversity in the workplace is a challenge that requires changes in the recruitment process, work organization, and team management. Supporting the functioning of neuroatypical persons in the labor market significantly improves their chances and creates an environment for them to develop their strengths. For years now, there have been companies that employ people on the autism spectrum. An example of such an initiative is the Danish *Specialisterne*, which provides IT services with the help of autistic employees. However, this does not mean that the situation of persons on the autism spectrum is simple. As Cowen (2011) notes, the skills of people on the autism spectrum are still undervalued, so it seems important to identify their potential and tap into their abilities so they feel appreciated. Understanding their limitations, as well as their strengths, will allow neuroatypical persons to develop to a greater extent and, consequently, participate much more widely in socioeconomic development.

Managing employee diversity that takes into account the different competencies resulting from atypical brain function could become another aspect of

DOI: 10.4324/9781032715407-10

employment heterogeneity. As the results of economic simulations indicate, employee diversity can be a positive phenomenon in terms of economic performance. In a report by the Polish Economic Institute on supporting persons on the autism spectrum to enter the labor market, Kutwa (2022) estimates that in Poland, under a moderate scenario (i.e., persons on the autism spectrum working for 6 hours a day), there would be an average annual boost in GDP growth of nearly PLN 17 billion (or more than USD 4 billion). This estimate applies only to people on the autism spectrum, but it should be noted that the implementation of appropriate strategies promoting neurodiversity and analogous support measures could also enable persons with dyslexia, ADHD, or other neurocognitive differences to operate more efficiently in the labor market.

The topic of neurodiversity in the workplace is still a new one. Currently, it is a significant, dynamic area of inquiry for researchers in various disciplines, including the medical sciences, social sciences, and management and quality sciences. Employers are looking for knowledge, and they want to implement appropriate solutions in the work environment. Research to date focuses on issues related to the strengths of neurodiverse persons, adapting the workplace to the special needs of the neurodiverse employees, for example, tailoring the recruitment and job selection process (Carrero et al., 2019), stereotyping risks (Whelpley et al., 2021, p. 283; Priscott & Allen, 2021), and preventing harassment (Mellifont, 2019).

There are still few studies comparing the effectiveness and engagement of neurodiverse and non-neurodiverse employees. It is also difficult to find research on productive behavior in a group of neurodiverse persons and their task engagement. The aim of this study, therefore, was to fill this cognitive gap and compare the productive behavior and task engagement of neurodiverse and non-neurodiverse persons in their workplace. While researchers have so far explored the issue of how neurodiverse persons function at work with qualitative methods (Walkowiak, 2021; Whelpley et al., 2021; Richards et al., 2019; Carrero et al., 2019; Richards & Sang, 2016; Mellifont, 2019; Austin & Pisano, 2017; Mpofu et al., 2019), this study uses a quantitative survey with a qualitative component.

## Specifics of Functioning of Neurodiverse Persons at Work

In management and quality sciences, diversity is usually associated with the diversity of human resources resulting from several variables that constitute human identity (Jeruszka & Wolan-Nowakowska, 2020, p. 15). Diversity in an organization can be defined as a variety of psychological and personality traits specific to individual employees, which should not become a cause of discrimination (Stroińska, 2017, p. 21). The diversity of employee groups is discussed in the literature, pointing to their differentiation based on race, gender, sexual orientation, physical fitness, religion, nationality, and lifestyle (Mazur-Wierzbicka et al., 2023, p. 40). Leoński et al. (2022, pp. 46–47) and Limaye et al. (2024) also point to disability as a differentiating factor for employee teams, defining it as a mental or psychological condition of a given employee that permanently or periodically hinders, limits, or prevents the fulfillment of social roles and, in particular, limits the ability to perform professional work.

Today, within the existing diversity paradigm, neurodiversity is a form of disability. This is because research on neurodiversity to date has largely originated from perspectives consistent with the medical model. Labeling neuroatypical persons in terms specific to this model involves drawing attention to their disabilities and related limited functioning, for example, in the social, cognitive, or other areas (Baron-Cohen, 2019). The medical model strongly emphasizes the deficits, limitations, and difficulties suffered by neuroatypical persons. What is overlooked, however, is the importance of the strengths and capabilities of such people.

Therefore, researchers (Maw et al., 2024) dealing with neurodiversity advocate not including it in the category of disability but treating it as a natural difference in human brain functioning.

Neurodiversity refers to the diversity in human cognition that is a natural phenomenon. The first use of the "neurodiversity" term is attributed to Judy Singer, an Australian sociologist working on the autism spectrum disorder, who used this term in her sociology thesis in the late 1990s (Corker & French, 1999). She believed that neurodiversity is a subset of biological diversity (or biodiversity). The researcher emphasized that people differ in terms of not only appearance, gender, background, social class, or sexual orientation but also mental status – they think differently, experience emotions, see colors, sense smells, or interact with the world (Singer, 1998). The sources of this diversity are both genetic variation and environmental factors, which, on the one hand, contribute to the barriers and limitations that neurodiverse persons face, and, on the other, foster the emergence of their unique abilities. Neurodiversity theory was developed by Temple Grandin, a renowned autistic scientist, author, and activist for people on the autism spectrum. In her research and publications, Grandin emphasized the diverse cognitive styles, brain functioning, and perception in people on the spectrum (Grandin, 2023; Musiałowska, 2023).

According to Armstrong (2011), *neurodiversity* is a concept that describes the diversity in the development and functioning of human brains in areas such as sociability, learning, attention, mood, and other mental functions, without pathologizing them. Neurodiversity is an increasingly visible phenomenon in social life as well. Statistics show that neuroatypical people make up about 15–20% of the population, including those on the autism spectrum with ADHD/ADD (attention-deficit hyperactivity disorder), dyslexia, dyscalculia, dyspraxia, or Tourette's syndrome (Doyle, 2020). Understanding the mechanisms of functioning of neurodiverse people, their needs, and abilities changes the way we think about recruitment, work organization, and team management.

With their minds functioning differently, neurodiverse people can use their individual talents and specialize at a high level (Becker & Murphy, 2020). In their model, Becker and Murphy describe the interactions between social forces and market behavior, which they refer to as "social exchange markets" (2020, p. 15). Their social economy model reveals social factors, that is, social networks, culture, abilities, differences, or norms that help determine what people want and how they navigate in a social environment. The model also indicates that the natural differences associated with the diverse functioning of the brains of individual people can and should be reflected in the formation of the conditions of their social functioning, including the conditions of the work environment.

The special abilities of persons on the autism spectrum include a high level of focus, detailed factual knowledge, and specialized analytical and technical skills. Reliability, low absenteeism, and loyalty can be added to this list. Employees with autism spectrum disorder are excellent at keeping records and have a high level of problem-solving skills (Tomczak, 2021, 2023). In turn, employees with dyslexia show creativity and ingenuity in their work. They identify patterns with ease. They can assess the bigger picture and think outside the box (Smith-Spark et al., 2023). Employees with dysgraphia present exceptional listening skills and the ability to recall verbal information. In the work environment, people with ADHD are often multitaskers, insightful, and able to take calculated risks (Musiałowska, 2023). Research suggests that teams with neurodiverse specialists can be 30% more productive than those without them (Austin & Pisano, 2017).

Supporting neurodiverse employees may prove to be a particularly good solution to the current and upcoming challenges related to the need for highly specialized services and products. One example of such areas is the technology industry, where it is often the potential associated with the presence of neurodiverse persons that significantly influences growth, thanks to the diversity of ideas generated by individual employees. Some international corporations even conduct a targeted recruitment process to acquire talented, neuroatypical employees on the autism spectrum (Hayward et al., 2019).

However, some managers fail to see the benefits of an inclusive work culture that embraces diversity of thought, different approaches to work, innovation, and creativity. A British survey of neurodiverse employees indicates a lack of understanding on the part of managers. In the survey, as many as 73% of respondents said that managers do not understand or are not aware of what diversity is, while 24% stated they sometimes understand, 2% said the managers usually understand, and only 1% admitted they always understand it (Hewlett et al., 2018). The results of this research show the importance of increasing knowledge among managers about the phenomenon of neurodiversity and awareness of the strengths and weaknesses of neurodiverse people. This will allow, first, for more effective inclusive measures and, second, for adequate support.

Over the past decades, tremendous progress has been made in combating cognitive discrimination and developing an inclusive and empathetic society.

However, despite increased awareness, there is still much work to be done. Diagnosed neurodiverse persons are usually covered by a standard support plan during their university studies, but their situation becomes more difficult after graduation. They are cut off from existing forms of assistance, suffer from a lack of counseling, and even outright disinterest in their further development and fate, which ultimately leads to loneliness and confusion. It should be noted that neuroatypical people experience unemployment, underemployment, and exclusion more often than neurotypical persons (Eden, 2019; Carter et al., 2012; National Autistic Society, 2016; Richards, 2012; Snowling et al., 2000). An approach focused on the strengths resulting from neurological differences provides opportunities for growth, entry into the labor market, and, ultimately, a greater sense of happiness and well-being. This is why inclusion policies and empowerment of the neurodiverse are so important, as they will foster the perception of neurodiversity not as a challenge but as a resource (e.g., Hayes et al., 2002; Holvino et al., 2004).

Concern for understanding and improving the professional functioning of neurodiverse persons and the mechanisms to effectively integrate them into organizations has resulted in studies addressing various aspects of this issue, such as the functioning of people with attention-deficit hyperactivity disorder (ADHD) (Moore et al., 2021), human resource management adjustments toward people with learning disabilities (Sumner & Brown, 2015), organizational inclusion of persons with autism from a philosophical perspective (Dobusch, 2021), and teaching neurodiverse students in a business communication course (Ortiz, 2020). The researchers also point out the still existing scarcity of research on neurodiversity, presenting proposals to deepen it (Spoor et al., 2021; Mellifont, 2019; Richards et al., 2019).

An important area seems to be the study of the productive behavior and engagement of neurodiverse persons and the identification of factors that influence their support in task completion. From the manager's point of view, knowledge in this area will benefit the implementation of the management process in planning and organizing tasks for neurodiverse employees. It will also improve the process of motivating them and building an inclusive environment.

## Research Methodology

The empirical research conducted aimed to identify differences between neurodiverse and non-neurodiverse employees in terms of productive behavior and task engagement. *Task engagement (behavioral engagement)* in this study is understood as the degree to which a person is absorbed in performing assigned tasks (see Saks, 2006; Ludwig & Frazier, 2012). Compared to the concept of work engagement defining the state of the employee – a positive, work-related, and rewarding state of mind that manifests itself in vigor, dedication, and preoccupation with the work performed (Schaufeli & Salanova, 2011; Schaufeli et al.,

2002) – *task engagement* refers exclusively to the observable behavior and effort put forth by the employee to achieve the set goals (Jurek & Olech, 2019, p. 48).

Engagement in performing tasks is a behavior that falls into the group of productive behaviors. Jurek and Olech (2019) define *productive behavior* as a comprehensive set of work-related behaviors that an employer expects from an employee. This set is most often written into a contract specifying mutual expectations. In some cases, productive behavior can be easily defined and measured, such as an employee doing a job with clearly defined tasks. In other cases, the productive behavior is more complex and much more difficult to assess, such as the work of an artist (Kmiotek & Piecuch, 2012).

This section attempts to answer the question of whether neurodiversity affects the level of productive behavior and engagement. The research undertaken will allow for the verification of the main hypothesis: Neurodiverse persons show similar levels of productive behavior and engagement to non-neurodiverse ones. Accordingly, the following specific hypotheses were adopted:

- H1. The task engagement of neurodiverse persons is similar to that of non-neurodiverse ones.
- H2. Neurodiverse persons provide the same level of support to colleagues in the work environment as non-neurodiverse employees.
- H3. Neurodiverse persons show similar levels of pro-organizational behavior to non-neurodiverse individuals.

The primary dependent variable in the study is productive behavior in the workplace, measured in terms of engagement in completing tasks, providing support to co-workers, and displaying pro-organizational behavior. In the study, productive behavior is the response variable, while the independent variables are the explanatory variables (Frankfort-Nachmias & Nachmias, 2001). The independent variables identified in the study are age, education, job experience, company size, neurodiversity, and non-neurodiversity.

The study used one of the KLIMAT4® Battery scales. The authors of the tool are Paweł Jurek and Maciej Olech. This battery is a comprehensive tool that helps diagnose organizational determinants of work engagement. The PRO scale, which is one of the scales in the battery, was used. It is intended to measure employees' perceived working conditions, their attitudes toward the organization, and the tasks they perform.

The procedure for creating the tool was based on rigorous methodological and psychometric standards. It meets all the criteria for tools used in psychology and management sciences. Validation studies on KLIMAT4® were conducted with a total of more than 12,000 employees. The tool's accuracy was confirmed by 14 studies. Both the factor structure of the scales and their relationship with key organizational attitudes and behaviors were analyzed, including work engagement, burnout, sense of justice, and employee silence. In turn, reliability was estimated with an Omega internal consistency coefficient of 0.77–0.91 for BEO scales, 0.81–0.91 for SAT scales, 0.88–0.94 for PNE scales, and 0.85–0.89 for PRO scales.

The PRO scale used in the study measures the behavior exhibited by employees in the workplace. The tool consists of 12 statements describing behavior beneficial to the organization. The subject's task is to rate on a one-point scale (from 1 – *definitely not* to 5 – *definitely yes*) the extent to which they agree with each statement. The PRO scale measures *engagement in performing tasks* (four items, e.g., "Sometimes, I am so absorbed in work that I lose track of time"), *providing support to co-workers* (four items, e.g., "I devote my time to help co-workers solve their problems"), and *pro-organizational behavior* (four items, e.g., "I participate in activities that go beyond my responsibilities").

The first subscale is inspired by a scale created by Saks (2006) measuring, among other things, employees' engagement in performing tasks arising from their professional function. The second and third subscales are inspired by a tool developed by Lee and Allen (2002), which measures other-oriented and organization-oriented behavior.

The survey's data collection process was conducted both on paper and electronically. The paper form required manual entry of responses into the database. Most of the data in the survey focusing on employees in various industries were collected online (with the Computer-Assisted Web Interview technique) using a publicly available platform (Google Form), which allowed for acquiring more respondents.

To verify the hypotheses, statistical analyses were carried out using the IBM SPSS Statistics 29 package. It was used to perform the analysis of basic descriptive statistics along with Shapiro–Wilk tests, the Mann–Whitney $U$ test, the Friedman test, the Wilcoxon test, and the Spearman rho correlation. The significance level in this section was set at $\alpha = 0.05$.

To give proper meaning to the results obtained in the survey, the raw scores were converted into Sten scores for each respondent. For this purpose, the standard tables provided in the test manual were used. Standardized results (calculated individually for each employee) indicate the level of the studied variables compared to a reference group – employees of various ages, hired in various organizations and different positions.

The surveys conducted were voluntary. The survey form consisted of a section containing the survey instructions, followed by the PRO scale statements, an open-ended question addressed to neurodiverse persons (*What kind of difficulties do you experience as a neurodiverse person (having the difficulties specified above) in your workplace?*), and survey demographics. The open-ended question was preceded by a filter question about having a formal diagnosis of a neurodevelopmental disorder.

A purposive sampling method was used, with particular emphasis on selecting survey participants with a formal diagnosis of a neurodevelopmental disorder defined as neurodiverse survey subjects and subjects without such a diagnosis. Purposive sampling provided detailed insight into the issues analyzed in this study. Finding neurodiverse subjects was a challenge of this research project, as neuroatypical employees make up a small percentage of the organization's total workforce for now, and not all of them are willing to share information about their diagnosis.

The survey sample included 107 respondents. Of the employees who consented to the survey, 107 persons (45 men and 62 women) between the ages of 25 and 65 returned completed forms. Considering age, the respondents represented the following demographic groups: The majority fell into the 26–35 age category (32%); another group was 36–45 years of age (27%). Those aged 46–55 and under 25 accounted for an equal share (19%); while the smallest group surveyed included respondents representing the oldest group of employees aged 55–65 (3%).

Analysis of the sample in terms of the respondents' education showed that more than half (51%) had a university degree (master's degree). Twelve percent of respondents had a higher education in the first cycle (bachelor's degree). In turn, 37% of respondents were employees with secondary education. Persons with primary education did not participate in the survey.

In terms of job type, the largest group was public sector professions (teacher, doctor, police officer, soldier, etc.), accounting for 35% of participants. Another group consisted of employees in administration, legal, HR, accounting, marketing, and so on, with 28% of respondents. Production workers accounted for 23% of those surveyed, and sales or customer service employees were present at 14%. The majority, that is, 57% of those surveyed, held specialist positions, while executive or ordinary positions were represented by 30% of the respondents. The smallest group, 13% of the respondents, held managerial positions.

Survey respondents reported working for organizations that varied in size. Nearly half, 44% of them, worked in corporations with more than 250 employees. Then, 30% of the respondents were employed in large companies with 50 to 249 employees. The medium-sized companies of 10–49 employees were represented by 21% of respondents. Only 5% of those surveyed were hired in small companies with up to nine employees.

In terms of length of service in the current job position, nearly 30% of the surveyed employees were in the range from 3 to 5 years and from 6 months to 2 years. Sixteen of respondents reported experience ranging from 11 to 20 years. In turn, the least represented group of respondents in terms of length of service were employees starting their jobs, declaring less than 6 months of service, and those who had worked for over 20 years.

The key element of the analyses was the information obtained from respondents regarding having a formal diagnosis of the neurodevelopmental disorders listed on the survey form. People on the autism spectrum account for 12% of respondents, and a similar group (13%) consists of persons diagnosed with learning disabilities (dyslexia, dysgraphia, dysorthography). The least represented group of neuroatypical respondents are those with attention-deficit hyperactivity disorder known as ADHD/ADD (3%). In the case of the autism spectrum disorder, an additional group was included – employees who do not have a formal diagnosis but identify themselves as being on the autism spectrum. This decision was based on the fact that many adults do not have access to an autism spectrum disorder diagnosis or, for various reasons, do not seek one. However, they may be experiencing difficulties at work specific to the autism spectrum while not receiving adequate support. Of those surveyed, 66% did not declare having neuroatypical and mental health diagnoses. These persons were referred to as non-neurodiverse in the research project.

Thus, the survey identified the following groups of employees:

- Persons with learning disabilities – ones diagnosed with dyslexia, dysgraphia, or dyscalculia, who at the same time did not have a diagnosis of autism spectrum disorder (or identify with this group) or ADHD/ADD
- Persons with ADHD/ADD – ones diagnosed with ADHD and/or attention-deficit disorder, except for those who declared a concurrent diagnosis or identification with the autism spectrum disorder
- Persons on the autism spectrum – all persons declaring a diagnosis of autism spectrum disorder or identifying as ones on the autism spectrum disorder (i.e., self-diagnosed persons)
- Persons not declaring any diagnoses in neuroatypicality and mental health

The survey was self-report-based. Respondents were not asked to document their diagnoses. The survey was anonymous and conducted on the premise that we were interested in the situation of persons who identify themselves as neuroatypical, even if they do not have a formal diagnosis. This fact should be taken into account when interpreting the data provided in this paper.

## The Impact of Neurodiversity on the Level of Task Engagement in the Workplace: Research Results

In the first step of the analysis, the distributions of quantitative variables were checked. This course of action is suggested by many researchers (Józefacka et al., 2023). In this study, it helped to decide what kind of statistical tests and other statistics should be used. For this purpose, basic descriptive statistics were calculated along with the Shapiro–Wilk test examining the normality of the distribution. Details of the analyses conducted are presented in Table 9.1.

As can be seen in Table 9.1, the Shapiro–Wilk test results indicate a distribution different from the normal distribution for most of the results. Therefore, it was decided to use non-parametric analyses to verify the research

*Table 9.1* Basic descriptive statistics of the studied variables with the Shapiro–Wilk test (for valid $N = 107$)

| *Dependent variable* | *M* | *Mdn* | *SD* | *Sk* | *Kurt* | *Min* | *Max* | *W* | *P* |
|---|---|---|---|---|---|---|---|---|---|
| *PRO scale results – productive behavior in the workplace* | | | | | | | | | |
| Task engagement | 14.13 | 14.00 | 3.27 | −0.13 | −0.56 | 5.00 | 20.00 | 0.97 | 0.039 |
| Providing support to co-workers | 15.24 | 15.00 | 2.86 | −0.47 | 0.61 | 6.00 | 20.00 | 0.95 | 0.003 |
| Pro-organizational behavior | 13.44 | 13.00 | 3.25 | −0.14 | −0.02 | 4.00 | 20.00 | 0.98 | 0.154 |
| Productive behavior | 42.80 | 42.00 | 7.59 | −0.29 | −0.21 | 22.00 | 57.00 | 0.98 | 0.301 |
| *Length of service* | | | | | | | | | |
| Total length of service | 13.78 | 14.00 | 9.53 | 0.60 | −0.50 | 1.00 | 36.00 | 0.93 | <0.001 |

Legend: *M* – mean; Mdn – median; SD – standard deviation; Sk – skewness; Kurt – kurtosis; Min – minimum value; Max – maximum value; *W* – the result of the Shapiro–Wilk test; *p* – the *p* value for the Shapiro–Wilk test

*Source:* Own research

*Table 9.2* Results of Mann–Whitney *U* test analysis comparing neurodiverse and non-neurodiverse persons in terms of intensity of productive behavior (for valid $N = 107$)

| *Dependent variable* | | *Non-neurodiversity (n = 59)* | *Neurodiversity (n = 48)* | *Z* | *P* | $\eta^2$ |
|---|---|---|---|---|---|---|
| **Task engagement** | Mdn | 15.00 | 13.50 | −1.73 | 0.084 | 0.04 |
| | IQR | 5.00 | 4.25 | | | |
| | Mean rank | 43.25 | 33.25 | | | |
| **Providing support to co-workers** | Mdn | 15.00 | 15.50 | −0.53 | 0.594 | <0.01 |
| | IQR | 2.50 | 5.25 | | | |
| | Mean rank | 39.66 | 42.73 | | | |
| **Pro-organizational behavior** | Mdn | 13.50 | 13.00 | −0.25 | 0.799 | <0.01 |
| | IQR | 4.00 | 6.50 | | | |
| | Mean rank | 40.91 | 39.43 | | | |
| **Productive behavior** | Mdn | 43.50 | 40.50 | −0.79 | 0.428 | <0.01 |
| | IQR | 10.25 | 12.00 | | | |
| | Mean rank | 41.77 | 37.16 | | | |

Legend: *n* – the number of observations; Mdn – median; IQR – interquartile range; *Z* – test statistic value; *p* – statistical significance; $\eta^2$ – the effect size index.

*Source:* Own research

hypotheses. It was then examined whether neurodiverse persons differed from non-neurodiverse persons in terms of the intensity of productive behavior in the workplace. For this purpose, the Mann–Whitney *U* test analysis was performed. The results are presented in Table 9.2.

The results revealed that neurodiverse and non-neurodiverse persons presented similar levels of intensity of productive behavior – for the overall level of productive behavior, as well as for its components, task engagement, providing support to co-workers, and pro-organizational behavior. This is evidenced by the lack of statistically significant differences between the compared groups.

Subsequently, it was examined whether any of the indicators of productive behavior in the workplace – task engagement, providing support to co-workers, and pro-organizational behavior – was more intense than the others among the neurodiverse and non-neurodiverse. For this purpose, the Friedman test analysis was performed. The results are presented in Table 9.3.

The analysis showed small differences in the intensity of productive behavior indicators, both among neurodiverse and non-neurodiverse persons. Further analysis using the Wilcoxon test showed that in the neurodiverse group, the intensity of providing support to co-workers was higher than the level of task engagement ($Z = -2.55$; $p = 0.011$) and pro-organizational behavior ($Z = -2.51$; $p = 0.012$). The intensity of task engagement and pro-organizational behavior was similar in the neurodiverse group ($Z = -0.09$; $p = 0.930$). For the non-neurodiverse group, the intensity of pro-organizational behavior was lower than the intensity of task engagement ($Z = -2.35$; $p = 0.019$) and providing support to co-workers ($Z = 3.93$; $p < 0.001$). Providing support to co-workers in the non-neurodiverse group was on a similar level to providing support to co-workers in the neurodiverse group ($Z = -1.81$; $p = 0.070$).

Next, it was examined whether the intensity of productive behavior in the workplace among the neurodiverse and non-neurodiverse depended on their age, education, length of service, and the size of the company in which the subjects worked. For this purpose, Spearman's rho correlation analysis was performed.

*Table 9.3* Results of the Friedman test analysis comparing the intensity of productive behavior in neurodiverse and non-neurodiverse persons (for valid $N = 107$)

| *Group* | *Variable* | *Mdn* | *IQR* | *Mean rank* | $\chi^2(2)$ | *p* | *W* |
|---|---|---|---|---|---|---|---|
| **Neurodiverse** | Task engagement | 13.50 | 4.25 | 1.82 | 10.49 | 0.005 | 0.24 |
| | Providing support to co-workers | 15.50 | 5.25 | 2.52 | | | |
| | Pro-organizational behavior | 13.00 | 6.50 | 1.66 | | | |
| **Non-neurodiverse** | Task engagement | 15.00 | 5.00 | 2.03 | 21.66 | <0.001 | 0.19 |
| | Providing support to co-workers | 15.00 | 2.50 | 2.40 | | | |
| | Pro-organizational behavior | 13.50 | 4.00 | 1.58 | | | |

Legend: *n* – number of observations; Mdn – median; IQR – interquartile range; $\chi^2$ – test statistic value; *p* – statistical significance; *W* – effect size index

*Source:* Own research

*Table 9.4* Results of Spearman's rho correlation analysis testing the co-variance of the productive behavior intensity in the workplace with age, education, length of service, and company size among neurodiverse persons (for valid $N = 107$)

| *Variable* | | *Task engagement* | *Providing support to co-workers* | *Pro-organizational behavior* | *Productive behavior* |
|---|---|---|---|---|---|
| **Age** | Spearman's rho | 0.07 | −0.33 | 0.31 | −0.02 |
| | Significance | 0.752 | 0.135 | 0.156 | 0.936 |
| **Education** | Spearman's rho | 0.14 | −0.34 | 0.17 | −0.02 |
| | Significance | 0.535 | 0.127 | 0.462 | 0.917 |
| **Length of service in current position** | Spearman's rho | 0.10 | −0.03 | 0.53 | 0.27 |
| | Significance | 0.668 | 0.885 | 0.012 | 0.218 |
| **Total length of service** | Spearman's rho | −0.10 | −0.39 | 0.27 | −0.12 |
| | Significance | 0.669 | 0.071 | 0.226 | 0.596 |
| **Company size** | Spearman's rho | −0.16 | −0.05 | −0.30 | −0.27 |
| | Significance | 0.477 | 0.810 | 0.174 | 0.230 |

*Source:* Own research

The results are presented in Table 9.4 (for neurodiverse employees) and Table 9.5 (for non-neurodiverse employees).

It turns out that among the neurodiverse, the intensity of pro-organizational behavior of the subjects increased with longer employment in their current position. Spearman'*s* rho value indicates that the relationship between the variables is very strong. For non-neurodiverse persons, the intensity of task engagement was higher the older the subjects were and the longer their employment in their current positions. The value of Spearman's rho correlation coefficient indicates a weak correlation between task engagement and age, as well as an average correlation between task engagement and length of service in the current position.

In the final step of the analysis, it was examined whether gender differentiated the intensity of productive behavior between the neurodiverse and non-neurodiverse subjects surveyed. For this purpose, Mann–Whitney *U* test analysis was performed. The results are presented in Table 9.6 – for the neurodiverse and non-neurodiverse groups.

The analysis showed similar levels of productive behavior in the workplace among the women and men surveyed. This applies to neurodiverse and non-neurodiverse persons, the overall level of productive behavior in the workplace, and its indicators – task performance engagement, providing support to co-workers, and pro-organizational behavior. This is evidenced by the lack of statistically significant differences between the compared groups.

In response to an open question about the types of difficulties experienced by neurodiverse persons in their workplace, respondents most frequently mentioned severe stress and pressure exerted by their employer and an inappropriate

*Table 9.5* Results of Spearman's rho correlation analysis testing the co-variance of the productive behavior intensity in the workplace with age, education, length of service, and company size among non-neurodiverse persons (for valid $N = 107$)

| *Variable* | | *Task engagement* | *Providing support to co-workers* | *Pro-organizational behavior* | *Productive behavior* |
|---|---|---|---|---|---|
| **Age** | Spearman's rho | 0.29 | 0.04 | 0.16 | 0.21 |
| | Significance | 0.027 | 0.764 | 0.237 | 0.120 |
| **Education** | Spearman's rho | 0.24 | 0.02 | 0.16 | 0.13 |
| | Significance | 0.076 | 0.892 | 0.236 | 0.315 |
| **Length of service in current position** | Spearman's rho | 0.34 | 0.01 | 0.20 | 0.25 |
| | Significance | 0.009 | 0.945 | 0.135 | 0.063 |
| **Total length of service** | Spearman's rho | 0.24 | −0.02 | 0.12 | 0.15 |
| | Significance | 0.077 | 0.856 | 0.379 | 0.276 |
| **Company size** | Spearman's rho | 0.01 | −0.21 | −0.20 | −0.13 |
| | Significance | 0.913 | 0.109 | 0.123 | 0.349 |

*Source:* Own research

work environment. In addition, problems with task performance and feeling safe in the workplace during high-stress periods were reported, as well as a belief that one's potential was not being realized. Among people on the autism spectrum, the most common reflections concerned difficulties with sensory load. For example, respondents wrote: "I miss peace and quiet at work. I am constantly tired of the sounds of noise, coffee making and other activities near my desk. It is unbearable. I told my employer about it, he laughed"; "distraction with the noise outside the window, too bright lighting (although compliant with occupational health and safety regulations)"; "trouble concentrating, coping with excess stimuli." There were also statements about the difficulties in building interactions and communicating with people around the office. One person with autism spectrum disorder wrote:

> in contact with employees and interpreting their intentions, I try to be sociable and smiling, but I fake it, I feel that I behave oddly at times and people misperceive my body language and intentions. I don't understand intrigue/gossip and things that are not literal.

Neurodiverse respondents with dyslexia most often complained that their slower pace of work was not understood by their employer. They also mentioned having trouble confusing dates and times of meetings, typos in writing, swapping tags in code when programming, and reduced focus on topics that do not interest them during lectures/training sessions. They would like their employer to take chronobiology into account in the work schedule. It means adjusting working hours to when they function best, that is, morning to noon and/or at night, as this would promote the efficiency of their work. One person with hyperkinetic disorder wrote: "ADHD doesn't help me. I have to try harder. Sometimes I forget something and I get very stressed." Obtained answers to the question about the specifics of the difficulties a neurodiverse person experiences in their workplace allowed us to tentatively show the barriers that neurodiverse employees face, and then isolate factors that can help overcome these barriers (see Table 9.6).

## Discussion and Inferences

The main hypothesis that neurodiverse persons achieve similar levels of productive behavior and engagement compared to the non-neurodiverse has been confirmed. The specific hypotheses have also been confirmed: The distribution of the variables studied in both groups was similar. The results showed that the task engagement of neurodiverse persons was similar to that of non-neurodiverse ones. Furthermore, neurodiverse persons provide the same level of support to colleagues in the work environment as non-neurodiverse employees. It was also found that the pro-organizational behavior of neurodiverse persons is similar to that of non-neurodiverse persons.

In the literature, behavior related to providing support to co-workers and pro-organizational behavior are categorized as a type of organizational "off-role" behavior, that is, such activities that are performed additionally (Rożnowski & Fortuna, 2020). Podsakoff defines helping behavior as voluntary actions for the benefit of other employees, helping them solve work problems, and preventing them from "creating" additional problems at work (Podsakoff et al., 2000). Following this way of thinking, it can be concluded that neurodiverse people exhibit this kind of attitude. This is perhaps a compensation effect for the difficulties they face. Proving oneself in the area of collective action, performing additional activities for the organization may be related to a strong need for acceptance and belonging in the work environment. The fact that neurodiverse persons' task engagement is at a similar level to that of the control group may be due to both neurodiverse employees' positive emotional attitudes toward the organization and a sense of extension of the self in the workplace.

Based on an analysis of an open-ended question addressed to neurodiverse respondents, Table 9.6 shows both factors that hinder task performance and suggestions for human resource management support measures that take diversity management into account.

When taking into account these characteristics and activities, the workplace can become more inclusive and supportive for neurodiverse persons, which will contribute to their engagement and career success.

Jenara Nerenberg (2022) proposes introducing a neurodiversity footprint at work, which will help neurodiverse employees avoid failure in the work

*Table 9.6* Factors supporting and hindering the work of neurodiverse people

| *Hindering factor* | *Supporting factor* |
|---|---|
| Workplace that prevents effective work | Designing an inclusive space tailored to the needs of the neurodiverse, including quiet zones, a desk tailored to the type of neurodiversity, open spaces, and cozy rooms. |
| Working hours not adapted to the employee's chronotype and limitations | Contract with an employer providing for the option of adjusting working hours: in line with chronotype, hybrid work option. |
| Cognitive and behavioral limitations with complex tasks that prevent their completion | Building a support network, peer tutoring, possibly assisting a neurodiverse person. |
| Communication difficulties | Adapting the type of communication to the psychophysical capabilities of a neurodiverse person. Email and direct contact agreed with the employer. |
| Reactions of staff team members inappropriate to the situation, such as ridicule, overprotectiveness, lack of acceptance | Training of the entire staff team on knowledge of the strengths and weaknesses of neurodiverse people. |
| Challenges related to completion and complexity of tasks | Assigning tasks adapted to the employee's psychophysical capabilities. Delegating tasks in stages, long-term projects with support from team members. |
| Employer's ignorance of the difficulties related to pathomechanism of the disorder, focusing only on the employee's strengths | Getting to know the employee, deepening the employer's knowledge of the disorder. Task mediation enables success at work, in the form of managerial consultations with psychologists, and discussions with employees on difficulties and opportunities. |

*Source:* Own research

environment. Her suggestions complement the findings of this study and focus on training all employees in the neurodiversity language and thinking and creating physical areas – quiet, secluded, or open spaces conducive to different work styles. In addition, she suggests holding regular small group meetings to talk about mental health, burnout, communication, boundaries, and organizational tips and tools.

Analysis of the results indicates the need for further research related to neurodiversity in the workplace. This research should allow for further, more detailed identification of factors that can increase the engagement of neurodiverse people and the use of their potential. It seems that in-depth interviews may allow for a broader exploration of this topic.

## Conclusion

The section has presented an analysis of the productive behavior and task engagement of neurodiverse persons (i.e., those with autism spectrum disorder, ADHD, dyslexia, and other neurodiversity) in their workplaces, compared to non-neurodiverse ones. The section shows the results of the author's own research, which was based on methodological triangulation. The quantitative research conducted allowed for addressing the formulated research hypotheses. The results obtained from the survey of neurodiverse and non-neurodiverse employees do not indicate the greater engagement of neurotypical persons. Research conducted in various professional environments has shown that the level of productive behavior of the two groups is similar. These findings challenge stereotypes suggesting that neurodiversity impedes professional performance. However, to fully realize the potential of neurodiverse employees, it is necessary to properly assign tasks and adjust workplaces. These adjustments can range from physical modifications (e.g., quiet rooms, adjustable lighting) to changes in organizational processes (e.g., flexible work hours, clearly specified tasks, and expectations). As a result of the literature review and analysis of the own research, a number of recommendations for management practice were prepared. Their implementation can significantly impact the engagement of neurodiverse persons. Here are some key workplace features that can support this group:

- Friendly environment: The workplace should be designed to be friendly to people with various neurological profiles. This means eliminating excessive sensory stimulation, providing space for relaxation, and using colors and lighting that are not intrusive to employees with sensory hypersensitivity.
- Flexibility in working hours: For many neurodiverse persons, fixed working hours can be a challenge. Providing flexible working hours allows employees to better adapt their schedules to their needs and constraints.
- Social support: Building community in the workplace can be crucial for neurodiverse people. Creating space for collaboration and integration, as well as promoting open communication and understanding, can help build social support.
- Workstation adjustments: They can be crucial for people with different neurological profiles. This could include adjusting work tools, rearranging the office layout, and providing ergonomic equipment or individual technical support.
- Understanding and training: Providing neurodiversity training to all employees can help increase understanding and acceptance. This may contribute to better support for neurodiverse persons and create a more inclusive work environment.
- Managing communication challenges: Communication may be hard for some neurodiverse employees. Providing clear communication guidelines, enabling various modes of communication, and training on effective communication can help manage these challenges.

The results also highlight the importance of managers' awareness in the context of managing neurological diversity. Managers should be trained and prepared to recognize and understand the unique needs of neurodiverse employees. This will allow managers to adequately manage the work of diverse employee groups and provide psychosocial support. Based on the data obtained, it can be concluded that an inclusive approach and flexible management practices can contribute to better use of the skills of neurodiverse persons, which can ultimately benefit both individuals and entire teams and organizations.

However, it should be emphasized that without the involvement of all employees in creating a workplace that supports effective diversity management, one cannot count on its effective implementation (Gross-Gołacka, 2018, p. 218). Single actions, such as training, will not be sufficient to achieve the expected results. As Rosenberg stated (in: Sonnenschein, 1997, p. 24): "Diversity has to be managed. It just does not manage itself."

## Note

1. The term neurodiverse person in this section is used interchangeably with the term neuroatypical or neurodivergent person.

## References

Armstrong, T. (2011). *The power of neurodiversity: Unleashing the advantages of your differently wired brain*. Da Capo Lifelong.

Austin, R. D., & Pisano, G. P. (2017). Neurodiversity as a competitive advantage. *Harvard Business Review*, *19*, 96–103.

Baron-Cohen, S. (2019). *The concept of neurodiversity is dividing the autism community*. https://blogs.scientificamerican.com/observations/the-concept-of-neurodiversity-is-dividing-the-autism-community/

Becker, G. S., & Murphy, K. M. (2020). *Ekonomia społeczna. Co wpływa na zachowanie jednostki?* PWN.

Carrero, J., Krzemińska, A., & Härtel, Ch. E. J. (2019). The DXC technology work experience program: Disability-inclusive recruitment and selection in action. *Journal of Management & Organization*, *25*(4), 535–542.

Carter, E. W., Austin, D., & Trainor, A. A. (2012). Predictors of postschool employment outcomes for young adults with severe disabilities. *Journal of Disability Policy Studies*, *23*, 50–63. https://doi.org/10.1177/1044207311414680

Corker, M., & French, S. (1999). *Disability discourse*. McGraw-Hill Education.

Cowen, T. (2011). An economic and rational choice approach to the autism spectrum and human neurodiversity. *GMU Working Paper in Economics*, *11*(58). http://dx.doi.org/10.2139/ssrn.1975809

Dobusch, L. (2021). The inclusivity of inclusion approaches: A relational perspective on inclusion and exclusion in organizations. *Gender Work and Organization*, *28*(1), 379–396.

Doyle, N. (2020). Neurodiversity at work: A biopsychosocial model and the impact on working adults. *British Medical Bulletin*, *135*(1), 108–125. https://doi.org/10.1093/bmb/ldaa021

Eden, P. (2019). *Corporate America must invest in neurodiversity* (p. 48). University Business.
Frankfort-Nachmias, Ch., & Nachmias, D. (2001). *Metody badawcze w naukach społecznych*. Zysk i s-ka.
Grandin, T. (2023). *Visual thinking: The hidden gifts of people who think in pictures, patterns, and abstractions*. Riverhead Books.
Gross-Gołacka, E. (2018). *Zarządzanie różnorodnością. W kierunku zróżnicowanych zasobów ludzkich w organizacji*. Difin.
Hayes, B. C., Bartle, S. A., & Major, D. A. (2002). Climate for opportunity: A conceptual model. *Human Resource Management Review*, *12*, 445–468. https://doi.org/10.1016/S1053-4822(02)00050-5
Hayward, S. M., McVilly, K. R., & Stokes, M. A. (2019). Autism, and employment: What works. *Research in Autism Spectrum Disorders*, *60*, 48–58.
Hewlett, K., Cooper, R., & Jameson, M. (2018). *Neurodiverse voices: Opening doors to employment*. Westminster Achievability Commission for Dyslexia and Neurodivergence.https://www.achieveability.org.uk/files/1516612947/wac-neurodiverse-voices-opening-doors-to-employment-report_2018_interactive.pdf
Holvino, E. H., Ferdman, B. M., & Merrill-Sands, D. (2004). Creating and sustaining diversity and inclusion in organizations: Strategies and approaches. In M. S. Stockdale & F. J. Cosby (Eds.), *The psychology and management of workplace diversity* (pp. 245–276). Blackwell.
Jeruszka, U., & Wolan-Nowakowska, M. (2020). *Zarządzanie różnorodnością w organizacji. Aspekty psychopedagogiczne*. Difin.
Józefacka, N. M., Kołek, M. F., Arciszewska-Leszczuk, A., & Iwankowski, P. (2023). *Metodologia i statystyka Przewodnik naukowego turysty*. PWN.
Jurek, P., & Olech, M. (2019). *Klimat4. Bateria diagnozy i klimatu pracy*. Pracownia Testów Psychologicznych i Pedagogicznych.
Kmiotek, K., & Piecuch, T. (2012). *Zachowania organizacyjne. Teoria i przykłady*. Difin.
Kostrzewa, A., Wasilewski, J., & Leszczyńska, Z. (2023). *W drodze do idei*. UN Global Compact.
Kutwa, K. (2022), *Droga do otwarcia rynku pracy w Polsce dla osób autystycznych*. Polski Instytut Ekonomiczny.
Lee, K., & Allen, N. J. (2002). Organizational citizenship behavior and workplace deviance: The role of affect and cognition. *Journal of Applied Psychology*, *87*(1), 131–142.
Leoński, W., Pluta, A., & Wieczorek-Szymańska, A. (2022). *Zarządzanie różnorodnością w organizacji*. CeDeWu.
Limaye, S., Johnstone, C. J., & Kayama, M. (2024). *Disability as diversity in India: Theory, practice, and lived experience*. Routledge India.
Ludwig, T. D., & Frazier, C. B. (2012). Employee engagement and organizational behavior management. *Journal of Organizational Behavior Management*, *32*, 75–82.
Maw, K. J., Beattie, G., & Burns, E. J. (2024). Cognitive strengths in neurodevelopmental disorders, conditions and differences: A critical review. *Neuropsychologia*, *197*.
Mazur-Wierzbicka, E., Wieczorek-Szymańska, A., & Leoński, W. (2023). *Zarządzanie zasobami ludzkimi. Wrażliwe na różnorodność*. CeDeWu.
Mellifont, D. (2019). DESerting clients? A study investigating evidence-based measures supporting the longterm employment of neurodiverse Australians. *Management and Labour Studies*, *44*(4), 455–466.
Moore, C. B., McIntyre, N. H., & Lanivich, S. E. (2021). ADHD-related neurodiversity and the entrepreneurial mindset. *Entrepreneurship Theory and Practice*, *45*(1), 64–91.
Mpofu, E., Tansey, T., Mpofu, N., Tu, W., & Li, Q. (2019). Employment practices with people with autism spectrum disorder in the digital age. In I. L. Potgieter, N. Ferreira, &

M. Coetzee (Eds.), *Theory, research and dynamics of career, wellbeing* (pp. 309–326). Springer International Publishing.

Musiałowska, D. (2023). *Mam ADHD, autyzm i całe spektrum możliwości. Psychoporadnik dla kobiet neuroatypowych.* JK.

National Autistic Society. (2016). *Autism facts and history.* https://www.autism.org.uk/about/what-is/myths-facts-stats.aspx

Nerenberg, J. (2022). *Neurorożnorodne. Jak żyć w świecie skrojonym nie na naszą miarę.* Wydawnictwo Krytyki Politycznej.

Ortiz, L. A. (2020). Reframing neurodiversity as competitive advantage: Opportunities, challenges, and resources for business and professional communication educators. *Business and Professional Communication Quarterly*, *83*(3), 261–284.

Podsakoff, P. M., MacKenzie, S. B., Paine, J. B., & Bachrach, D. G. (2000). Organizational citizenship behaviors: A critical review of the theoretical and empirical literature and suggestions for future research. *Journal of Management*, *26*, 513–569.

Priscott, T., & Allen, R. A. (2021). Human capital neurodiversity: An examination of stereotype threat anticipation. *Employee Relations*, *43*(5), 1067–1071.

Richards, J. (2012). Examining the exclusion of employees with Asperger syndrome from the workplace. *Personnel Review*, *5*, 630–646. https://doi.org/10.1108/00483481211249148

Richards, J., & Sang, K. (2016). Trade unions as employment facilitators for disabled employees. *International Journal of Human Resource Management*, *27*(14), 1642–1661.

Richards, J., Sang, K., Marks, A., & Gill, S. (2019). "I've found it extremely draining" emotional labour and the lived experience of line managing neurodiversity. *Personnel Review*, *48*(7), 1903–1923.

Rożnowski, B., & Fortuna, P. (2020). *Psychologia biznesu*. PWN.

Saks, A. M. (2006). Antecedents and consequences of employee engagement. *Journal of Management Psychology*, *21*(7), 600–619.

Schaufeli, W. B., & Salanova, M. (2011). Work engagement: On how to better catch a slippery concept. *European Journal of Work and Organizational Psychology*, *20*(1), 39–46.

Schaufeli, W. B., Salanova, M., Gonzalez-Romá, V. A., & Bakker, A. B. (2002). Te measurement of engagement and burnout: A two-sample confirmatory factor analytic approach. *Journal of Happiness Studies*, *3*, 71–92.

Singer, J. (1998). *Odd people in: The birth of community amongst people on the "autistic spectrum": A personal exploration of a new social movement based on neurological diversity*. University of Technology.

Smith-Spark, J. H., Gordon, R., & Jansari, A. S. (2023). The impact of developmental dyslexia on workplace cognition: Evidence from a virtual reality environment. *Behaviour & Information Technology*, *42*(3), 269–277.

Snowling, M. J., Adams, J. W., Bowyer-Crane, C., & Tobin, V. A. (2000). Levels of literacy among juvenile offenders: The incidence of specific reading difficulties. *Criminal Behaviour and Mental Health*, *10*, 229–241. https://doi.org/10.1002/cbm.362

Sonnenschein, W. (1997). *The practical executive and workforce diversity*. NTC Business Books.

Spoor, J. R., Flower, R. L., Bury, S. M., & Hedley, D. (2021). Employee engagement and commitment to two Australian autism employment programs: Associations with workload and perceived supervisor support. *Equality Diversity and Inclusion*. Retrieved May 14, 2024, from https://doi.org/10.1108/EDI05-2020-0132

Stroińska, E. (2017). Blaski i cienie zarządzania wiekiem – raport z badań. In K. Wojaszczyk (Ed.), *Zarządzanie różnorodnością w teorii i praktyce* (pp. 19–38). Wydawnictwo SIZ.

Sumner, K. E., & Brown, T. J. (2015). Neurodiversity and human resource management: Employer challenges for applicants and employees with learning disabilities. *The Psychologist-Manager Journal*, *18*(2), 77–85. https://doi.org/10.1037/mgr0000031

Tomczak, M. (2021). Employees with autism spectrum disorders in the digitized work environment: Perspectives for the future. *Journal of Disability Policy Studies*, *31*(4), 195–205.

Tomczak, M. (2023). *Neuroróżnorodność w miejscu pracy.* https://swps.pl/oferta/warszawa/podyplomowe/psychologia-psychoterapia/neuroroznorodnosc-w-miejscu-pracy-inkluzywna-rekrutacja-i-zarzadzanie

Walkowiak, E. (2021). Neurodiversity of the workforce and digital transformation: The case of inclusion of autistic workers at the workplace. *Technological Forecasting and Social Change*, *168*, 1–11.

Whelpley, Ch. E., & Perrault, E. (2021). Autism at work: How internal and external factors influence employee outcomes and firm performance. *Journal of General Management*, *46*(3), 210–219.

# 10 Remote Work Engagement

## How to Support It?

*Justyna Pawlak and Renata Winkler*

### Introduction

In the era of digital transformation and flexible work models, work performed away from the seat of the organization, using information and communications technologies (ICT) has become an indispensable element of the modern business environment. Depending on its various forms, it may be called telework, home office, work-at-home, mobile work, virtual work, remote work, or distance work. In the context of this dynamic transformation, the issue of remote employee work engagement and especially of how organizations can provide efficient support to group of workers has become essential for the success of the organization. The research on work engagement conducted thus far was mainly directed toward non-teleworkers (see Lesener et al., 2019). The literature offers a series of paper on the issue (Van Roekel et al., 2023; Bakker, 2022; Fortuin et al., 2021; Borst et al., 2020; Eldor, 2016; Tims et al., 2011; Christian et al., 2011; Hakanen & Roodt, 2010). Relatively little, however, is known about the ways to enhance the work engagement of employees who show up at the offices of their organizations rarely or never.

In spite of its advantages, remote work can lead to the emergence of numerous challenges for managers who attempt to increase work engagement of their employees. The lack of direct contact with the team, difficulties in communicating, and a sense of isolation can negatively impact the sense of belonging to the organization and performance of teleworkers. Hence, there is an urgent need to develop an understanding of the determinants of work engagement among people who work outside the organization's premises and create efficient management strategies for this aspect of work.

In light of the above, this chapter aims to gain an in-depth insight into the phenomenon of engagement in remote work and identify the factors influencing the level of this engagement. To accomplish this goal, a two-step research method has been developed. First, a systematic literature review was conducted. This enabled the authors to determine the variables that influence the work engagement of remote employees, established in the research conducted to date.

DOI: 10.4324/9781032715407-11

Subsequently, the qualitative research was designed and carried out with the use of in-depth, semi-structured interviews aimed to identify and understand the factors significant from the point of view of organizational strategies and practices for the components of engagement in its respective dimensions. Consequently, it became possible to develop a catalog of proposals and recommended solutions for managerial problems related to stimulating and maintaining remote work engagement.

## Determinants of Remote Work Engagement in Light of Previous Research

For the purpose of the considerations presented here, work engagement is understood according to the account of Schaufeli and Bakker (2004), who outlined engagement in terms of its three main aspects, defined as positive work-related mental and physical states of employees. These are vigor, dedication, and absorption. Vigor, that is, energy and resilience toward work tasks, refers to employees' willingness to undertake activities for the benefit of the organization and expend effort on the duties assigned to them, as well as their perseverance in spite of difficulties. Dedication, that is, positive attitude and loyalty toward one's responsibilities, determines employees' identification with the goals and values of the organization, their enthusiasm, sense of meaning, inspiration, and pride. Absorption, that is the level of employees' immersion in job tasks, corresponds to how much employees are absorbed in their work, how hard it is for them to detach themselves from it, and the extent to which they do not perceive the passage of time at work.

To realize the goal set out in the study, as a first stage of the work, a systematic review of literature (Lenart-Gansiniec, 2021) was conducted to identify the output on topics related to remote work engagement. It was performed in two bibliographic and bibliometric databases: Scopus (by Elsevier) and Web of Science (WoS) (by Clarivate Analytics). Within the WoS database, the review was performed in the range of Core Collection within the SSCI. On the basis of a preliminary analysis of the literature on the subject, a subset of headwords was compiled for each of the main issues (engagement and remote work). Considering the study objective, a search string was developed in such a way so as not to include publications focused directly on pandemic-related issues in the pool of search results. The review was limited to open access papers published in English in academic journals in the fields of Psychology, Management, Economics, and Sociology. The detailed account of the search query is presented in Table 10.1. The search did not specify publication date limits. Eventually (June 04, 2023), having verified abstracts and eliminated papers whose content did not align with the review goal, the authors qualified 13 items.

The literature review conducted allowed for the selection of crucial factors for successful remote work. Panteli et al. (2019), while researching the work of

*Table 10.1* The data on the systematic literature reviews

| *Inclusion criteria* | | *Scopus* | *Web of Science* |
|---|---|---|---|
| **(I)** Subset of headwords (for ***engagement***) | "employee engagement" OR "work* engagement" OR "job engagement," OR "orgni?ational engagement" | *Article title* (4443) | *Title* (3809) |
| *AND* | | | |
| **(II)** Subset of headwords (for ***remote work***) | "telework*" OR "telecommut*" OR "e-commut*" OR "home office" OR "based work*" OR "work*-at-home" OR "work* from home" OR "WFH" OR "mobile work*" OR "virtual work*" OR "mobile virtual work*" OR "MVW" OR "work* from anywhere" OR "WFA" OR "remote work*" OR "work* remotely" OR "e-work*" OR "digital work*" OR "new ways of work*" OR "newWoW" OR "job 2.0" OR "distance work*" | *Article title, Abstract, Keywords* (131) | *Topic* (126) |
| *AND NOT* | | | |
| **(III)** Subset of headwords (for pandemic) | "COVID*" OR "pandemic" | *Article title* (98) | *Title* (95) |
| *AND NOT* | | | |
| **(IV)** Subset of headwords (for pandemic) | "COVID" OR "pandemic" | *Keywords* (87) | *Author Keywords* (90) |
| **Exclusion criteria** | | | |
| Document types | Limited to *Article* | (72) | (83) |
| Languages | Limited to *English* | (71) | (81) |
| Publication stage | Limited to *Final* | (64) | (75) |
| Open access | Limited to *all open access* | (42) | *(48)* |

(*Continued*)

*Table 10.1* (Continued)

| *Inclusion criteria* | | *Scopus* | *Web of Science* |
|---|---|---|---|
| Subject area | Limited to:<br>* Social Sciences, Psychology, Business, Management and Accounting, Economics, Econometrics and Finance, Engineering<br>** Psychology Applied, Management, Psychology Multidisciplinary, Business, Social Sciences Interdisciplinary, Engineering Manufacturing, Psychology, Sociology, Economics, Psychology Social | * (30) | ** (25) |
| **Preliminary base – duplicate items removed** | | 36 | |
| **Articles selected after abstract analysis** | | researcher A (14): 12 *selected, 2 inspiring*<br>researcher B (15): 14 *selected, 1 inspiring* | |
| **Base of publications selected for content analysis** | | **17** | |
| **Final base of publications (after content analysis)** | | **13*** | |
| Gerards et al. (2018), Panteli et al. (2019), Vayre and Vonthron (2019), Duque et al. (2020), Toth et al. (2020, 2021), Canavesi and Minelli (2022), Mäkikangas et al. (2022), Sanhokwe (2022), Wang et al. (2022), Hizam et al. (2023), Ugwu et al. (2023), Wang et al. (2023) | | | |

*Source:* Own work

temporary virtual teams (VT), as the most important determinants identified the following: salary and supportive behavior of the leader. They identified the key role played in such teams by leaders who can actively promote work engagement through the effective use of resources that support employee development. Such support can take the form of various kinds of encouragement and adequate feedback. These scholars further claimed that "developing work engagement is not a one-off practice, but instead, requires ongoing effort that should be evident and supported across the different phases of the VT lifecycle." In the context of VT, they also considered communication media to be important, because these can play "an essential role in supporting work engagement, because it is through them that information exchange, explaining, and general support through communication occurs."

The research by Wang et al. (2023) demonstrated the major role of leadership in fostering work engagement. By analyzing how and when remote work has a negatively impacts work engagement, these researchers were able to demonstrate that the higher the level of family supportive leadership, the lesser the negative influence of home-based telework on work engagement. Furthermore, according to the results obtained by Wang's team, home-based telework has an indirect negative influence on work engagement through the chain mediating path "workplace isolation – negative emotions" and through the chain mediating path "telepressure – negative emotions." The factor that limited the observed association turned out to be family supportive leadership, which weakened the chain mediating path of "workplace isolation – negative emotion" and "telepressure – negative emotions" between home-based telework and work engagement.

The importance of effective leadership in sustaining and nourishing a high level of engagement was also pointed out by Canavesi and Minelli (2022, pp. 428–429). They believe servant leadership style to be the most desirable, as it is directed toward appreciating, strengthening, and supporting subordinates. It manifests itself in respecting the autonomy of employees, showing them recognition, providing with personal and team support, as well as encouraging them to take on new challenges and improve their work performance on a daily basis. They also single out as significant the level of team cohesion and intra-team support.

The context of leadership was also apparent in the research conducted by Gerards et al. (2018). According to them, a significant direct influence on engagement can be observed for such variables as transformational leadership and social interactions. It seems interesting, at this juncture, that in light of the results of their research on five key characteristics of the New Ways of Working (NWoW) – namely, (i) work independent of time and place, (ii) flexible work–life balance, (iii) autonomy in work delivery methods, (iv) open access to organizational knowledge, and (v) open, accessible workplace – engagement is only influenced by autonomy. No significant association was detected between engagement and work independent of time and place or flexible work–life balance. Nonetheless, the authors of the study acknowledge that access to organizational knowledge and an open, accessible workplace (albeit in and of themselves not promoting work engagement) may contribute to stimulating social interactions and transformational leadership, which are, in fact, significant for engagement. In addition, good social interactions (and, indirectly, good leadership too) proved of importance according to the results of research by Toth et al. (2020). They demonstrated that the development of remote employee work engagement is crucially dependent on virtual community trust.

Meanwhile, Hizam et al. (2023), on the basis of their research, singled out the following four major predictors of work engagement: employees' willingness to share their knowledge (Knowledge Sharing: KS), genuine organizational support aimed at improving the digital literacy of teleworking staff (Training and Development: TD), freedom (autonomy) in choosing the place where the employees decide to perform work (Employee Mobility: EM), and the level of personal sense of agency (Psychological Empowerment: PE).

The importance of the psychosocial context, including non-work resources and demands, was also pointed out by Sanhokwe (2022). His research demonstrated that non-work resources were positively associated with work engagement, whereas non-work demands had a negative correlation with work engagement. The important element here was the presence or absence of external support, as it had mitigating effect on the relation between non-work demands and work engagement. External support for non-work demands significantly lowered their negative influence on work engagement. External support played an especially significant role when variables related to gender and parenting were introduced. The relationship between gender and work engagement was insignificant when the variable of external support was introduced to the model, whereas the relationship between parenting and engagement remained negative and significant, but it approached zero with external support present.

Meanwhile, Mäkikangas et al. (2022), who analyzed longitudinal profiles of work engagement (respondent participated in the study three times over a period of 10 months), identified the following as contributors to high engagement:

- *Functionality of the house* (i.e., availability of a quiet space, appropriate equipment for virtual remote work, ergonomics, and work–life balance)
- *High level of organizational support* (encompassing: technical support for remote work and instruction on new technologies, help in creating conditions for telework, and open communication)
- *Positive assessment of one's efficacy with regard to the job performed (perceived self-efficacy)* (individuals' certainty that they possess the necessary skills to do job-related tasks and tackle professional challenges)
- *High level of workload optimization* (streamlining and/or simplifying work processes to effectively perform work, for instance, by seeking new ways of working)

The assessment of the connection between the attributes of the New Ways of Working (NWoW), Physical Environment Factors, and engagement was conducted by Duque et al. (2020). In their research, these researchers defined NWoW by attributing to it the following qualities: access to organizational knowledge, time and space flexibility, flexibility in labor relations, independent Production Management (i.e., autonomy in defining the way and pace of delivery of demands). Among Physical Environment Factors (PEF), they listed air quality, temperature, ergonomics, noise level, and lighting quality. It was established that both NWoW and PEF have a direct and positive influence on work engagement. However, even though the significance of PEF for NWoW attributes can be attested to, PEF do not moderate the relationship between NWoW and engagement. At this point, it is worth to take note of the results by Ugwu et al. (2023), who demonstrated that work engagement is positively related to home demands. At the same time, both home demands and work engagement are negatively related to work–life balance (WLB). Moreover, home demands negatively mediate the relationship between work engagement and WLB. The study points to the importance of implementing solutions that foster employees' WLB. This fact was also corroborated by Vayre and Vonthron (2019), who determined that a negative impact of work on non-working life contributes to a lower level of engagement, whereas a positive impact of work on non-working life is responsible for a higher level of engagement.

The issues related to the ability to maintain WLB with remote work and deal with WLC (work–life conflict) were also identified by Wang et al. (2022). They demonstrated that work-to-family conflict has a negative impact on both employee engagement and their innovative behaviors. Furthermore, in the light of the results they obtained, stress in the mobile workplace exacerbates work-to-family conflict. Under greater stress, employees were more prone to neglect creative work, which lowered their innovation inputs and was not insignificant for their engagement.

The significance of other factors that foster work engagement was established by Toth et al. (2021). They studied the relationship between the entrepreneurial passion for inventing (EPI) and work-related well-being, manifested as work engagement. In their research, EPI was regarded as an antecedent of work engagement, particularly in the case of modern knowledge-based work. The results of their research revealed that the impact of EPI on engagement is higher for teleworkers, for example, tech entrepreneurs and digital freelancers. The findings that an increase in work demands may have a highly positive impact on well-being, which then manifests as engagement, can be of particular value for management practitioners. In the case of high performing people with passion for inventing, the research showed great importance of judicious task allocation, as increased work demands mediated the relationship between passion for inventing and work engagement, enhancing the latter.

The literature review allowed us to determine that there are some factors in the domain discussed thus far as significant for remote work should be highlighted.

Supportive leadership behaviors and the ability to maintain WLB were indicated most often. Additionally, there was focus on the importance of: salary, autonomy in choosing the place of work, optional availability of space within the premises of the organization, access to organizational knowledge, access to training activities aimed at improving the digital literacy of teleworking staff, technical support for remote work, a level of workload optimization (streamlining and/or simplifying work processes to effectively perform work, for instance, by seeking new ways of working), adequate feedback, autonomy in work delivery methods, knowledge sharing among employees, as well as issues related to the physical environment of work settings. It should be emphasized, however, that some of the shortlisted factors, as far as employees' position within the company and coordination of remote work is concerned, may largely depend on the decisions of superiors. This means that leaders' influence is not only limited to their relationship with their subordinates but also reflected in their organizational decisions that shape the work environment.

## Determinants of Remote Work Engagement in Light of Original Research

At the second stage of the study, it was decided to conduct qualitative research using an in-depth, semi-structured interview. The choice of this type of interview was dictated by its relatively high psychometric quality, while at the same time providing flexibility and the ability to establish a deeper connection with the person under study (King et al., 2018; Oltman, 2016). The procedure entailed the following steps: (i) developing the strategy for participant selection, (ii) designing the interview script, (iii) conducting the interview, (iv) transcribing the interviews, (v) analyzing the data obtained.

Nine respondents were selected to be recruited for the study. The conditions for inclusion in the study were defined in the following way: having experience with remote work outside of the pandemic period (of at least two years), current remote employment in a large- or medium-sized enterprise, high level of remote work engagement. Due to the explorative character of the study, it was concluded that taking into consideration a variety of contexts for remote work would allow for a more comprehensive picture of the factors influencing work engagement among remote workers. During the recruitment process of respondents, therefore, attempts were made to include the largest variety possible in terms of age, family commitments, the scope of remote work, and organizational structures for remote work. The level of candidates' engagement was evaluated using the Utrecht Work Engagement Scale (UWES) questionnaire.

The respondents qualified for the study (cf. Table 10.2) worked remotely from their places of residence, with seven people working on a full-time basis (100%), one on a semi-full-time basis (80%), and one on a hybrid basis (20%, i.e., a day of remote work per week).

*Table 10.2* Background characteristics of respondents

| *Identification no.* | *Gender* | *Age* | *Percent of the time working remotely* | *Team** | *Children* |
|---|---|---|---|---|---|
| K48/100/3 | K | 48 | 100% | V | + |
| M45/80/4 | M | 45 | 80% | H | + |
| M45/20/2 | M | 45 | 20% | V/H | + |
| K45/100/2 | K | 45 | 100% | V/H | + |
| M43/100/2 | M | 43 | 100% | V | + |
| K41/100/0 | F | 41 | 100% | V | - |
| F32/100/0 | F | 32 | 100% | V | - |
| F31/100/0 | F | 31 | 100% | V | - |
| F21/100/0 | F | 21 | 100% | V/H | - |

***V = everyone remote, H = everyone hybrid, V/H = someone hybrid/someone remote**

*Source:* Own research

In the selected group of respondents, four people were childless, while five had children. The number of children ranged from two to four, while the age difference between offspring living with respondents was 16 years. Importantly, five respondents worked in completely virtual teams, whereas four people in teams with some colleagues worked on a hybrid basis. All respondents exhibited high or very high levels of engagement. As for the components of engagement (vigor, dedication, and absorption), five interviewees recorded their highest scores for dedication, two for vigor, and another two for absorption. An overwhelming majority of respondents opted for a remote form of employment because they felt that the range of opportunities for adjusting work to their personal preferences and lifestyle presented by this type of work was greater.

In the context of the study goal, the definition of engagement adopted, and in light of the analysis of the results yielded by the literature review, the set of questions for the interview script was centered on: (i) *evaluating the respondent's employment circumstances*, (ii) *diagnosing the respondent's individual level of engagement* (to exclude disengaged employees), and (iii) *exploring the factors significant for remote work engagement*. Employment circumstances were assessed in terms of each of the respondents' job description, their remote working hours, the place and conditions in which they performed their professional duties, the scope of the autonomy granted to them by their organizations with regard to the selection of place and remote working hours – and whether or not their family situation was assessed as favorable for remote work. The battery of questions aimed at exploring the factors significant for remote work engagement referred to the aspects of engagement identified in the UWES instrument, that is, vigor, dedication, and absorption. The respondents were asked to both describe situations in which they experienced the states of engagement specified in the questionnaire[1] and indicate what they believed to be the crucial, important, and supportive elements of a given issue. They were also asked to elaborate on the significance of the activities performed by the organization, the executive staff, and colleagues, and of the material aspects of the workplace for promoting work engagement in its three dimensions.

Depending on the respondents' availability, the interviews were conducted in-person or remotely. Each interview was recorded. A single interview lasted approximately 70 minutes. The material collected was transcribed, and the transcripts were then subject to qualitative content analysis. The transcripts of respondents' statements were analyzed by two researchers independently. They endeavored to evaluate the factors significant for each of the specified aspects of engagement and isolate the leadership behaviors that the respondents recognized as stimulating for their work engagement.

### *Engagement Determinants: Vigor*

In the context of the analysis of this dimension of engagement, what the respondents identified as crucial were mainly the issues related to flexibility in a broad sense (both understood as the freedom in managing their time, and the unrestricted choice of the workplace) and the autonomy at work (in the way of performing job tasks).

> Well. . . , I'm motivated to get up and start working remotely when I can, say, visit my mum and telework from her home. Yeah, I appreciate that this kind of work gives me greater mobility.
>
> (K41/100/0)

> Breaking this effort into various times of day, or the ability to – I don't know – take a break from work altogether, or adjust its character, really, to the other things that one may need to do during the day. . . . After all, some meetings are held later in the day, so with remote work I'm better able to adjust to any such demands.
>
> (M45/20/2)

> We don't have to get up at eight in the morning and start working, instead, we can get up at ten and work till eight in the evening.
>
> (K21/100/0)

> Whether it is me who works from the office and some members of my organization from home or the other way around, it gives me a great flexibility in deciding on, well, both the tasks and the time when to carry them out. So, in a way, this is something that motivates me to remote work.
>
> (M45/20/2)

Additionally, in the context of the factors that significantly help to maintain high levels of vigor, the respondents stressed the importance of the trust that they are given in remote work.

> When someone offers me their trust and I have much freedom on my hands, it awakens in me the responsibility for my task.
>
> (K31/100/0)

> That I am not evaluated in terms of the hours that I work but the tasks I complete.
>
> (K41/100/0)

> [He] gives us so much freedom, quite simply, with everything . . . that we can feel at ease, that we don't get those calls, saying "have you finished, already?" or "have you figured it out?"
>
> (K21/100/0)

> Trust. For we have complete trust here. . . . To tell you the truth, I am not monitored at all.
>
> (M43/100/2)

The respondents also pointed to the relational aspect that influences their work performance. It involved highlighting the significance of whether or not they feel treated as individuals, whether others express interest in them, which prevents them from feeling isolated. Another thing that they considered important was the degree to which they could experience appreciation both as direct praise and though how others (especially their leader) react to the results of their work. Also mentioned was the role of receiving (but also providing) interpersonal support.

> If a manager really did show such a positive interest in what I do and was aware that, say, on a given day I do this and that.
>
> (K32/100/0)

> If someone asks how you're doing or if you're working with someone on something, it's easier then. . . . If someone would text me: "Out of bed, already?" – generally, anything that has something to do with human interaction.
>
> (M45/80/4)

> Conversations with the chairman of the board, above all, or with the people who I cooperate with and who tell me "It's great that you've covered that!"

and "We really owe you on this one!" generally, things like that, well . . . for me it's conversation in the first place.

(K21/100/0)

A sense that I am not alone, that I've not been left with the problem to my own devices and just have to deal with it, all by myself. That there is someone – whether the manager or, or . . . other members of the team, that you can, quite simply, count on them.

(K21/100/0)

Support from the team or from the manager. Mostly, any interest taken in what I do.

(K32/100/0)

The respondents also raised the issue of conditions of the physical work environment – including a stable internet connection, equipment that works, and good acoustics for work.

I find that I work better when I'm somewhere where . . . like in this separate apartment, where I know that no-one will interrupt me anymore. After all, children can be a little distracting.

(M43/100/2)

The content and characteristics of their job tasks were also of importance for the respondents. It is worth noting that task content and meaning are among the key factors for work engagement in studies analyzing the traditional (i.e., office-based) forms of work. In this research, the respondents paid particular attention to the issues related to the meaning and reasonableness of tasks and how clearly the task itself and the demands of its completion were specified.

#### *Engagement Determinants: Dedication*

The analysis of the answers to the questions exploring the aspect of *dedication* revealed that among the most important determinants study participants ranked the sense of self-efficacy (which is itself associated with the experiences of autonomy and trust).

The feeling that you've accomplished something when you've completed a project milestone or . . . or when you've closed the entire process and see that something is working.

(M43/100/2)

When I'm able to maintain {inaudible} a high level of work productivity.

(M45/20/2)

> The fact that I know that my manager knows me and trusts me. It is all really trusted-based and he knows that I usually make good decisions, so he leaves the issue to me and this way he strengthens my belief that I'm doing ok.
>
> (K32/100/0)

They also found vital a supportive reaction of their community to the way they perform their job tasks, manifested in appreciation and positive feedback both from the leader and from colleagues.

> It has a positive influence on me that someone appreciates my work.
>
> (K32/100/0)

> Well, it's also motivating when you hear that . . . that it's great, and that you've one something really cool.
>
> (M43/100/2)

> It has a positive effect on me when someone acknowledges my work. . . , when they come back with this positive feedback, saying they are really pleased with me, that I committed to something and actually helped them.
>
> (K32/100/0)

> People tell me they enjoy working with me, that they feel comfortable, that they appreciate the atmosphere I created, the freedom I grant them, that they value my management style.
>
> (K41/100/0)

Furthermore, the persons studied also valued their flexibility understood as the ability to manage their own time and the freedom to "arrange their lives," which they defined as the ability to successfully combine their personal lives with work.

> This job suits me, because I'm able to organize my life; . . . as far as time management is concerned. And organize my days in general – without wasting much time. This really is a great advantage here.
>
> (M43/100/2)

> It's when I can perform my work whenever I want and in whatever conditions I want.
>
> (K21/100/0)

> Flexibility is the decisive factor, alongside the possibility to adjust my working hours to the rest of my day.
>
> K41/100/0

Another factor that enhances engagement in terms of dedication were employee relationships of providing one another with mutual support because of the ability to give support and receive the support from others, as well as task qualities, which, according to the studied group, should be interesting, meaningful, and useful.

#### *Engagement Determinants: Absorption*

The analysis of the research results on the determinants of the final of engagement, that is, absorption, demonstrated that the respondents indicated as the most significant their sense of self-efficacy, that is, the sense that there are visible effects of their actions, that there is process, and that subsequent tasks are getting closed.

> When I have the results.
>
> (M45/20/2)

> Supposing there is a huge cumulation of work and I plan everything out so that I am really able to, well . . ., to complete all my tasks, at the moment when I have, all that pressure goes down and I feel genuinely happy.
>
> (K32/100/0)

> When I go into this overdrive mode . . . this period of very intense work, I don't think about anything else, I just focus on what I'm doing. Then, afar I've completed such a heavy, heavy workload, I have this feeling that . . . that I've done what I was supposed to do, and suddenly there's no backlog, everything is up-to-date, and I can get some peaceful rest.
>
> (K21/100/0)

At this juncture, some described having the experience of flow (or zone) and a total immersion in work.

> I have this thing that when I start tinkering with something, I tinker on and on until . . . I've figured the thing out. Sometimes, I catch myself that it's already one in the afternoon, and I haven't had breakfast, even though I sat down to work at nine.
>
> (M43/100/2)

> When nothing else distracts me . . . and I don't have to split my time between work tasks and other things and can allow myself instead to, as it were, get carried away by it.
>
> (K21/100/0)

Respondents further emphasized that in order to be able to experience such profound absorption, one needs to be allowed silence and an uninterrupted course of work. Some of them also found it crucial to have a well-organized workplace, as well as seamlessly working equipment and internet connection.

The type of tasks performed, as expected, proved significant with regard to this aspect too, as these should be meaningful, interesting, and at times, additionally, stimulating development.

> Challenging me with these non-trivial problems that fall either on the limit or slightly beyond the limit of my knowledge and my comfort zone.
>
> (M45/80/4)

In light of the respondents' statements, another major factor identified was that of positive feedback from colleagues and a sense that what one is doing has a good effect on others. Some mentioned "cheering each other on." Other things highlighted were the availability of colleagues and their readiness to help, that is, a sense of being able to count on their support. What is significant, some of the persons interviewed stated that this aspect of engagement stems from their aptitude.

> It's this sense of responsibility of mine.
>
> (K41/100/0)

> It is not their task, it is, in my opinion, absolutely my task.
>
> (K32/100/0)

> My mental condition, my attitude.
>
> (M45/80/4)

It should be noted that, although the study participants identified slightly different issues for each factor, they tended to give shorter answers to subsequent questions, indicating that they had already mentioned some related items.

### *The Leader's Role*

After a series of questions aimed at exploring the situations in which the persons under study experience engagement in its three dimensions discussed, and having identified the critical factors in these domains, the questionnaire moved on to ask about the role of the leader in nurturing work engagement. The analysis of the responses revealed that with regard to vigor, the study participants predominantly identified making space for autonomous activities and flexibility:

> I have this little advantage that my work is subject to no control whatsoever . . . so I don't feel much pressure, I don't feel treated like a caged animal, I'm not subject to any exaggerated outside monitoring. . . . [My manager]

> could simply remain the way he is, showing me trust and treating me like a partner, by which I mean evaluating my tasks for their completion, not in terms of a specific time frame of my performing them.
>
> (K41/100/0)

> [The manager] gives us so much freedom, quite simply, with everything . . . that we can feel at ease, that we don't get those calls, saying "have you finished, already?" or "have you figured it out?" – just the regular self-discipline. . . . We have no supervisor poring over our work . . . checking whether we completed the task, instead we can be our own masters and, so to speak, settle the accounts ourselves.
>
> (K21/100/0)

The respondents stressed the importance of support, manifest as showing friendly interest and exercising tolerance of errors.

> Above all, some interest in what I do . . . if a manager really did show such a positive interest in what I do and was aware that, say, on a given day I do this and that.
>
> (K32/100/0)

> Well, yes, the manager could simply write: "Hello, Kowalski, so how are you doing out there?" Some form of small talk with the manager.
>
> (M45/100/4)

> The most important thing is a kind word from the superiors, and the fact that I can do it, that I know that I can have this support.
>
> (K/45/100/2)

It should be pointed out that with a dispersed team, the manager often working from abroad, and at times even from another continent, such an interest also means their readiness to delve into the context of an employee's work:

> If only [my manager] had the knowledge of the market and of what I specifically do; it would be so helpful.
>
> (K32/100/0)

> It's like, people from different countries have different attitudes to certain activities, because these may look very different there, and they are different here too.
>
> (K45/100/2)

As far as dedication is concerned, the support for engagement can be carried out on several levels. Most importantly, the leader should make effort to build the team, which in the case of remote and dispersed teams presents a far greater challenge both in terms of ensuring concurrent availability and applying the same fair rules to everybody.

> It is a challenge to build the team when it's dispersed.
>
> (M45/20/10-14)

> Paying attention to the people who work remotely. Because sometimes people who work remotely do not have a sense of . . . belonging to the organization.
>
> (K41/100/0)

> And this is also a matter of . . . non-discrimination, so that teleworkers are not discriminated against in any way, i.e., in that they do not get promoted, etc.
>
> (M43/100/5-5)

The study participants also pointed to elements of management style that supports engagement, which should be characterized by offering autonomy and trust, and "the lack of excessive formalization and control," as well as "*good task scheduling*, clearly defined demands, precisely determined execution time" (M45/20/13), and "delegating things that will truly prove useful over time" (K41/100/0).

Other things that the respondents highlighted were the importance of feedback and the indication of the results of an employee's activity that sometimes could be imperceptible through "revealing my actual influence" (M45/80/4). The respondents also mentioned having personalized conversations about the opportunities related to their career paths (M45/80/4; K32/100/0) and support from the direct supervisor (K45/100/2).

Manager–employee relationships based on trust also proved vital for enhancing engagement in the domain of absorption:

> [The manager] gives me total freedom and in a way shows having trust in me, that I will accomplish what I'm supposed to. . . . No one likes being put under the microscope.
>
> (K41/100/0)

> It would certainly entail lowering or reducing the number of control points to the absolute minimum.
>
> (M45/20/2)

Furthermore, there were mentions of providing opportunities to build the team and a sense of belonging, for example, by holding informal team meetings or providing a platform for expressing opinions.

> I see that sort of climate and culture building here.
>
> (M45/100/4)

> I like, for instance, being informed about various things. When someone calls me and, say, wants to get to know my opinion about something. And then .... I no longer feel so excluded, not knowing what goes on in the organization.
>
> (K21/100/0)

The answers given by the respondents to the questions about absorption mainly highlighted the importance of comfortable working conditions that promote concentration. Hence, managers were expected not to overload employees with an excessive number of tasks and but to safeguard their uninterrupted work time.

> Being aware that, say, when I focus on a very important task, which may engross me, the leader could say to all my colleagues, something in the vein of: "Give her a moment, as it were, give her some space – she needs it right now – so try not to involve her in anything else, because she's busy, end of story."
>
> (K21/100/0)

Thus, the results gathered obtained that regarding the leader's behaviors and support is crucial for triggering and maintaining remote work engagement. The following crucial tasks that leaders face have been established:

- Making space for autonomy and flexibility
- Showing friendly interest and readiness to delve into the (social – legal – economic) context the person works in
- Building the team and a sense of belonging
- Offering trust
- Good task scheduling
- Providing adequate and supportive feedback
- Effort made to ensure comfortable work conditions that foster concentration

The undertaking of these tasks was recognized by the study participants as supportive for their engagement in all its dimensions.

## Discussion and Recommendations

The results of the study enable us to draw some very interesting conclusions. The data obtained from the responses of the interviewees partly overlap with those gathered at the stage of SLR, focused squarely on remote work, and the results reported by studies on the determinants of work engagement (regardless of whether or not they covered remote work).

According to Van Roekel et al. (2023), it has thus far been established that the pool of factors significant for on-site work as crucial determinants of work engagement includes both qualities of the work environment (e.g., support from colleagues, nature of tasks, and autonomy) and the leadership style (positive relationships with superiors, transformational leadership). The role of engaging leadership, defined as a leader's behavior that facilitates, strengthens, unites, and inspires employees in order to enhance their work engagement, was also emphasized by Schaufeli (2021). Also, the research work by Tims et al. (2011) demonstrated the importance of manager's support and transformational behaviors for work engagement, underscoring the significance of stimulating employee autonomy. In studies dedicated to remote work, meanwhile, the value of leadership was validated by Canavesi and Minelli (2022) and Wang et al. (2023).

Additionally, Halbesleben (2010) pointed to the importance of feedback, positive organizational climate, and the sense of self-efficacy. Graham et al. (2023) complemented this perspective by placing emphasis on the role of a sense of community and social support in generating high levels of work engagement. For remote work, the importance of feedback was attested to by Panteli et al. (2019), of self-efficacy by Mäkikangas et al. (2022), whereas of the presence of good social interactions by Toth et al. (2020).

All the above factors did appear in the casual answers given by the respondents in our survey; however, also observed was the emergence of new factors, which modern managers should take into consideration. Thus, in light of the analysis of the collected responses provided by the study participants, a set of activities can be recommended for stimulating and maintaining high remote work engagement (both in the aspect of *vigor*, *dedication*, and *absorption*).

On the organizational level, we should first note a contextual aspect of work itself, one that possibly constitutes a necessary – albeit not sufficient – condition for remote work. Namely, the issue of resources such as the equipment and tools, that is, software, provided. It should be emphasized here that in this case, employee equipment gradually comes to play a vital role not only for the technical problem of efficient (tool-oriented) performance of the employed staff but also in the domain of subjective feelings toward the perceived degree of personalized contact with the employer. A similar role came to also be attributed to the access to formal and constant technical support for the remotely employed workforce. In both these instances (equipment and technical support), it is recommended to acknowledge an increase in the rank of the two factors. For some workers, the introduction of financial assistance to cover the additional costs incurred by working from home may have not as much a financial as personal dimension to it.

What should be underscored regarding the actual organizational aspect is the need to develop a culture of remote work based on trust. The implementation of elaborate forms of employee control is detrimental to remote work engagement. Personal experiences and expectations of the respondents indicated their preference for tasked-based systems. The task-based working system is positively evaluated by the respondents also as a facilitator of maintaining work–life balance (as indicated above, the majority of participants saw this aspect as the basic motivation for undertaking the studied form of employment). Within the discussed aspect, it seems reasonable to additionally implement regular activities to: (i) increase the degree of employees' personalized contact with the employer, and (ii) minimize their sense of isolation. The introduction of tasks of this kind, aimed at facilitating (group or pair) interactions, for example, as meetings devoted mainly to team (relationship) building, should not be of a "purely" professional (task-oriented) nature. Forms to be considered include micro-training sessions, series of one-on-one meetings, and conducting social micro-projects.

The use of communication media and the structure of the communication system should be seen as factors that can significantly support work engagement. It must be stressed, however, that without being directed toward support, without activity within the interpersonal system, they cannot perform their function. Hence, the spotlight here is on the leader.

The research conducted has certain limitations, which should be considered. First, it should be noted that, even though the study was conducted among persons employed predominantly in large international corporations, it included only Polish respondents, which in and of itself may be a barrier to universalizing its results. Second, because of the exploratory character of the study, its conclusions should be interpreted with caution. In the future, it is worth considering the need to conduct quantitative research in the said field aimed, among other things, at ranking the importance of the factors identified for enhancing engagement in all three of its aspects separately.

## Conclusion

This chapter discussed the influence of factors stimulating work engagement on remote work, considering each of the three dimensions suggested by Schaufeli and Bakker (2004): absorption, dedication, and vigor. The SLR conducted revealed that the literature and research work on the topic have thus far been relatively scarce. It also allowed for the identification of the scope of it that had already been researched and the factors that should be recognized when interpreting the qualitative data. The qualitative research conducted in this field both corroborated the existing results of the studies on the determinants of engagement and helped identify new domains of significance for fostering remote employees work engagement. It attested to the importance of building and supporting dispersed teams and nurturing a sense of team belonging, while at the same time safeguarding autonomy. Furthermore, the research highlighted the value of support for remote employees' ability to focus on their work and of responding to the needs of flexible work scheduling and workplace selection, as these contribute to the increased capacity to maintain work–life balance. The provision of an adequately equipped workplace (including software), access to organizational knowledge, and effective communication channels also turned out to be crucial factors.

The research is significant for two major reasons. First, faced with the increase in remote work, the understanding of the factors supporting work engagement within this form of employment becomes indispensable for organizations to successfully manage human resources and achieve the desired results. Second, they indicate new areas for intervention and managerial practices which may prove crucial for maintaining work engagement among teleworkers. Thus, they may offer practical implications for companies striving to enhance the levels of engagement of their remote workers.

## Note

1. "What situations make you . . . ": . . . feel bursting with energy; . . . feel strong and vigorous; . . . enthusiastic about yours job; . . . feel inspired by your job; . . . get up in the morning, feeling like going to work; . . . feel happy when you are working intensely; . . . proud of the work that you do; . . . feel immersed in yours work; . . . get carried away when you are working.

## References


Bakker, A. B. (2022). The social psychology of work engagement: State of the field. *Career Development International*, *27*(1), 36–53. https://doi.org/10.1108/CDI-08-2021-0213

Borst, R. T., Kruyen, P. M., Lako, C. J., & de Vries, M. S. (2020). The attitudinal, behavioral, and performance outcomes of work engagement: A comparative meta-analysis across the public, semipublic, and private sector. *Review of Public Personnel Administration*, *40*(4), 613–640. https://doi.org/10.1177/0734371X19840399

Canavesi, A., & Minelli, E. A. (2022). Servant leadership and employee engagement: A qualitative study. *Employee Responsibilities and Rights Journal*, *34*, 413–435. https://doi.org/10.1007/s10672-021-09389-9

Christian, M. S., Garza, A. S., & Slaughter, J. E. (2011). Work engagement: A quantitative review and test of its relations with task and contextual performance. *Personnel Psychology*, *64*(1), 89–136. https://doi.org/10.1111/j.1744-6570.2010.01203.x

Duque, L., Costa, R., Dias, Á., Pereira, L., Santos, J., & António, N. (2020). New ways of working and the physical environment to improve employee engagement. *Sustainability*, *12*, 6759. https://doi.org/10.3390/su12176759

Eldor, L. (2016). Work engagement: Toward a general theoretical enriching model. *Human Resource Development Review*, *15*, 317–339. https://doi.org/10.1177/1534484316655666

Fortuin, D. J., van Mierlo, H., Bakker, A. B., Petrou, P., & Demerouti, E. (2021). Team boosting behaviours: Development and validation of a new concept and scale. *European Journal of Work and Organizational Psychology*, *30*(4), 600–618. https://doi.org/10.1080/1359432X.2020.1854226

Gerards, R., de Grip, A., & Baudewijns, C. (2018). Do new ways of working increase work engagement? *Personnel Review*, *47*(2), 517–534. https://doi.org/10.1108/PR-02-2017-0050

Graham, M., Lambert, K. A., Weale, V., Stuckey, R., & Oakman, J. (2023). Working from home during the COVID 19 pandemic: A longitudinal examination of employees' sense of community and social support and impacts on self-rated health. *BMC Public Health*, *23*(1), 11.

Hakanen, J. J., & Roodt, G. (2010). Using the job demands-resources model to predict engagement: Analysing a conceptual model. In A. B. Bakker & M. P. Leiter (Eds.), *Work engagement: A handbook of essential theory and research* (pp. 85–101). Psychology Press.

Halbesleben, J. R. B. (2010). A meta-analysis of work engagement: Relationships with burnout, demands, resources, and consequences. In A. B. Bakker & M. P. Leiter (Eds.), *Work engagement: A handbook of essential theory and research* (pp. 102–117). Psychology Press.

Hizam, S. M., Akter, H., Sentosa, I., Ahmed, W., Masrek, M. N., & Ali, J. (2023). Predicting workforce engagement towards digital transformation through a multi-analytical approach. *Sustainability*, *15*, 6835. https://doi.org/10.3390/su15086835

King, N., Horrocks, Ch., & Brooks, J. (2018). *Interviews in qualitative research* (2nd ed., pp. 1–360). Sage.

Lenart-Gansiniec, R. (2021). *Systematyczny przegląd literatury w naukach społecznych.* Wydawnictwo Naukowe Scholar.

Lesener, T., Gusy, B., Jochmann, A., & Wolter, C. (2019). The drivers of work engagement: A meta-analytic review of longitudinal evidence. *Work & Stress*, *34*(3), 259–278. https://doi.org/10.1080/02678373.2019.1686440

Mäkikangas, A., Juutinen, S., Mäkiniemi, J.-P., Sjöblom, K., & Oksanen, A. (2022). Work engagement and its antecedents in remote work: A person-centered view. *Work & Stress*, *36*(4), 392–416. https://doi.org/10.1080/02678373.2022.2080777

Oltman, M. S. (2016). Qualitative interviews: A methodological discussion of the interviewer and respondent contexts. *Forum: Qualitative Social Research*, *17*(2), 1–16. https://doi.org/10.17169/fqs-17.2.2551

Panteli, N., Yalabik, Z. Y., & Rapti, A. (2019). Fostering work engagement in geographically-dispersed and asynchronous virtual teams. *Information Technology & People*, *32*(1), 2–17. https://doi.org/10.1108/ITP-04-2017-0133

Sanhokwe, H. (2022). The influence of nonwork resources, nonwork demands and external support on work engagement and productivity: A moderated mediation model. *SA Journal of Industrial Psychology/SA Tydskrif vir Bedryfsielkunde*, *48*, a1957. https://doi.org/10.4102/sajip.v48i0.1957

Schaufeli, W. (2021). Engaging leadership: How to promote work engagement? *Frontiers in Psychology*, *12*, 754556. https://doi.org/10.3389/fpsyg.2021.754556

Schaufeli, W. B., & Bakker, A. B. (2004). *UWES. Utrecht Work Engagement Scale. Preliminary manual. Version 1.1.* Occupational Health Psychology Unit. https://www.wilmarschaufeli.nl/publications/Schaufeli/Test%20Manuals/Test_manual_UWES_English.pdf

Tims, M., Bakker, A. B., & Xanthopoulou, D. (2011). Do transformational leaders enhance their followers' daily work engagement? *The Leadership Quarterly*, *22*, 121–131.

Toth, I., Heinänen, S., & Blomqvist, K. (2020). Freelancing on digital work platforms – Roles of virtual community trust and work engagement on person–job fit. *VINE Journal of Information and Knowledge Management Systems*, *50*(4), 553–567. https://doi.org/10.1108/VJIKMS-12-2018-0124

Toth, I., Heinänen, S., & Puumalainen, K. (2021). Passionate and engaged? Passion for inventing and work engagement in different knowledge work contexts. *International Journal of Entrepreneurial Behavior & Research*, *27*(9), 1–25. https://doi.org/10.1108/IJEBR-09-2020-0632

Ugwu, F. O., Enwereuzor, I. K., & Mazei, J. (2023). Is working from home a blessing or a burden? Home demands as a mediator of the relationship between work engagement and work-life balance, applied research in quality of life. *International Society for Quality-of-Life Studies*, *18*(1), 341–364.

Van Roekel, H., Wigger, E. F. J., Veldkamp, B. P., & Bakker, A. B. (2023). What is work engagement? A text mining approach using employees' self-narratives. *Applied Psychology, 73*, 1071–1102. https://doi.org/10.1111/apps.12501.

Vayre, E., & Vonthron, A.-M. (2019). Identifying work-related internet's uses – At work and outside usual workplaces and hours – And their relationships with work-home interface, work engagement, and problematic internet behavior. *Frontiers in Psychology, 10*, 2118. https://doi.org/10.3389/fpsyg.2019.02118

Wang, H., Xiao, Y., Wang, H., Zhang, H., & Chen, X. (2023). "Who knows me understands my needs": The effect of home-based telework on work engagement. *Psychology Research and Behavior Management, 16*, 619–635. https://doi.org/10.2147/PRBM.S402159

Wang, X., Zhang, Z., & Chun, D. (2022). How does mobile workplace stress affect employee innovative behavior? The role of work–family conflict and employee engagement. *Behaviora Sciences, 12*(2). https://doi.org/10.3390/bs12010002

# Conclusions

*Małgorzata Adamska-Chudzińska and Justyna Pawlak*

In a rapidly changing business environment, employee engagement becomes one of the crucial factors influencing the success of the organization. Indeed, a high level of engagement leads to increased productivity, creativity, and loyalty, which has a positive bearing on the organization's competitiveness. It is, therefore, more and more often that companies create work environments that support building and maintaining engagement. However, this task has become all the more difficult in light of the fact that organizational attachment has recently been observed to fall whereas employee attachment to increasingly fluctuate, which leads to various forms of the "quiet quitting" phenomenon, manifesting itself in reduced employee efforts and performance limited to the bare minimum requirements. In response to these challenges, organizations must seek adequate methods to support engagement and motivate their teams. Thus, it has become essential to assess the effectiveness of the tools and practices used so far and to develop and appraise new ones.

It should be emphasized, however, that it would be short sighted to focus solely on developing more or less advanced motivation, reward, or monitoring systems, as employee engagement is a phenomenon rooted in the personality traits of an individual and closely related to their system of values, this way influencing their work behavior. The level of such engagement is largely determined by a complex interplay of psychosocial factors, such as, among others, the experience of well-being in the workplace (including a sense of meaningfulness of work tasks), organizational culture, quality of relationships with superiors, psychological person–job fit, and the alignment of employees' organizational goals with their personal goals. Understanding these factors is vital for maximizing employee potential and building a productive and harmonious workplace.

In the account of engagement selected in this contributed volume, namely, work engagement, it is defined as work engagement as a positive state of mind that is characterized by high levels of energy for long-term work. It is a multi-component construct, which emerges in the context of employees' dynamic relations with various aspects of their work environment. Work engagement develops within the emotional sphere of an employee and is shaped by

DOI: 10.4324/9781032715407-12

the social relations and the material and physical conditions in a work environment that impact well-being. It is conditioned by the organizational methods of employee engagement management, including transformational leadership style and creating a suitable work environment. All these levels, when appropriately synchronized, enable employees to experience psychological presence at work, which is crucial for generating the engagement of the human capital.

This contributed volume addresses the problem of building and maintaining work engagement in the context of what the authors believe to be the most important psychosocial determinants, which constitute currently the most interesting factor regulating and supporting the employee–organization relationship. It has been assumed that the experience of positive emotions in the workplace is nowadays the aspect that tends to shape the level of engagement. First, the model that defines the indicators of work engagement was developed to analyze the complex dynamics of how psychosocial support influences building employee well-being and work engagement, with the latter being determined as an intense mental state, characterized by high levels of energy, dedication, and absorption in the task at hand. This model indicates the key conditions and stimulating factors that play a major role in creating these states both on the individual level and in the organizational context. Both the preconditions – that is, job resources such as positive work climate, managerial support and supportive team atmosphere, experience of autonomy, transformational leadership, and respectful treatment – and the stimulating factors – including, among others, individual resources, human-centered organizational culture, and flexibility to allow for life circumstances – are understood as the fundamental structural and cultural elements that may influence employee well-being and, in turn, their level of engagement.

These aspects of human resource management create the framework within which employees can perform their tasks, while an adequate adjustment of these has a direct impact on their well-being, performance, and job satisfaction. Thus, through a suitable design and implementation of measures, organizations are able to actively enhance the level of work engagement among their workers, which contributes to better job performance. The model presented outlines the concept of work engagement as a result of a complex interaction between structural and procedural aspects of the organization, individual resources, and carefully designed purposeful stimulating activities. It should be underscored that the factors indicated in the model are by no means a complete list; instead, they demarcate the scope of the main psychosocial determinants of work engagement.

Starting with this model, the contributed volume discusses the various forms of psychosocial support that can significantly influence employee well-being and work engagement. Based on an in-depth analysis of literature and the results of empirical research, the book chapters present the key dimensions of such support and the ways it is manifested. Among the issues analyzed, there are both systemic measures, such as the establishment of supportive organizational culture and climate, and the care for employee work–life balance, as well as elements of an individualized approach that enables organizations to recognize and understand employee needs, support them in their current tasks, and develop their potential through suitably chosen training events. The role of managers was also highlighted as those of them who exhibit a transformational leadership style and a high level of emotional intelligence – empathy, in particular – may become a great source of support for employees and thus contribute to enhancing their work engagement too. Some attention was devoted to various perfectly tailored forms of support for various employee groups, such as remote and neurodivergent workers.

The authors stress how important it is in modern managerial practice to comprehensively understand employee needs and not only implement solutions focused on controlling the quality of the tasks performed and monitoring the accomplishment of organizational goals but, above all, also successfully build the organizational culture that, by providing adequate support, enables the activation and the best possible use of the potential of employees and then be able in a greater extent to identify themselves with these goals, the organization, and its culture.

The most important conclusions to be drawn from the research conducted shed light on the complexity of work engagement, which is a result of dynamic activity on many levels – from individual traits conceived of as personal predispositions, through organizational structures and processes, all the way to social contexts, broadly understood. Psychosocial support emerges as one of the key pillars of both well-being and engagement, which highlights the fact that successful employee management cannot exist without an in-depth understanding and addressing their emotional and social needs.

The contributed volume further demonstrates that employee well-being is the effect of both internal predispositions of the individual and the external conditions of work. The determinants of well-being are complex and require the organization to be flexible in adjusting the management practices to individual and collective employee needs. Successful management of the variety of employee needs and adjustment of the work environment contribute to improve both well-being and work engagement. Employee well-being, identified as a priority for organizational strategies, requires mangers not only to understand but, above all, also to be flexible, empathetic, and open to change. It is the response to the challenges associated with the adjustment of organizational policies to the ever-changing expectations and working conditions. Organizational culture, through its rituals, internal language, and cultural diversity management, plays a key role in shaping the organizational identity and supporting work engagement of its employees on the solid foundation of values and norms.

A significant role in building engagement is also played by transformational leadership, which is focused on inspiration, motivation, and support. Empathetic leaders, who act to the needs of their subordinates, are also able to successfully create teams with high levels of satisfaction and engagement. Meanwhile, flexibility in work organization (e.g., possibility for remote work, task-based assessment, and adjustable working hours) is a key tool that fosters employee well-being, as well as their engagement. These allow for effective management of work–life balance, which is becoming increasingly important in the rapidly changing conditions of the modern world of work. Organizational flexibility also facilitates adaptation to the needs of employees with idiosyncratic predispositions and forms of work.

In conclusion, the contributed volume provides a wealth of convincing evidence that modern management cannot limit itself to being reactive but must, above all, embrace proactivity, adjusting itself to the variety of employee needs and developing the ability to integrate employee diversity to achieve both employee well-being and work engagement. It highlights the importance of focusing not solely on organizational goal but also on the employee as a person with their individual predispositions, situational context, and personal needs, as well as on seeking opportunities to adequately and fully satisfy those needs. For this is the way to release intrinsic motivation, that is, enable employees to experience positive mental states (well-being), on which the level of employee engagement depends.

The contributed volume also identifies the direction for future investigation, which should start from further specifying the set of factors, as outlined here, that shape employees' psychological presence in the organization and then provide a way to rank the importance of the factors indicated above for building engagement. It is also worth verifying the lasting effects of the influence of a given factor on employee well-being and engagement with the use of longitudinal methods.

In the contributed volume, a range has been outlined of organizational determinants and solutions that may impact the creation of such an organizational context that will provide all employees with psychosocial support, broadly understood. Based on an analysis of the available data and the research conducted, the crucial factors that influence the generation of positive emotions in the workplace and the enhancement of work engagement have been identified. Hence, the implementation of the solutions offered may help to harmonize and satisfy the needs of both employees and the organization, and successfully accelerate organizational adaptation to the ongoing changes in the world around us.

# Index

Note: Page numbers in *italics* indicate figures, and page numbers in **bold** indicate tables in the text

For Product Safety Concerns and Information please contact our EU
representative GPSR@taylorandfrancis.com
Taylor & Francis Verlag GmbH, Kaufingerstraße 24, 80331 München, Germany

www.ingramcontent.com/pod-product-compliance
Ingram Content Group UK Ltd.
Pitfield, Milton Keynes, MK11 3LW, UK
UKHW022353190926
475702UK00015B/2264

* 9 7 8 1 0 3 2 7 1 5 3 9 1 *